On the Doorstep of Europe

THE ETHNOGRAPHY OF POLITICAL VIOLENCE

Series Editors: Daniel J. Hoffman, Tobias Kelly, Sharika Thiranagama

A complete list of books in the series is available from the publisher.

ON THE DOORSTEP OF EUROPE

ASYLUM AND CITIZENSHIP IN GREECE

HEATH CABOT

With a new preface by the author

PENN

UNIVERSITY OF PENNSYLVANIA PRESS

PHILADELPHIA

Originally published in 2014 by the University of Pennsylvania Press

Published by
University of Pennsylvania Press
Philadelphia, Pennsylvania 19104-4112
www.upenn.edu/pennpress
Printed in the United States of America on acid-free paper
10 9 8 7 6 5 4 3 2 1

Paperback ISBN: 978-1-5128-2521-3
eBook ISBN: 978-1-5128-2522-0

A Cataloging-in-Publication record is available from the Library of Congress

Peace be forever on the houses and citizens of Athens.

—Aeschylos, *The Eumenides*

Contents

Preface to the 2023 Edition

Seeking Refuge

How do legal processes become venues for producing and shifting boundaries between self and other, and what does that boundary look like? How does advocacy—at base, working to help someone else—become ameliorative or dangerous? And how do people navigate, manage, and compensate for broken systems without themselves falling apart? This book was, and is, an ethnography of refugee advocacy in Greece. In it I approach the political asylum process as a site of encounter, where lawyers, asylum applicants, and decision makers together work out the meaning of refuge on Europe's borders in the context of radical power inequalities. While much has changed since this book's initial publication (2014), key patterns persist across specificities of time and space that this study makes clear. These include both the necessity and perhaps impossibility of refuge (Ramsay 2017), and how global, perduring formations of law and rights find expression in everyday ethics.

The "tragedies" of asylum in Greece, as I call them here, refer not to the spectacular and sometimes heartrending violence often experienced by noncitizens but instead to moral-ethical dilemmas. This is the problem of "damned if you do, damned if you don't"—the impossibility of making an innocent, just, even good decision (see Nussbaum 2001; Calabresi and Bobbitt 1978). Tragedy shapes the search for refuge everywhere. Asylum is a form of refuge grounded in exclusion: on political and legal frameworks that carve out spaces of protection *through* the claimant's otherness and alienage. This founding tension shapes the experiences of, and encounters between, various persons engaged in seeking or "making" refuge (Besteman 2016). The costs of these tragedies are felt differently by different actors, depending on their relative positions of power. Still, asylum seekers, advocates, and decision makers alike are caught in dilemmas that impact them all in ways that go far beyond the capacity for individual action and agency.

The tragedies that I discuss here have aesthetic and affective dimensions that shape how decision makers, advocates, and claimants approach each other and the asylum process itself. This book is thus also an account of how anxiety, uncertainty, "not-knowing" (Cabot 2016), and even phantasmagorical modes of knowledge production dominate in contexts of great power asymmetry, where otherness is foregrounded (such as asylum processes). These aspects—which one might call informal factors in asylum advocacy—were crucial in how my research participants related to and encountered each other, and they concretely impacted formal factors, such as claims making, documents, and decisions. As I illustrate in Chapter 2, for instance, the informal uses of identity documents often subsumed their official meanings for claimants and advocates alike. Uncertainties also emerged in how advocates sought to imagine, and narrate, the life stories and experiences of asylum claimants (Chapters 3 and 4)—and, in turn, how claimants sought to make sense of the legal and bureaucratic systems in which they were caught (Chapter 7). These ambient feelings of uncertainty and anxiety were shared (though differently) by various participants in the asylum process—also by me—and they formed the ground on which asylum claims were made, examined, interpreted, and decided on.

This book first came out in 2014—just a year before the European Refugee Crisis threw images of Greece onto newspaper frontpages everywhere. Most of the research on which this study is based dates from well before that—between 2004 and 2011. This ethnography is thus a window into a still-recent (as of 2023) but very different era: when Greece was just coming into the limelight as a European border of global significance. So many things have changed since then: the specific politics and policies that shape border governance; the legal subtleties and institutional arrangements of the Greek asylum process; and European approaches to migration management. Still, Giuseppe Tomasi de Lampedusa's well-known statement (1959) is particularly prescient when it comes to the search for refuge on European borders: *For things to remain the same, everything must change.*

During the period of my research, the numbers of people entering Greece peaked in 2010–11 at around 100,000 estimated crossings, primarily via the land border with Turkey in the North, in the region of Evros. These numbers have only grown since the publication of this book. During the "long summer of migration" from 2015 to 2016, over a million people crossed into

Europe through Greece, mostly via the Aegean Islands between Greece and Turkey (specifically Lesvos, which appears at various points in this study). Greece, known primarily among global publics for its ancient landscapes and amazing vacation spots, thus emerged as one of Europe's frontlines of border politics, humanitarian disaster, and "militarized global apartheid" (Besteman 2019). Greece is one of those contested sites where the countries of Europe and the Global North seek to defend themselves against the "mobility of people from the global south" (S26).

Just as crossings skyrocketed during the 2015–16 refugee crisis, the number of humanitarian actors in Greece also exploded. Grassroots networks and collectives who greeted the initial arrivals became more diverse and numerous (Kirtsoglou 2020; Papataxiarchis 2016a, 2016b; Rozakou 2016). International and non-Greek civil society organizations also arrived, establishing offices in Athens, the islands, and later in the North. My primary interlocutors in this study, legal advisors, became the hardened voices of experience in this emergent asylum and refugee industry. Dimitris, a crucial interlocutor throughout this book (and now, even closer friend), told me in 2017 that many of his lawyer colleagues used to laugh at him when he first became an asylum lawyer. They said he would never make any money. But with the crisis, he posited, people increasingly became asylum lawyers precisely to make money and further their careers. A new generation of asylum lawyers was born, so to speak. In the world and times of this book, however, asylum was still a niche area of expertise in Greece relegated to specific legal professionals and a few formal organizations working in the field—including my primary fieldsite, the Athens Refugee Service (ARS, a pseudonym), at that time the largest and oldest refugee advocacy organization in Greece.

In 2015–16, the refugee and migration industries (McGuirk and Pine 2020; Andersson 2014) became crucial employment venues not just for lawyers but for many Greeks. This was also among the most difficult periods of the Greek economic crisis and the punitive austerity policies that decimated pensions and social services. Yet the refugee crisis also brought certain opportunities for a struggling Greek populace. People who had been unemployed for years suddenly found unskilled jobs at refugee camps and NGOs. Precariously employed educators and artists found work in initiatives for refugee children and teenagers. Like many sectors of the Greek workforce, Greek academics also suffered deeply under the lasting effects of austerity: massive pay cuts; closures; and the obliteration of positions, research funding, and other resources—all in a climate of ongoing neoliberalization and even hostility toward the academy. The field of asylum (both state and extrastate institutional forms) also provided academics with opportunities for (somewhat) stable employment. A great many people from the European and Global Norths also found volunteer experience and even paid work in Greece.

The lines between the refugee and migration industries and the business of academic work became increasingly blurred (Cabot 2019): or more likely, they had always been permeable—I was just finally able to see their porosity as I, too, was increasingly imbricated in these spheres. Greece (and the topic of migration to Greece) had been a notably peripheral area of expertise when I began my doctoral work in 2003 and, later, published this book. But after 2016 I received invitations for keynote addresses and was asked to make a number of written commentaries as the "refugee crisis" was increasingly deemed a necessary, crucial, or "hot" topic. Academic conference themes, even in anthropology, increasingly focused on mobility, displacement, and crisis. There was an explosion of new projects, and even earmarked research funds, for research on European borders through which more established and early-career scholars alike acquired funding. Some senior academics leaned on local scholars and students (Greek, often in precarious positions) for help conducting research, crafting grant applications, and even writing articles.

Some important scholarship has come out of this ferment of interest in Greece. Still, the boom of the refugee industry in Greece also produced a sense of dysphoria that I and others I know experienced as the currencies of knowledge and research changed in such a short period of time (Rozakou 2019). This dysphoria highlighted for me how knowledge production is subject to the changing tides of public interest, attention, funding, and "relevance" (Greenhouse 2011). And the politics of relevance may also set the stage for even greater forms of exploitation: of other scholars, of "locals," and of marginalized people themselves—in particular, border crossers (Khosravi 2018; Sukarieh and Tannock 2019).

Today, as I write, Ukraine demands attention and concern, while movement across the Mediterranean has taken a backseat; it will be something (and somewhere) else tomorrow. The issue of asylum in Greece counted very little before the crisis. Still, readers will learn in this book about the difficult challenges faced by asylum claimants and advocates even in earlier times—and how those earlier challenges remain important and illustrative today. This book shows how Greece (and by extension the EU) was utterly unprepared for even dramatically fewer border crossers and asylum claimants—let alone the unprecedented numbers who arrived just a few years later.

An advocate I quote in Chapter 1 noted (from an interview in June 2008), "Everyone knew terrible things were happening in Greece, but no one was talking about it." This comment highlights the profound invisibility that reigned in earlier times when publicity and attention on Greek migration management were lacking. Still, my research participants had known for years that European migration governance in Greece was fundamentally flawed and often violent. And plenty of them had made this patently clear to various publics: state agents, governing bodies, and decision makers at Greek and European levels. Through their legal advocacy casework, they outlined in detail the violent effects of the very legal frameworks meant to protect. And finally, refugees and asylum seekers themselves recounted in striking detail the violence they faced on their journeys, once they arrived in Greece, and elsewhere in Europe. They did so in various venues: via legal processes and civil society frameworks, but increasingly through grassroots political mobilizations, as discussed in Chapter 7. I too witnessed many of these things. I also heard them described, sat in on meetings, read reports, and watched them discussed in the European Parliament. And I wrote about them—here.

Crises-in-the-making often become visible when it is already too late. Invisibility is not an accident nor necessarily the result of blind spots or lack of knowledge; it is also a politics, often strategic, that governs attention while violence remains unchecked elsewhere. The events of 2015–16 were both extraordinary and not wholly unexpected for seekers of refuge and anyone who had been working in the field of asylum in Greece. Wider truths, as well as answers to emergent (if not yet visible) problems, can be found even in sites that are not yet on the map, so to speak, of relevance, interest, and attention. Even as many things have changed, violence remains a pervasive feature of refuge (see Munyikwa 2021). As such, the search for refuge must be a steady process, not subject to the boom and bust cycles of government- and foundation-funded initiatives and academic research.

Seeking refuge must also be much more than a legal process or social project focused on the Other. Owing to modes of dislocation and dispossession meant to extract labor and resources from bodies and territories, diverse populations around the globe find their lives increasingly unlivable (Anderson 2021; Cabot and Ramsay 2021). As I was completing this book, the debt crisis and austerity had increasingly come to define Greece and my interlocutors there, and Greek citizens and long-term residents—not just asylum seekers and recent migrants—also began seeking help at voluntary organizations and NGOs. At the very end of the book, I ask the wider question of what would happen to the meaning of belonging in Greece as the rights of citizenship were thrown increasingly into question. Would the insides and outsides of the body politic change, sharpen, or bleed together? All of the above? And as the presumed safety of citizenship fell apart (for those whose legal right to belong had never been in question), how did this change the meaning of displacement—and likewise, refuge?

Refugees and citizens alike may face similar struggles—though in different ways. Refuge may be difficult to find in one's own country, neighborhood, house, home, or family; just as one can be displaced from the terrain of rights and livable livelihood without ever being driven across borders. Those who try to help those seeking refuge may themselves lack a stable place to stand as they, too, navigate systemic factors that produce triage, scarcity, mistrust, and uncertainty (Caldwell 2017). Legal protection matters—as does the freedom to move without fear of arrest and deportation. But just as the rights of citizenship without the capacity to thrive lack teeth, the right to asylum with nothing else is, in many ways, nothing. Seeking refuge must be a collective endeavor—imperfect and riven with challenges, dilemmas, tragedies—to create spaces of safety, well-being, and flourishing for all.

References

Anderson, Bridget. 2021. "Methodological De-Nationalism: De-Exceptionalizing Displacement, Re-Exceptionalizing Citizenship." *Humanity: An International Journal of Human Rights, Humanitarianism, and Development* 12 (3): 300–311.

Andersson, Ruben. 2014. *Illegality, Inc.: Clandestine Migration and the Business of Bordering Europe*. Berkeley: University of California Press.

Besteman, Catherine. 2016. *Making Refuge: Somali Bantu Refugees and Lewiston, Maine*. Durham, NC: Duke University Press.

———. 2019. "Militarized Global Apartheid." *Current Anthropology* 60 (S): S26–S38.

Calabresi, Guido, and Phillip Bobbitt. 1978. *Tragic Choices: Fels Lectures on Public Policy Analysis*. New York: Norton.

Cabot, Heath. 2019. "The Business of Anthropology and the European Refugee Regime." *American Ethnologist* 46 (3): 261–75.

———. 2016. "'Refugee Voices': Tragedy, Ghosts, and the Anthropology of Not Knowing." *Journal of Contemporary Ethnography*. 45 (6): 645–72.

Cabot, Heath, and Georgina Ramsay. 2021. "Deexceptionalizing Displacement: An Introduction." *Humanity: An International Journal of Human Rights, Humanitarianism, and Development* 12 (3): 286–99.

Caldwell, Melissa L. 2017. *Living Faithfully in an Unjust World: Compassionate Care in Russia*. Berkeley: University of California Press.

Greenhouse, Carol J. 2011. *The Paradox of Relevance: Ethnography and Citizenship in the United States*. Philadelphia: University of Pennsylvania Press.

Khosravi, Shahram. 2018. "Afterward: Experiences and Stories Along the Way." *Geoforum* 116: 292–95.

Kirtsoglou, Elisabeth. 2020. "'We Are All Human': Cosmopolitanism as a Radically Political, Moral Project." In *An Anthropology of the Enlightenment*, edited by Larry Wolff and Marco Cipolloni, 133–50. London: Routledge.

Lampedusa, Giuseppe Tomasi di. 1959. *Il Gattopardo* [*The Leopard*]. Milan: Feltrinelli.

McGuirk, Siobhán, and Adrienne Pine, eds. 2020. *Asylum for Sale: Profit and Protest in the Migration Industry*. Oakland, CA: PM Press.

Munyikwa, Michelle. 2021. "Locating Refuge: Racialized Displacement and the Spatial Politics of Belonging." *Humanity: An International Journal of Human Rights, Humanitarianism, and Development* 12 (3): 312–23.

Nussbaum, Martha. 2001 [1986]. *The Fragility of Goodness: Luck and Ethics in Greek Tragedy and Philosophy*. New York: Cambridge University Press.

Papataxiarchis, Evthymios. 2016a. "Being 'There': At the Front Line of the 'European Refugee Crisis'—Part 1." *Anthropology Today* 32 (2): 5–9.

———. 2016b. "Μια μεγάλη ανατροπή: Η 'ευρωπαϊκή προσφυγική κρίση'και ο νέος πατριωτισμός της αλληλεγγύης" [A Big Upheaval: The European Refugee Crisis and the New Patriotism of Solidarity]. Σύγχρονα Θέματα [*Contemporary Issues*] 132–33: 7–28.

Ramsay, Georgina. 2017. *Impossible Refuge: The Control and Constraint of Refugee Futures*. London: Routledge.

Rozakou, Katerina. 2016. "Socialities of Solidarity: Revisiting the Gift Taboo in Times of Crises." *Social Anthropology/Anthropologie Sociale* 24 (2): 185–99.

———. 2019. "'How Did You Get In?': Research Access and Sovereign Power During the 'Migration Crisis' in Greece." *Social Anthropology/Anthropologie Sociale* 27 (S1): 68–83.

Sukarieh, Mayssoun, and Stuart Tannock. 2019. Subcontracting Academia: Alienation, Exploitation and Disillusionment in the UK Overseas Syrian Refugee Research Industry. *Antipode* 51 (2): 664–80.

Preface

This book is about the regime of political asylum in Greece and how asylum seekers, aid workers, and bureaucrats alike have sought to make sense of the dilemmas, often insurmountable, posed by both human rights law and European governance. It has been almost ten years since I first began research on this project. My first research trip to Athens was during the lead-up to the Olympics of 2004, when the city had been polished, cleaned, and marketed as a revived European capital. Athens now faces economic instability and increasing poverty, often brutal policing, and race-related violence. The story of asylum in Greece precedes the inception of the current Greek financial crisis, but many of the themes are similar, including Greece's marginality in Europe, the disciplining forces of Europeanization, and the ways persons and communities navigate seemingly impossible situations. I believe there are important lessons to be learned through what I will later describe as the "tragedies" of asylum in Greece: about ethical life, the work of judgment, and new possibilities for belonging and citizenship in the wake of political violence. There is also something ineffable but equally crucial that may be found: the haunting, but often powerful ways in which people come together, perhaps only fleetingly, to create attachments, intimacies, and even justice.

Three particular dilemmas of writing deserve mention at the outset. The first is the problem of how to take appropriate account of the Greek sovereign debt crisis without making it the assumed telos of all the events I convey in this book. The institutional instabilities and sociopolitical ferments that have emerged in Greece since 2008 have demanded that Greek, European, and international publics rethink the impacts of Europeanization on both migration management and fiscal policies. Here I show that while the financial crisis was certainly not predictable, it invokes and even replicates longstanding discourses and patterns of governance, which have been similarly problematic in the arenas of immigration and asylum. I also hope that my analysis will show that there are other pasts and potential futures beneath the dominant one of crisis that are equally important to note. The "crisis" is certainly a crucial set of events at the present moment, and just as importantly, it is a powerful trope through which many have come to describe and apprehend their worlds. But the future is open: no one knows what will happen next—economically, socially, or politically—and chances are it will be something that none of us can imagine.

Second, I attempt to highlight the dramatic, even artistic components of ethnographic practice and writing without simply celebrating them. I seek to recount stories in a way that, like tragic drama, will bring the reader in, and spark active emotional and intellectual engagement. Biehl and Locke (2010: 336) liken ethnography to art in its capacity "to invoke neglected human potentials and to expand the limits of understanding and imagination." Perhaps most importantly, they underscore (drawing on Deleuze 1998) how ethnography (like all art) must speak to an audience that has not yet emerged but which perhaps is emergent: "a people yet to come." I do not hope to accomplish such a feat, yet I take this as an important reminder of what we are really doing here and why writing can be important. As Iain Chambers (2008: 19) articulates, writing "seeks to open a fold in time to be invaded by other times, by others," with the potential to create openings not just into overlapping and divergent histories but also into possible futures. I thus also draw on the potential of ethnography to chronicle worlds yet to come: thresholds into possible lives and futures, into larger sociopolitical transformations, which may have already begun to take shape through the seeds of a nascent critical consciousness (Gramsci 1992). These points of movement and opening may never materialize into "history," or they may already be remaking the world in ways that are not yet visible. Either way, they matter deeply in the lives that Athenians have woven and continue to weave out of broken synapses of the polis.

Finally, this book is critical in that it is focused on analyzing and even exposing aspects of governance, rights discourse, and humanitarian practice that might otherwise remain uninterrogated. But it is not critique. Throughout, I speak to the powerful, but nondeterminative, force of structural violence in placing both asylum seekers and decision makers in profoundly difficult situations. This is not to disregard individual and collective agency; on the contrary, I will later suggest that agency can be found even in moments of hard silence and apparent immovability. But I do not spend a lot of time trying to highlight what my interlocutors have done wrong or could do better. The NGO workers who are such important figures throughout this book are well aware of most critiques that could be made of their own humanitarian practice—and indeed, could launch a few devastating critiques of their own. In my experience, aid workers and human rights professionals in Greece are deeply, even painfully, aware of everything wrong with the asylum process, asylum advocacy and aid work, and rights frameworks more broadly. What I seek to do here, then, is consider how these workers, and the asylum seekers whom they encounter, deal with a broken system without being swallowed whole; why they do it; and what their engagements might say regarding the possibilities and limits of asylum advocacy, aid, and rights-based protection.

Transliterating Greek is a complex matter, with a complex political history, particularly for an Anglophone like me. My goal in transliteration is to render Greek phrases legible to those who do not speak Greek. Rather than making use of the Modern Greek Studies Association transliteration guidelines, which are certainly useful but can be somewhat opaque for non-Greek speakers, I have chosen a style that is focused on phonetic consistence, so as to preserve the musicality of the speech. The downside to this approach is that it does not adequately convey the spelling of Greek words, which also has a complex history (some of which I discuss in Chapter 6), not to be dismissed. Thus, I have also often included the Greek characters, not simply for their elegance, but so as to engage both English and Greek-speaking audiences. Where I diverge from these transliteration norms is in regards to place names. For those places that have a recognizable rendering in the Latin alphabet, I have spelled them the way that is most legible for wider audiences (for example, Lesbos instead of Lesvos; Syntagma, instead of Sintagma).

A Greek friend of mine, on reading through a draft of the manuscript, commented that I should have done more to expose "the real bad guys." He was referencing the deep patterns of violence and colonial speculation in the Balkans and Asian Minor, including not just Ottoman rule but its aftermath: the ongoing involvement of Northern European and US powers in shaping the futures of the region. Others may object that I do not give significant attention to those in the Greek government, and others in the driver's seats of the Euro-global "troika" (the European Commission, International Monetary Fund, and European Central Bank) that have contributed greatly to Greece's marginalization and the exclusion of foreigners within Greece and Europe. This is not a book about them. What you will find here are all sorts of people, who defy easy classification as insider or outsider, "good" or "bad," but who are seeking to live tolerable, even ethically engaged, lives in ways that are often undone through forces outside their control; in a city that traverses the mythic and the quotidian, the underworld and the world of the living, the laws of blood, the sovereign, and the gods. This is a book about citizens of Athens.

Introduction. The Rock of Judgment

> Stavros led me on a leisurely and circuitous route up the Acropolis, the winter lights of Athens below us, and the monuments of the ancient city in sharp relief against the night sky. Eventually we arrived at an outcropping of stones on the northwest side of the Acropolis, which lay in darkness, except for the cigarettes of those who sat atop the rocks chatting quietly. We climbed up, my feet finding slippery grooves in the stone polished smooth from wear as I forsook the ladder that had been placed there for visitors, and we sat looking out at the Athenian night. The clusters of pine trees below us, with their green scent of darkness, opened outward into an unruly city that tumbled over and over upon itself: streets, apartment buildings, the whir of traffic, and lights. This rock, Stavros explained, was Areios Paghos: the high court of the ancient city. The supreme court of civil law in contemporary Greece also bears its name. Here—according to myth—Ares god of war was tried for murdering the son of Poseidon, hence its epithet (rock of Ares). And in Aeschylos's *Eumenides*, this is where Athena set up the very first court, with a human jury, to weigh the guilt of Orestes, avenger of his father and murderer of his mother.

To do fieldwork in Athens is always to encounter the mythic city, as it is perpetually reanimated and remade in both topographies and conversations. Stavros himself is a lawyer, who at that time worked at an NGO for asylum seekers in Athens, where we met and shared important conversations. He explained that he often came to this ancient rock of judgment to think: to work through dilemmas of life, love, and law. Despite my occasional vantage point from atop this rock, where I too would sometimes come to think, I generally looked *up* at the Acropolis, which is visible even from dark and cramped corners of the city center. An oasis of air, stone, and green, the Acropolis rises above the fray like a great rocky head, sitting in watch and perhaps also in judgment over the city. For many Athenians (students of their own mythic histories, retold through popular culture, across generations, and in school), and certainly for many foreigners like myself, the great rock ruptures the topography of the contemporary polis, calling up the ghosts of what was or is imagined to have been: the mythic past then collides with the quotidian, the city of particular routines and practices (see Hamilakis 2007; Yalouri 2001).

From the narrow city center streets, or from my fifth-floor balcony where I could view just a sliver of the Parthenon if I positioned myself just right, during my fieldwork in Athens I looked to the Acropolis as a symbol of judgment but also of refuge. As an undergraduate student of classical religion, I was captivated when an older, particularly brainy friend explained to me that beneath the Acropolis, the center of the polis, reside the *Erinyes* or Furies. In the very last scene of Aeschylos's *Eumenides,* which defuses the dilemmas that have ensnared characters throughout the tragic cycle of the *Oresteia,* Orestes is acquitted of the charges against him, thanks to Athena, who casts the deciding vote in an otherwise "hung" jury. Yet the Furies, who have chased him all the way from Argos to Athens, threaten to torment the city in retribution: they are ancient goddesses of night, they claim, and they demand recognition. And so Athena issues another judgment, a sovereign act before the audience of the court, but really more of an afterthought, outside the formal space of the law. She offers the Furies refuge beneath the Acropolis, so they might "look over the city as terror watches over the mind." Thus granted recognition and refuge, the persecuting Furies are transformed, becoming the Eumenides, "the kindly ones," to be honored for eternity by the citizens of Athens. And as they vanish in a procession of lights into the dark spaces beneath the great rock, the city also is transformed.[1]

This image of judgment, refuge, and their potential for transformation serves as a mythic backdrop for this book, which explores Greece's emergence as a country of refuge for persons seeking political asylum. I consider the asylum system in Greece much in the vein of Susan Coutin's (2000) "ethnography of a legal process," through which she tracks the asylum claims of Salvadorans in the United States from their inception to their abandonment. Yet, even more, this book is about that which spills over from the formal space of asylum law: the encounters, social interactions, forms of knowledge, and ethical engagements that have their genesis in formal law but are not reducible to it. I argue that judgment and refuge, while eminently necessary, are also impossible within the formal confines of the asylum procedure. Rather, those elements that exceed or even undermine the asylum process have powerful and even transformative effects in claims for protection and the lived experiences of those who make, mediate, and adjudicate such claims. These asides, afterthoughts, and correctives to processes of adjudication serve, in always partial ways, to remake Athenian citizenship's topographies.

The "Krisi" of Asylum

As I write in 2013, Greece is currently characterized as the lynchpin of a worldwide financial "crisis," which has thrown into question the stability of European and global markets, the possibility of economic integration, and the futures of global economies. This small country on the periphery of Europe is thus at the center of deeply contested questions over sovereignty, financial viability, governance, and democracy. In 2004, however, when I first began my research in Athens, Greece was riding the dizzy wave of prosperity following its initial accession to the Euro and, perhaps even more important, the long-awaited "return" of the Olympic Games. With massive "cleanups," infrastructural improvements, and sidewalks that had been polished slippery-smooth, Athens achieved some visibility as a renewed European capital worth visiting on the way to the islands. Yet overall, for international audiences, Greece continued to connote an entrenched quality of marginality, appearing largely as a benign, tourist friendly, and somewhat disorganized country on the Mediterranean peripheries of Europe and the West.

In the European context, however, in the early 2000s Greece was fast acquiring notoriety as a problem zone with regard to questions of immigration and asylum. This was largely owing to its geopolitical position on EU land and sea borders, changing patterns of violence and poverty (notably the wars in Iraq and Afghanistan), and increasingly militarized policing measures in other regions of Europe's Mediterranean coast. These multiple factors contributed to rapidly increasing numbers entering Greece's own territorial borders, reconfiguring also the routes of smuggling through which people make their ways to Europe. Greece is often more accessible than other EU Mediterranean countries for persons coming from the Middle East, because of its proximity and its shared land and sea borders with Turkey. Most cross the river and mountain-drawn borders in the North. Others enter in rubber dinghies, crossing the short but dangerous distances from the Turkish coast to islands in the Aegean. Larger boats from North Africa often initially head for

Italy (or passengers may be told that this is where they are bound), but many boats are redirected and abandoned in Greek territorial waters. In the current climate of economic instability, many migrants are returning voluntarily to home countries in the Middle East, Africa, and South Asia; others, many of whom have lived in Greece for a number of years, have left for other locations in Europe. Since 2011 there has been an overall decrease in undocumented migration to Europe, owing largely to more militarized and rigorous policing measures on all external borders. Still, as of 2013, the Greek borders, and in particular, the Evros River between Greece and Turkey, are among the most trafficked borders of the European Union.[2]

A few years before the financial collapse, the Greek asylum process thus emerged as a growing area of "crisis" for the EU. Only a fraction of those who entered Greece applied for asylum, very often owing to difficulty accessing the asylum system, and just as often because many traveled elsewhere in Europe or remained undocumented. Beginning in 2004, however, Greece had one of the fastest rising rates of asylum application in Europe, combined with staggeringly low refugee recognition rates. According to official statistics compiled by the Ministry of Public Order and Citizen Protection (Ipouryio Dhimosias Taksis kai Prostasias tou Politi; Υπουργείο Δημόσιας Τάξης και Προστασίας του Πολίτη),[3] the number of asylum applications in Greece grew by more than five times between 2004 and 2007, from 4,469 to 25,113 (see Table 1). Meanwhile, only a small fraction were recognized as refugees each year. In 2006, only 64 persons acquired refugee status; in 2007, 140.[4] In 2008, there was an increase in the number of positive decisions to 415 but this number remained extremely low in comparison to other EU member states (see Table 2). Just as striking as the high number of rejections was the extraordinarily high number of cases that remained pending. In 2010, according to data released by the UN High Commissioner for Refugees (UNHCR 2010), Greece was globally the country with the fourth highest number of backlogged asylum cases (48,201), behind South Africa, the United States, and Ecuador. For European and international audiences, then, the "crisis" of asylum in Greece was not just a question of volume but lay also in the spheres of law and bureaucracy: in Greece's incapacity to document, register, and process claims to protection. Moreover, given Greece's status as a European external border, asylum in Greece also threw into crisis the EU capacity both to protect European territories and citizens from "alien" threats and to comply with international laws guaranteeing protection for persons fleeing violence and persecution.

Table 1: Number of Asylum Applications in Greece by Year, 2004–2010

Year	*Number of new applications*
2004	4,469
2005	19,884
2006	12,267
2007	25,113
2008	19,884
2009	15,928
2010	10,273

Source: Greek Ministry of Public Order and Citizen Protection.

Table 2: Comparative Table of EU Asylum Decisions, 2008 (EU countries issuing highest numbers of decisions)

EU country	*Total decisions issued*	*Positive decisions (refugee status)*
France	56,115	11,470
Germany	30,405	10,650
Greece	30,915	415
Italy	20,260	9,740
Sweden	31,220	8,670
United Kingdom	33,525	10,190

Source: Data provided by national authorities and by Eurostat (www.europa.eu); rounded to nearest 5.

Krisi [κρίση], in Greek, refers not just to "crisis" (its clear English equivalent) but also to the work of judgment in the context of law and, more loosely, in the sense of critique or criticism. This book examines a number of sites where judgment is carried out. Within the asylum procedure, and through detailed examinations of encounters between workers and aid candidates at an Athenian asylum aid NGO, I consider how processes of decision making give rise to prototypes (Coutin 2000: 107) of credible asylum cases, and accompanying figurations of which persons and lives are (or are not) eligible for protection. More broadly, however, "crisis" invokes a narrative of historical time punctuated by turning points and critical shifts (Redfield 2005). Such narratives also accomplish moral work, enacting forms of judgment by demarcating certain territories, persons, and moments as sites of potential danger. I thus explore how European and more global narratives of crisis reinscribe long-standing, even structurally entrenched histories of exclusion and marginality. These include both the marginalization of Greece in Europe and the ongoing exclusion of asylum seekers and refugees, who—in Greece, in the EU, and on a more global scale—are perpetually relegated to the edges of the body politic. I consider how crisis narratives both assert and legitimate structural violence, which in Greece plays out not only in the fraught arena of asylum, but in increasing poverty, civil unrest, state brutality, and the breakdown of bureaucratic and civic entitlements. Finally, I show that the *krisi* of asylum in Greece, like the financial crisis, simultaneously enacts a rupture in these marginalizing configurations, throwing them into contestation, and creating possibilities for change in sociopolitical and legal spheres as well as in ethical life.

The asylum process in Greece, as I approach it here, is a venue for a series of "social dramas" (Gluckman 2006 [1965]; Llewellyn and Hoebel 2002; Turner 1967, 1974) currently taking place in Athens around questions of governance, citizenship, rights, and ethics. While I recognize the limits of "social drama" as an analytical device, including its potentially teleological character and tendency to convey a stage-based theory of social change, this model highlights some important elements of the relationship between formal law and the wider sociopolitical processes that it both reflects and affects. For Turner (1974: 37), "social dramas" entail the "contestation" and, in many cases, transformation of dominant frameworks of social organization; they are "aharmonic or disharmonic processes, arising in conflict situations." This analytical framework underscores how legal processes are often venues for the exposure and contestation of prevalent forms of structural pressure and violence, which often go unacknowledged.

Turner (1974: 39) writes that particularly during periods of "crisis," when dominant social and political formations are turned upside down, it is "least easy to don masks and pretend that nothing is rotten in the village." The *krisi* of asylum makes visible a number of underlying and perhaps irresolvable tensions in Europeanization and rights politics more broadly: how to reconcile humanitarian and security concerns, how to distinguish refugees from other kinds of migrants, how to rearticulate the insides and outsides of the Greek nation-state, and the question of what kind of polities Greece and Europe are becoming. Asylum claimants, bureaucrats, and service providers engage these dilemmas through their face-to-face encounters with each other. Some of these tensions are peculiar to Greece at this particular historical moment. These include the problems of EU governance in the arenas of immigration and asylum, and the often untenable positions in which Greek institutions currently find themselves in sites of entrenched geopolitical and economic marginality.

More deeply, however, the dramas I explore highlight how ethically engaged individuals face the tensions embedded in an international regime of rights-based protection that, even in supranational contexts, depends on nation states for its realization. This tension is endemic to the "national order of things" that Liisa Malkki (1995b) so artfully elucidates, and which Hannah Arendt (1976 [1951]) outlines with striking clarity. At least in theory, asylum, based on the framework of international human rights, is for those who have been driven from home countries and must now seek protection in the territory of a foreign nation state. Yet in practice, this national order persistently goes awry. People fleeing violence often cannot make it across borders, giving rise to that anomalous category of the "internally displaced person." Meanwhile, barring the willingness or capacity of nation states to offer protection, there has been a proliferation of no-man's lands, camps, and other non-nationalized spaces, where refugees are confined to zones of limbo as they await resettlement, processing, and the distribution of services (Agamben 1998; Hyndman 2000). When claimants do, however, find a way to cross borders, to a nation state deemed by the international community to be "safe" and capable of providing protection, refuge is awarded by the very virtue of their being "alien": a citizen of another nation where citizenship has failed. Thus, while the law of protection is grounded on an ahistorical vision of humanity, a "universal" citizenship invoked through the regime of international human rights, this framework simultaneously reinscribes the refugee's "alien" origins. At stake in asylum law, then, is the question of who among these "alien" subjects are worthy of or entitled to refuge.

I explore how this problem at the heart of asylum law is expressed and engaged both through the encounters of everyday life and in the practical concerns of asylum claimants, adjudicators, and those who take on the mediating role of service provision. I argue that the asylum procedure, in its formal application, presents applicants and decision makers with "tragic" dilemmas. "Tragedy," as I discuss it both later in this Introduction and in greater detail in Chapter 3, entails the material, legal, and political constraints that limit claims to protection (see Calabresi and Bobbitt 1978), as well as conflicting ethical commitments in the rendering of these judgments (Nussbaum 2001 [1986]). Decision makers who assess asylum applications, in both governmental and nongovernmental spheres, must balance material limits to their capacities to offer protection with the demands of law and policy, as well as more fluid ethical concerns that may reflect cultural practices, affective modes, and dominant notions of right action.

These problems of ethics are also about citizenship: who gets to make claims to belonging and entitlement and on what grounds—a question that has powerful implications for the claimant's quality of life and even life itself. As adjudicators, claimants, and service providers negotiate the tragedies of asylum in Greece, they also redelineate the insides and outsides of the body politic. These ethical engagements, generated in the space of law, reflect changing notions of who inhabits the viable center of the polis, and who is cast to its margins or beyond. They also point to new possibilities for who might be brought into the topography of the city itself, becoming "kindly" rather than merely "alien." As Gluckman (2006 [1965]) and more recently, Herzfeld (1982) and Ngai (2004) show, though in very different ways, it is the "alien" or "stranger" (in Greek, *ksenos*; ξένος) who forces the body politic to (re)constitute and rearticulate itself.[5]

Such reshaping of the body politic in relationship to the "other" occurs across multiple scales and entails a constantly shifting constellation of who or what is near or far, inside or outside. Writes Simmel (1950: 405): "The stranger is close to us, insofar as we feel between him and ourselves common features of a national, social, occupational, or generally human, nature. He is far from us, insofar as these common features extend beyond him or us." This telescopic reorienting of relationships between inside and outside, self and other, unfolds across global, European, and national scales, transecting the shifting topography of Athens and sites of face-to-face encounter. Greece—its own European membership on trial—has become a kind of test case for European dreams of the free movement of people and capital. The Greek asylum system thus speaks directly to the failures and potentialities of European citizenship: Who can make legitimate claims to belonging and entitlement in Europe, and what does this entail? And with a European migration "apparatus" that attempts the incongruous melding of security with the values of freedom and justice (Feldman 2011), what are the possibilities and limits of rights and international protection? Further, with regard to global landscapes of human rights and humanitarian intervention, are there ways of responding to claims for refuge that invoke a more flexible and inclusive image of the "generally human" that pays appropriate attention to both difference and common ground (Goodale 2009)? What alternative visions of humanity, ethics, and citizenship might tragedy unveil?

The asylum process and its adjudicative logics also entail a wealth of epistemic practices, through which both claimants and decision makers seek to make sense of each other, the law, the state, and bureaucracy, including bureaucratic tools such as documentation, interviewing, form filling, and file making. Yet far from being simply technocratic, these practices rely heavily on more indeterminate forms of knowledge production: storytelling and narrative; pictures, images, and other aesthetic forms; and rumor and fantasy. These creative and fluid knowledge practices emerge, I suggest, from profound epistemic problems embedded in the Greek asylum process. Gaps in power between decision makers and asylum seekers also entail gaps in knowledge of each by the other (Laing 1983 [1967]). Furthermore, as I highlight in Chapter 2, the Greek state and its tools of regulation are deeply mystified, even for service providers and bureaucrats, who may be even more perplexed than asylum seekers themselves. The asylum procedure thus readily weds bureaucracy with practices of what I describe as *mythopoesis* or myth-making, through which all parties seek to make sense of radical uncertainty, unpredictability, and even absurdity.

Asylum seekers, adjudicators, and service providers are engaged in trying to acquire usable knowledge of the asylum process, each other, and their everyday lives. Since the "real," however, frequently evades explanation, they often look to frameworks that, like myth, are said to underlie daily life and practice. Moreover, rather than emerging in contradistinction to law and bureaucracy, myth-making is crucial to the workings of asylum in Greece and unfolds *through* the technocratic values of transparency and bureaucratic accountability. Much as Charles Stewart (1991) argues that the demonic buoys up the Orthodox in contemporary Greek cosmology, I show that these knowledge forms at the margins of law and bureaucracy are in fact central to their everyday functioning. In the vein of Evans-Pritchard's (1937) analysis of Azande magic, my ethnography highlights how the search for sense, origins, causes, and effects beyond the visible or self-evident is, in its own way, deeply rational. Yet these more indeterminate forms of knowledge take on lives of their own: documents acquire their own agency; persons disappear or become phantoms and ghosts; bureaucratic processes become products of hearsay; and stories, true or not, come to form the ground of judgment.

While, for Turner (1967, 1974), social dramas often end in moments of reconstitution, when balance is restored and norms are reasserted, I emphasize their creative potential and radical indeterminacy. Paul Friedrich (1986) formulated the concept of "poetic indeterminacy" to highlight the role of individual imaginations in (re)shaping the structural dimensions of language and culture. By this, he sought to bring into view the processes by which individuals "integrate knowledge, perceptions, and emotions in some creative way . . . in order that they may enter into new mental states or new relations with their milieus" (18). I show here that in processes of decision making and adjudication, the enactment of judgment is accompanied by unofficial, often highly creative practices that have crucial consequences in the experiences of claimants and adjudicators. The forms of governance, sociality, knowledge, and ethical engagement generated through *krisi*, with their many dilemmas, take on new and unpredictable formations, with equally indeterminate effects. Projects of governance may lead to their own undoing, even as they enact regulation. Knowledge is wedded to myth. Socialities predicated on power inequalities, structural violence, and exclusion also generate attachment, humor, and intimacy. Ethics, while grounded in the binary dilemmas of tragedy, become kaleidoscopic and multilayered, as persons find myriad ways to manage and destabilize these dilemmas.

Such asides, afterthoughts, and finaglings could easily fall by the wayside if one were to focus only on the formal asylum process, Greece's apparent failures in implementing it, and the issuance—or denial—of refuge. Yet these excesses and even byproducts of law and judgment, with their elements of superfluity, are crucial to the asylum process and its lived effects on contemporary Greek citizenship. This book, in many ways, is an exploration of how certain persons and lives are constituted as superfluous,[6] cast out of home countries through multiple kinds of violence, and suspended in politicolegal precariousness in Greece. These forms of excess, however, also make possible productive encounters that have an important role in reshaping modes of social, political, and legal belonging. Those left out of dominant formations of citizenship are central to how the Athenian body politic, like the city, is remade and rearticulated.

An Office in Athens

On the loud central Athenian boulevard of Peiraios, a small "Chinatown" has sprung up in the past ten years—a row of Chinese wholesalers that supply many of the less expensive clothing shops in Athens. Both Greek and Chinese shop owners, as well as many street vendors, acquire their goods from these distributors (see Rosen 2013). Just in view of the Acropolis, and just outside the zones where tourists wander, a five to fifteen-minute walk in any direction will take you in very different trajectories.

Five minutes to the southeast, you could push your way through Psiri, the old meat-packing district, silent during the day with shuttered windows, but at night coming alive with bars and restaurants that open into the street. Psiri connects labyrinth-like with some of the back streets where long-standing Greek inhabitants and recent migrants live side by side, and the grilled fish, onion, garlic, and lemon smells of old *tavernes* mingle with the scents of curries, sour bread, and spicy eggplant. Or you could take a tourists' walk that Athenians also love, snaking through Psiri to Thisseio and Monastiraki, where the lines of the Acropolis vault above the narrow streets and faded shop fronts of old Athens. In a mixed sea of Greek speakers and fair-skinned tourists speaking German, English, or French, you could follow the tracks of the *ılektrico* (ηλεκτρικό), Athens's first public train system, which carves a moat on the side of the Acropolis, beneath the ancient Agora. You would also pass street vendors. Men from Bangladesh sell goods they have obtained from Chinese wholesalers—sometimes sunglasses and jewelry, but mostly knick-knacks, plastic toys such as windup dolls and windmill hats, and surprisingly useful items like whistles, key chains, and LED flashlights, which you can buy for 3 Euro. There are also West African traders selling "designer" purses—replicas of Louis Vuitton and Gucci spread out on soiled white sheets, which make for both a quick get-away and a quick way to reopen shop. When other vendors—or often customers—whisper warnings of "police" or *astinomia* [αστυνομία], sellers gather up their goods, only to lay them down again moments later, once danger has passed.

If you head five minutes to the southwest away from Chinatown, you will find Gazi, a relatively new center of Athenian nightlife, housing the temple of Athens's contemporary art scene, the "Technopolis," a converted factory that is now an exhibition space. Here, if you know where to look, you will also find the ancient gates of Athens and the ancient cemetery of Keramikos, an oasis of quiet green, replete with a small brook and the occasional snapping turtle. If you go a little to the southwest beyond Gazi, with its recently opened metro stop that has dramatically increased the crowds of club goers, you will find another crucial node in my map of Athens: the Boulevard of Petrou Ralli, and the Police Department for Aliens, where, until recently, people lined up in order to apply for asylum.[7]

If you take Peiraios in the other direction, to the northeast, in fifteen or twenty minutes you will reach Omonia Square, the Square of "Harmony," with its heavy traffic of people and cars. The walk I took most weekday mornings from September 2006 through July 2008, during my primary stint of fieldwork in Athens, involved just a few city blocks: from the metro stop in Omonia to a run-down office near Exarcheia Square. Dense with people, smog, and traffic, moped engines and car horns, Omonia is known among long-time Athenian residents for its heavy concentration of tourists, drug users, and migrants, but it is also a vibrant and buzzing neighborhood full of contradictions. Exiting in the direction of Eleutherios Venezelou Street, I would walk down a *pezodhromos* (pedestrian walkway), past shoeshine men, kiosks, professionals in suits and sunglasses drinking coffee, bakeries, street vendors, a mid-class hotel, and a legal brothel. Rounding the corner, I would cross a broad boulevard, then head down cramped and pitted side streets into the neighborhood of Exarcheia, where dense buildings frame a sky often tinged with the tarry film of smog. Exarcheia is the site of the *Polytechneio*, the Polytechnic University, where the student uprising against the military dictatorship on November 17, 1973, ended in the deaths of students, sparking a much wider series of protests that eventually contributed to ousting the Junta in 1974, in the face of the Cyprus crisis. Every November 17, crowds come here in memoriam and protest, then march across town to the American embassy, in angry remembrance of the U.S. support of the Junta. A bastion for anarchist and leftist politics, this neighborhood is also hospitable for migrants, and it houses a number of NGOs and community organizations devoted to assisting migrants and refugees. For me, Exarcheia is most significant as the site of the Athens Refugee Service (ARS, a pseudonym),[8] the largest and oldest asylum-related NGO in Greece.

The ARS signals its presence before one reaches the street where it is located. People speaking Arabic, Dari, Urdu, Bangla, or other languages make their way toward the office carrying files and papers; the public phone on the block often has a line. Each morning, I would find a crowd waiting at the entrance: sometimes twenty to fifty people, sometimes as many as one hundred or one hundred and fifty, some pressed against the door, others sitting on the sidewalk outside, some smoking, some just waiting. As I made my way to the entrance, the crowd would part, people tapping each other on the back to give me space, and embarrassed by their politeness, I would push through bodies and the sharp tang of old sweat. I would greet Luc, an African man who staffs the door and has worked at the ARS for a number of years. A few of those waiting most likely would be chatting with him, along with a couple of other regular visitors. A young Afghan man who loves French often practiced with Luc, and an elderly Vietnamese gentleman was usually asleep in a chair; he was homeless, and Luc let him nap there.

Climbing the tight staircase, near the second floor I would encounter the crowd of regularly scheduled clients waiting to see a social worker or a lawyer. Then I would make my way to the fourth floor, the Legal Service, which generally employed ten on-staff lawyers and a few rotating volunteers, though the staff changed multiple times even during my time there. Five staircase twists above the street, and two above the busy waiting area, this was usually one of the quietest parts of the building, but nonetheless, the shared offices were usually packed, with clients and an interpreter clustered around each lawyer's desk. The density of languages heightened the tightness of space: interpreters translating into Greek and English for clients speaking Farsi/Dari, Kurdish, Arabic, Urdu, Bangla, Amharic, and Somali—and maybe also a crying baby.

During much of my fieldwork I was based in this Athens office, where I conducted participant observation as a volunteer in the legal department. In addition to helping to produce and proofread documents in English, I assisted with clerical tasks like typing, photocopying, file making (and file finding), and registration, in exchange for the opportunity to speak with staff, watch them work, and observe meetings between aid candidates and workers. However, given the sheer amount of work to do, the ARS is not a place where one can simply observe, and as time went on, I was increasingly asked to become a more active and involved presence there: assisting lawyers with research on their cases, meeting with and advising clients, and conducting client interviews. Unlike many other EU countries, the Greek state allocates minimal direct funding and resources for legal aid (*nomiki aroyi*; νομική αρωγή) or assistance (*sindhromi*; συνδρομή) to asylum seekers. The ARS is one among just a handful of organizations throughout Greece that provide pro bono legal aid to applicants. Furthermore, it is the largest of just a few organizations in Athens devoted to this purpose, with full-time staff lawyers. With Greece's lack of state-funded legal support, and a significant gap in the NGO infrastructure as well, the ARS plays a crucial role in assisting applicants in navigating the asylum procedure. Through my presence there, I was able to access a central site in the asylum process in Greece.

For years, the ARS has been on what might be described as the front lines of the Greek asylum "crisis"—a central stopping point for many who enter Greece, whether or not they stay there. Newly arrived asylum seekers come to Athens to find work, to sell goods, to find each other, and also to find smugglers to help them travel elsewhere in Europe. As I discuss in Chapter 2, Athens is also the bureaucratic center of the asylum process, so applicants also come to file paperwork and for asylum hearings. Border communities play an enormous role in the reception of migrants and asylum seekers,[9] without adequate assistance from the state, and border police figure significantly in their apprehension and detention; once released, however, new arrivals are often funneled to Athens. On Lesbos, one of the island borders in the Aegean, newly released individuals (both those who do and those who do not express a desire to apply for asylum) are bused directly from the detention center to the ferry, where they are given tickets to the capital, sometimes paid for by a local group of supporters; as a woman who works at the port described the scene, "they round them up and send them away to Athens." Near Kavala, just a couple of hours by car from the northern land border, a local police captain described to me how officers had started to take up a collection to buy bus tickets to Athens for those recently released. When I asked this police captain, "Why Athens?" he shrugged and answered as if it were obvious: "What will they do *here*?" While this story may have functioned as a way to demonstrate how well police treat detainees (in case I was reporting this information back to someone), this account also highlights the centrality of Athens as an assumed destination or stopping point for all new arrivals.

Athens is an epicenter in the movements of asylum seekers and refugees in Greece, and many of those who come to Athens are among the crowds that I used to find each morning at the doorstep of the ARS. Asylum seekers are directed to the ARS by acquaintances, other organizations, and even police; one can find the address scribbled by police officers on the backs of documents issued not just at the central police station in Athens, but also at the airport, at detention centers, and in border areas. The ARS has thousands of official clients, and a great many more whom they advise informally. There are even more who do not return to the office once registered in the database. For some, the ARS is a central, even daily or weekly, stopping point; for others, it is just another office they visit once or twice; for others still, it is a waypost on the road to elsewhere in Europe.

As I describe in greater detail in Chapter 1, this NGO is an important locale in multiple migratory geographies that transect but also interact intimately with geographies of law, governance, policy, and advocacy. Through its many visitors, the ARS is tied to routes of movement stretching through and across the Mediterranean world and even toward southern and eastern Asia. But it is also an important site in wide-ranging routes of intra-European

Figure 1. Threshold of the ARS.

travel, and the entries and expulsions of asylum seekers across internal and external borders. This became powerfully evident to me while I was in Rome in July 2007, conducting a week of comparative research with an NGO that, at times, collaborated with the ARS. There I met with a large group of Afghans who had established an informal camp behind one of the central train stations. Many of them greeted me with recognition, in Greek, having seen me at the ARS. One of them I had met on three different occasions: first, months before, at a detention center in Mytilene, then at the ARS office, and finally at this unofficial camp in Rome. Another, who had just arrived, I had seen just the week before at the ARS office, but while I had come to Italy in a plane, he had taken the ferry from Patras to Ancona by smuggling himself into the bottom of a truck. This startling moment of recognition highlighted powerfully for me the smallness of the networks in which people move, despite the great distances they cross. The ARS and the people who work there are part of these networks, an important node in the movements of asylum seekers from many different countries of origin, whether these movements are more local or regional (primarily in Athens and Greece) or more broad, traversing multiple sites in Europe.

The ARS is a nexus for the various ethnographic threads that constitute this book: frameworks of governance, policy, law, and advocacy (at international, Greek, and EU scales); bureaucratic practices; dilemmas of knowledge, ethics, and judgment; and finally, the lives of asylum seekers in Greece, and their struggles for survival and recognition. In my field practice, I followed these threads outward from this small office, which took me from refugee apartments at the outskirts of the city center, to the borders with Turkey, to the European Parliament, and briefly to other NGOs in Brussels, Spain, and Italy. Still, at the center of this book is this Athens office, an ethnographic threshold into the asylum process in Greece and the lives that it makes possible: old PCs, fluorescent lighting and dusty floors, files piled on desks, crowds of people inside and outside, densities of different languages, the smell of sweat and cigarettes, and moments of humor, kindness, anger, and frustration.

I approach the ARS not simply as a site relevant to questions of asylum in Europe, nor even as an entry into broader patterns of movement, but also as the doorstep of a kind of possible city: a new Athens emerging in and through the "crises" of immigration and asylum. Just as I was recognized in Rome by this group of Afghan asylum seekers, ARS workers often spoke of being recognized in Athens, by people and in places many of their Greek compatriots did not even notice—being addressed on the street, in buses, in parks, on the beach by peripatetic vendors or other "foreigners." While these moments of encounter outside the office were often unnerving for workers, they were also, like my meeting in Rome, moments of surprise and often warmth. When I walked with Stavros past a Bangladeshi street vendor who spoke to him with recognition, Stavros greeted him with a wide smile and said to me, ironically but with kindness, *ine dhikos mas* (είναι δικός μας), "he is one of ours" or "one of us." This phrase also has strong kinship associations—"he is one of our own." Stavros certainly did not mean that this man is, indeed, "family"; instead, he was highlighting that this man had likely visited the ARS. Yet the statement speaks to forms of tolerance and even intimacy (Papataxiarchis 2006) fostered in the space of the office, creeping outward uncertainly onto the streets of the city. Even in their fleetingness, the social and ethical engagements that emerged at this office, around often profound dilemmas of judgment, also point to new kinds of relationships, reconfigurations of emotion and language, changing notions of inclusion and exclusion, and new conceptions of belonging that are becoming possible to imagine and even talk about.

A Moving Target

After my primary fieldwork, I returned for follow-up research in the summers of 2009, 2010, and 2011, through which I was able to address, in focused ways, the rapid developments taking place around asylum, Greek politics, and the financial crisis. Just after my exit from the field in 2008, doing research about Greece suddenly became like following a moving target: a fifteen-year-old Athenian youth, Alexandros Grigoropoulos, was shot by a police officer during a night out in Exarcheia, on a street just around the corner from the ARS, and protests exploded in Athens. Migrants also took an active role in these protests, which those on the Radical Left cited as a small victory for democracy and others on the Right recounted in terms of a growing internal "alien" threat. The militarized response to this unrest also highlighted how the state, particularly as represented in the armed figures of riot police or MAT (Units for the Reinstatement of Order; Μονάδες Αποκατάστασης Τάξης), was increasingly violent toward *both* Greeks and migrants. In 2010, when the financial crisis propelled Greece into the global limelight, the sociopolitical ferments accompanying these economic instabilities made radical protest and police violence dominant aspects of life in the city center. Before, the burn of tear gas could be expected on just a few days a year—primarily, the annual protests on November 17. Now, it permeates Athenian daily life, from Exarcheia to the Parliament and beyond, while the city burns, often literally.

Somewhat ironically, however, as I recount in Chapter 1, these widespread sociopolitical and economic instabilities have been accompanied by significant (and by many accounts, positive) reforms of the asylum process. I outline these transformations alongside the forms of violence that have emerged in Athens at large. I also explore how these emergent developments around the crisis have produced a new politics of race in Athens and accompanying forms of race-related violence, which my interlocutors have recounted for me in profound and disturbing ways. While Athens, and Greece more broadly, has long been shaped through powerful metaphors (Herzfeld 1997) of blood and nation, this sharply delineated politics of race has exploded into the Athenian public sphere in just the past few years. In particular, there has been a rapid diffusion of Fascist and neo-Nazi ideologies, largely through the increasingly visible political party, Khrisi Avyi (Χρυσή Αυγή), or "Golden Dawn," which explicitly targets migrants and other persons of color. Yet such forms of violence are also accompanied by more visible and articulated political claims among foreign residents of Athens, who increasingly demand entitlements and recognition.

It may seem incongruous to herald new forms of inclusion in the Athenian body politic alongside such dramatic forms of exclusion and violence, yet I suggest that both processes are taking place simultaneously. Whether we can induce something broader about social change in general is beyond the purview of this book or my intentions. Yet this is certainly what I have observed, and continue to observe, in Athens. The moments of urban transformation I gesture to here include extraordinary violence and rapid closure, inscriptions of old patterns, anger and disappointment, and nostalgias for and rearticulations of an imagined earlier Greek nation-state, with more solid boundaries and borders. Likewise, the ARS is not just a site of extraordinary diversity but also one of inequality based on race, class, gender, national and ethnic origin, legal status, language, and knowledge. There, NGO workers, through their assessments of legal aid applicants, make crucial judgments regarding who is and is not deserving of protection in Greece. These decisions have very real consequences in the lives of aid candidates, but despite the violence they enact, they are not one-sided. How asylum seekers engage in these encounters matters deeply in their own legal and social futures, with important impacts on the judgments lawyers make. Likewise, the new ways in which "alien" residents articulate claims to belonging shape how Greeks themselves approach citizenship.

Notes on Form: Law and Tragedy

The ethnographic material I present in this book highlights law's dramatic and tragic qualities through the heuristic of the case. The "case" is a knowledge form common to multiple diagnostic sciences: law, medicine, psychoanalysis, and even social scientific research. Rather than drawing on the diagnostic use of the case, however, which seeks to examine and thus unveil the root[s] of a set of symptoms, I emphasize its dramatic potential. Llewellyn and Hoebel (1941) denote "trouble cases" as moments of "hitch, dispute, grievance, or trouble . . . that dramatize a 'norm' or 'conflict of norms' which may have been latent" (21). The usefulness of the "trouble case," for both participants and ethnographers, lies in how it "forces conscious attention, forces the defining of issues" (21), making normative structures and practices "present at hand" (Heidegger 1962). All the cases I explore in this manuscript are, in their own ways, troublesome to NGO workers, aid applicants, agents of the state, and policy makers (indeed, Greece itself could be framed as a "trouble case"). They demand active engagements from multiple participants who must produce judgments in the face of uncertainty, doubt, and "the ghost of the undecidable" (Derrida 1992: 24), entailing anxiety, difficult ethical work on all sides, and decisions that are in many ways impossible. Yet such cases also disrupt law's normative and regulatory properties: through "crises" in the fabric of law, legal and sociopolitical orders become open to redefinition and transformation. These are what Agamben (1998: 19) describes as "thresholds": liminal spaces, openings, between the "normal" situation and that of crisis, between the world that is and one that may (or may never) emerge.

At stake in this discussion of tragedy is the precious yet often troublesome gap between self and other, inside and outside, and the ways in which a political body may or may not find ways of recognizing otherness without domesticating it. Law has a tendency either to cast the other out or "reduce outsider to insider" (Douzinas and Warrington 1994: 223), often simultaneously. Indeed, the paradox of refuge is that laws of protection simultaneously incorporate and reinscribe alienage. Both rights frameworks and the practice of humanitarianism demand that claimants, adjudicators, and service providers do the impossible: render suffering visible, pasts accessible, and stories legible, even as suffering, like the past, always exceeds speech, narration, and visibility (Papailias 2004; Scarry 1985). Those who fail may be cast to the margins of the city or beyond. Yet beneath the formal veneers of rights discourse and humanitarian practice, there are elements that persistently exceed such domestication, which are not redemptive but are crucial to making lives livable and may even have revolutionary potential.

Tragedy, as a dramatic genre, entails an encounter with that which is at once self and other, inside and outside the body politic. The tragic hero is often taken to represent a vision of universal humanity, but as Butler (2000) highlights in her analysis of *Antigone*, there is much that marks the hero as a perversion of the social order (such as Antigone's entwinement in incestuous kinship ties, or in Orestes's case, a family prone to cannibalism and the murder of kin). The tragic hero is thus, in part, a "stranger," cast out of the polis or even condemned to death, a "dangerous person" (Panourgia 2009), through whom the body politic, as a normative order, is destabilized or even turned inside out. Pollution may follow him, the Furies at his heels, threatening to bring destruction and suffering to the city; or like Antigone, she may threaten to expose the social order itself as perverse by revealing the pollution that lies at the seat of sovereignty. It is no accident that these dangerous heroes are so often seekers of refuge: Oedipus invokes the laws of hospitality at Colonus; Orestes seeks protection at the living image of Athena; Antigone, perhaps, finds refuge in the tomb. Yet as Neni Panourgia (2009: 7) writes, this figure, in her very dangerousness, "transcends the polis; she becomes a part of it; she knows its inner workings, makes hiding places in its buildings, learns and produces a topography that is also a topology completely unimagined and unsuspected by the sovereign who suspects her."

The moment of judgment marks the intervention of human and divine power in attempting to reorganize and set to right the city and the cosmos (Douglas 1966; Malkki 1995a). Orestes is cast out by the laws of both humans and gods until he is finally brought to judgment. Meanwhile, Antigone, the willing victim (Butler 2000) of an unjust verdict, is removed to the space of the tomb even in life. There is an inherent violence to this form of intervention, and its penal character is unmistakable, yet it also has creative elements. Judgment entails no simple resolution, but rather, incites an opening into a possible (though often thwarted) transformation: of self and other, of both the hero and the city itself. The dramatic action of the trial, the judgment, and its aftermath brings the audience "in," an engaged participant (Nussbaum 2001 [1986]) in the suffering and struggle unfolding on the stage. Reason, here, is insufficient. Rather, tragedy engenders in the audience what Aristotle, following Plato, describes as *catharsis*: an encounter with suffering that catalyzes a cleansing of the self through the release of a spirit of excess (Lacan 1992). This point of crisis, then—the hero taken to judgment—presents an opening, a threshold, which does not erase the gap between self and other but deeply confounds it. The stranger is revealed as the hero who, in a way, she has always been: the beating heart of the polis. The Furies, with their fearful countenances, both persecuted and persecuting, make their way into the darkness beneath the city. Neither stranger nor citizen, neither actor nor audience, remains the same. This transformative potential of tragedy—an ineffable line of excess and flight—is at once the *pnevma* (spirit) of this book and the ghost that haunts it.

ACT I

Governance

For they will hunt you
Through all the length of the earth, as you stride onward,
Over the ground worn by your feet,
Over the seas, and then, over the island cities. . . .
Go to the city of Pallas Athena;
There clasp your arms around the ancient image,
And sit. In that place you will find judges.

—*The Eumenides*, 74–81

Chapter 1

European Moral Geographies

On January 21, 2011, well into the fallout from the Greek debt crisis, the European Court of Human Rights (ECHR) issued a judgment on *MSS v. Belgium and Greece*, a case brought by an Afghan asylum seeker, Mohamed Samir Samimi, against these two EU member states. According to the list of "facts" recorded in the court's decision, "MSS" was apprehended by Greek police after his initial crossing via sea to Lesbos, just a few kilometers of sea from the Turkish coast. There, his fingerprints were taken, and after a week he was released and issued an order to leave the country.[1] He "transitioned" through France to Belgium, where he applied for asylum; he never applied for asylum in Greece. Under the auspices of the 2003 Dublin II Regulation, however, asylum seekers are obliged to apply for protection in the country where they first enter European territory, and if apprehended elsewhere in the EU, they are subject to removal to the country of entry. Thus, when Belgian authorities discovered MSS's fingerprints registered in the Eurodac system, a trans-European database of biometric material, he was deported back to Greece, despite a number of attempts to contest his removal. Through a series of text messages to his lawyer in Belgium, he then documented in detail the squalid reception conditions he faced, the impossibility of finding housing and social support, his difficulty obtaining access to the asylum procedure, and his near expulsion *back* across the Turkish border by Greek authorities.[2]

The decision itself attests to the deeply creolized legal terrain that characterizes the case of just one asylum seeker. After this brief account of MSS movements in EU territory, the decision goes on to cite in detail "relevant" European and international law,[3] then turns to "Relevant Law and Practice" in both Greece and Belgium. The section on Greece cites not just formal law but also references reports issued by the UN High Commissioner for Refugees and various NGOs, which present the on-the-ground situation facing asylum seekers. The court ultimately indicts Greece for violating MSS's rights on two counts: for failing to guarantee access to the asylum procedure (in violation of Article 2 of the European Convention on Human Rights and Fundamental Freedoms guaranteeing the right to life), and for exposing MSS to cruel and degrading treatment (in violation of Article 3). Belgium, meanwhile, is indicted for not providing the claimant with a way to contest the potential threat to his life and freedom in Greece (in violation of Article 13, which guarantees an "effective remedy before a national authority" to challenge rights violations). In its structure and content, the decision emphasizes the international and supranational legislative contexts of MSS's case, yet in the end invokes member state obligations for upholding European rights-based legislation. Through its failure adequately to provide dignity and protection to MSS, Greece emerges as a kind of proxy for the challenges and failures entailed in safeguarding the rights of asylum seekers in the European Union.

I begin here with this ECHR decision, because it is emblematic of EU governance practices through which a particular EU member state, its government, and its citizens are held responsible for failures on a European scale. The EU relies on techniques of governance that keep unruly members states in line through legal, political, and—especially—moral forms of marginalization. The crisis of asylum in Greece—much like the current financial crisis—is not just a national predicament affecting a state on Europe's geopolitical and economic peripheries; it is also seen to undermine the EU's *moral* integrity as an area of "freedom, security, and justice." Such narratives of crisis in turn grant moral legitimacy to Greece's continued political, legal, and financial marginalization within Europe. The power of the ECHR decision lies perhaps even less in its material effects than in its articulation of a particular configuration of value on a European scale. Not only does the decision reassert the European commitment to safeguarding rights, but it also highlights how Greece deviates from and actively undermines these values.

In this chapter, I show that the very real shortcomings of the Greek asylum procedure must be understood within the broader context of European governance mechanisms, including legislative, policy, and advocacy trends; regional histories of displacement; and often more global forms of violence and inequality that have positioned Greece on the margins of Europe. I undertake my analysis through a kind of mapping, which underscores the relationship between EU moral logics of governance and a European spatial politics of marginality. When it comes to managing migration and asylum, Greece's moral and political marginality in Europe is inextricable from its position on Europe's land and sea borders. Concrete geographical and topographical factors play a crucial role in determining which member states become sites of crossing (Mitchell 1997), but these are reinforced and further complicated through EU legislation. Take, for instance, MSS's story, rendered in chronological brevity in the court's decision, which speaks to multiple scales of law, complex routes of migration, and various geopolitical and topographical boundaries, which intersect, collide, and are transgressed on Europe's borders. Likewise, the overlapping enforcement measures that characterize the border regime in Greece, and the various sites where they are enacted, invoke EU, regional, and national territorialities. Policies and practices aimed toward safeguarding the EU as an area of "freedom, security, and justice" interact with internal Greek policing and legislative practices and migrants' own routes of movement. The *krisi* of asylum in Greece reflects the entwinement of legal and moral geographies.

The MSS judgment implies that the Greek state's poor adherence to EU law at the level of individual asylum seekers undermines the EU as a territorial, legal, and moral entity. Recent ethnographic scholarship has shown how the formalities of legal processes reflect and reinstantiate notions of ethics and morality that operate simultaneously across multiple scales (Fassin and Rechtman 2010; Kelly 2011): individual, national, regional, transnational, global, and in this case, supranational. Such moral configurations are particularly powerful in the context of international human rights law, which, as Sassen (1996) has shown, can function to undermine, or even threaten, national sovereignties. Yet even in the EU, the success of international rights regimes depends on nation-states. In the domestic enactment of rights law, states find ways of simultaneously complying with and resisting such infringements on sovereignty, also through the regulation of moral and ethical life. For instance, Fassin and Rechtman's (2010) work on asylum in France shows how the moral dispositions that greet asylum seekers at the tribunal, suspicion in particular, reinvigorate the French state's restrictive approach toward offering protection as part of a broader, exclusionary, policy on immigration. Through the reinscription of rights in European Community law, the judgments that uphold them, and European instruments for safeguarding these values (in particular, the court), the moral power of rights becomes even more tightly wedded to supranational governing mechanisms which simultaneously reassert and challenge member state sovereignties.

Such forms of moral governance, and the tensions of sovereignty that they reflect, have long been endemic to the European management of immigration and asylum across more formal venues of law, zones of civil society advocacy, media accounts, and the multiple sites where such phenomena overlap. Arendt (1976 [1951]) shows how the post-World War I refugee crisis in Europe exposed a fundamental tension between international protection and the sovereignties of nation-states. In the supranational context, these dilemmas do not vanish but proliferate, particularly through the coupling of asylum processes to broader projects of EU migration management (Menz 2009). The EU is both a territorial polity with borders that must be regulated and a supranational zone formally devoted to freedom of movement, human rights, and humanitarian values. At the EU level, as the international obligation to offer protection has become entwined with the regulation and defense of European territory, a number of powerful tensions have emerged. These tensions are perhaps best exemplified in the twin, yet contradictory, EU policy goals of ensuring that Europe's borders are *both* "secure" and "humanitarian." Greece, as we have observed, is said to fail on both of these counts.

Given this set of tensions, EU asylum-related legislation is often deeply contradictory. The MSS decision betrays a juridical sleight of hand that invokes European sovereignty (and the EU's capacity to indict, monitor, and discipline individual member states) while simultaneously reasserting member state responsibilities. Through Dublin II, Mediterranean member states must—owing to accidents of geopolitics—shoulder a greater responsibility for maintaining EU borders in the name of collectively sharing the "burden" of protection. Such contradictions have their uses, however: EU governance can draw selectively on EU and member state sovereignties and responsibilities to engage the tensions embedded in the collective management of migration and asylum. Yet such techniques of governance further inscribe the morally marginal, even dangerous, qualities associated with member states like Greece.

Marginalities

Unlike a number of more longstanding migration destinations in Europe, Greece does not have recent colonial ties with the home countries of those now seeking protection within its borders. France, the United Kingdom, Belgium, the Netherlands, Spain, and even Italy, with its brief foray into colonial projects in East Africa, all negotiate complex colonial histories and their legacies through immigration (Gilroy 2004; Hall 1990; Ticktin 2011), as well as ongoing forms of intercultural and linguistic exchange (Chakrabarty 2000; Cooper and Stoler 1997). Greece, in contrast, underwent its own, deeply fraught experience of Ottoman imperialism (Kostopoulou 2009), the aftermath of which continues to shape Greece's relationship with Islam (Antoniou 2005, 2010; Triandafyllidou and Gropas 2009), its immediate neighbors, and the "East." Moreover, powerful symbolic and political tensions have long characterized Greece's relationship with the European west and north. During the Greek bid for independence from the Ottoman Empire in the early 1800s, Greece was transformed into a kind of "Ur-Europa" (Herzfeld 1982), largely thanks to northern European intellectuals who revivified and mythologized its ancient history. Yet having been an Ottoman territory for centuries, Greece was also subject to Orientalizing tendencies. Thus, even as ancient Greece was framed as the font of European civilization, Modern Greece has often been characterized—even by Greeks themselves—as backward, bastardized, and corrupted by the influences of the East. Such tensions have combined to grant the Greek nation state a particularly marginal relationship with the European core, which in turn has been repeatedly invoked to legitimate the ongoing involvement of outside interests in Greece.

Herzfeld (2002a: 901) coins the term "crypto-colonialism" to describe "the curious alchemy whereby certain countries, buffer zones between the colonized lands and those yet untamed, were compelled to acquire their political independence at the expense of massive economic dependence." This former territory of the Ottoman Empire has been subject to enormous outside economic and political involvement: first by the "philhellenes" of Britain, France, and Germany; later, by the warring powers of World War II; and finally, in the Cold War period, by the United States in its support of the Junta. With the twinning of geographical and political marginality embedded in crypto-colonialism, similar patterns are evident in Greece's contemporary relationship with the European north, despite the EU's formal commitment to transcending national and regional interests. Greece is now subject to intervention by EU governing bodies, individual EU member states, speculating investors, the IMF, and the World Bank. As the constantly unfolding news on the Greek financial crisis makes compellingly clear, "building Europe" (Shore 2000) has produced new systems of inclusion and exclusion and vast asymmetries of power between the European north and south. Through these ongoing crypto-colonial relationships, the contemporary Greek nation state acquires its status as a kind of political and moral "pariah" (19), an allegedly corrupt, undisciplined, and renegade member of the European Community that is transgressive and potentially dangerous.

In the debates surrounding the Greek asylum process, law and judgment work to invoke and reassert similar forms of marginalization. Just as the symbolic and political marginalization of Greece has been deeply grounded in its peripheral geographical position, the marginalizing effects of EU migration and asylum law are inextricable from Greece's location on Europe's borders. Étienne Balibar (2004: 5) suggests that patterns of inclusion/exclusion that have emerged as the EU was fashioned into being are most conspicuous at the borders. Likewise, the moral logics of European legislation and policy are embedded in a political geography concentrated primarily around the negotiation and management of external borders. Wallace (2000: 375) describes how the European continent has long been fraught with the tensions of managing "neighborness" through the regulation of borders, including both intra-European territorial zones and a variety of "near-abroads" by land and sea. With the shift in sovereignty from internal to external borders accompanying Europeanization, Greece—like other member states on Europe's Mediterranean coast—has become a crucial site where the boundaries of Europe are persistently transgressed and redrawn. Yet through the intensified management of European territorial borders, the marginality of these border states is asserted even more powerfully.

Doorsteps

It was only 8 a.m., but it was already hot. I had recently stepped off the plane from Athens for the June 21, 2008, World Refugee Day celebration in Mytilene, on the island of Lesbos. I was sitting at a portside café across from Stefan, a refugee advocate, drinking a much-needed coffee. Stefan is the primary brains, imagination, and labor behind one of the more influential asylum advocacy NGOs in northern Europe. In collaboration with Greek lawyers, he had recently published a report on sea deaths in the Greek Aegean, one of the more powerful critiques of Greek asylum and border management, which just a few years later was to be cited in the MSS decision. He was also in the process of establishing a border project in Mytilene, in collaboration with local service providers, to improve reception conditions for the many who arrive there—most often in small, leaky rubber boats.

A tall, broad-shouldered man with piercing eyes, Stefan chain-smoked as he answered my question about why he had chosen to begin an advocacy project in Greece. After citing his love of the Aegean and dramatically closing his eyes and gesturing at his surroundings, he said: "I *knew*. It was not an exact calculation, it was not a master plan, but it was clear that if someone wanted to do a successful project, it would be Greece." He went on, explaining that unlike Italy and Spain, which had more recently been in the spotlight, "everyone knew that Greece was a mess, but no one was talking about it."

Greece, of course, is no longer a place no one talks about. Until relatively recently, Italy and Spain had indeed dominated the limelight as border areas of pan-European concern, as Lampedusa and the Canary Islands generated powerful and contradictory images of sun, sea, destitute bodies, and sunbathers giving water to washed-up migrants. Italy, Spain, and also Malta (DeBono 2011), remain sites of concern, not just owing to the displacements of people affected through the 2011 "Arab Spring" and its aftermath; in October 2013, over 300 people were estimated dead when a boat sank off the coast of Lampedusa. Greece, however, has emerged as an increasingly problematic border country at the center of controversies over the security, humanitarianism, and solvency of Europe (see Green 2010). Since my meeting with Stefan at the edge of the Aegean, the EU has produced increasingly powerful apparatuses of migration management (Feldman 2011), both in the sea and in Evros, in response to the continued spike in crossings on the Greek borders. In 2010, following a request from the Greek government, Frontex, the EU's border management agency, deployed its first "RABITS" (Rapid Deployment Border Intervention Teams) to assist in deterring undocumented crossings along the Greek borders. On the face of it, Frontex signifies a powerful assertion of EU involvement in policing Greek borders, yet in practice it also bespeaks a more messy set of allegiances and sovereignties. Rather than staffing its own forces, so to speak, Frontex hires, retrains, and redeploys border guards from EU member countries; this also applies to the equipment and forms of transport employed in Frontex operations, which often bear the emblems of other European states.[4] The former Papandreou government also initiated a plan to build a fence along the Evros border with EU funding; on a visit to Turkey in January 2011 to discuss the border fence, minister of citizen protection Christos Papoutsis, explicitly referenced the U.S./Mexico border as a model.

Regional and national legislation also have an important role in shaping the Greek border context. A readmission agreement with Turkey (signed in 2001) has encouraged ad hoc expulsions, where migrants are often simply pushed back across the border without being returned to their home countries; this was the danger MSS faced on his return to Greece. The legality of this agreement is questionable, as the deportees include, almost always, "mixed flows" of migrants and asylum seekers (see Feldman 2012), and neither side does an effective job of identifying those wishing to apply for asylum.[5] Greece is obliged under both international and EU law to hear the claims of applicants for protection. However, as reported by many asylum seekers and some local inhabitants in border regions, during the time I was in the field the Greek police allegedly undertook widespread deportations of "mixed" groups of migrants and asylum seekers to Turkey.[6] For many deportees, however, such practices encourage new strategies of crossing: some enter Europe via new routes and others attempt successive crossings at the Greek borders. I met many during my fieldwork who underwent multiple entries and expulsions.

Borders are not just territorial, however; they are also manifested and negotiated in the domain of law, which produces its own spatial politics and geographies (see Coutin and Yngvesson 2006; Coutin 2007; Darian-Smith 1999, 2007; Rouse 1991; Volpp 2012; Zilberg 2011). Legalization processes are most often initiated in urban centers, primarily Athens and Thessaloniki, making entry into the *legal* territory of Greece often dependent on further internal movement and travel. Yet access to legalization processes—whether through the asylum procedure or through routes of economic migration—is itself circumscribed by aggressive forms of internal policing, which have only increased with the sociopolitical instabilities accompanying the Greek financial difficulties (Xenakis and Cheliotis 2012; Cheliotis 2013 in process). In Chapter 2, I highlight the police violence that, during the period of my research, impinged on access to asylum through an account of activities at "Allodhapon," the Athens "Aliens Police," at that time in charge of examining most first-instance asylum applications. The fact that the threshold of the asylum procedure was, quite literally, the doorstep of a tightly and often violently guarded police compound incited many would-be applicants to remain in spaces of legal limbo (Cabot 2012) or "nonexistence" (Coutin 2000), without the protection offered by papers. Increasingly powerful enforcement measures throughout the Athens city center target individuals through a clear reliance on racial profiling. In areas of the city known to have heavy foreign populations (Omonia Square and its environs, Attiki, and Exarcheia), it is common to find a gun-toting MAT (SWAT) officer stationed on street corners, while less visibly armed patrols accost persons of color and demand their papers. In the summer of 2009, for instance, I found a rather gregarious group of police playing cards outside an unlicensed Sudanese restaurant that asylum seekers, undocumented migrants, and smugglers alike were known to frequent. In response to this increasing militarization of the Athens city center, many asylum seekers and migrants look for work and refuge in the countryside (Lawrence 2007; Verinis 2011) and in the islands, even—interestingly—in border regions (Cabot and Lenz 2012), where policing is focused more on safeguarding the border from without than targeting threats from within. The asylum procedure is a particularly charged element of the Greek border scenario. The question of asylum inflects broader Greek and European anxieties over responses to immigration, humanitarianism, security, and Greece's capacities to handle (or not) the movements across its borders.

Asylum in Greece

Despite its symbolic and legal significance, the MSS decision only emerged a number of years after the Greek asylum process began to raise red flags for European and international advocacy communities. It is difficult to account fully for the exclusionary and sluggish qualities of the Greek asylum system. With the bureaucratic inefficiencies that have plagued the Greek process (particularly evident in the overwhelming backlog of cases), rejections of asylum cases have also, perhaps inadvertently, provided ways of streamlining through "buck passing" via appeals and encouraging attrition among applicants. Though the appeals process was suspended between 2009 and 2010, during most of my research for this book the asylum process entailed two "instances" or *vathmi* (levels [βαθμοί]).[7] Claimants lodged first-instance applications at a central police station (in most cases, in Athens, though also in Thessaloniki) and underwent asylum interviews there. Rejected cases could then be appealed to the second instance, involving a more detailed hearing in front of an advisory committee at the Ministry. Second-instance rejections could only be contested through an application to the Simvoulio tis Epikratias (Council of State [Συμβούλιο της Επικρατείας]), the highest court of administrative law in Greece, which ruled not on the substance of the asylum case but on the procedural integrity of the asylum hearing.[8]

The vast majority of cases were rejected at first instance, almost as a matter of routine. The appeals process, which would usually take months or even years, entailed a high level of attrition: some asylum seekers left Greece for elsewhere in the EU, while others may never have received notifications of their hearings; even then, there were often problems of language and literacy. The second-instance examination committees consisted of six individuals: a chairperson of the committee, who was from the Legal Council of the State (Nomiko Simvoulio tou Ktratous [Νομικό Συμβούλιο του Κράτους]); one representative from the Aliens Department (Dhiefthinsi Allodhapon [Διεύθηνση Αλλοδαπών]) of the Ministry of Public Order; two representatives from the Ministry of Foreign Affairs; one from the UNHCR; and one from the Athens Bar Association. While a greater number of positive decisions were issued at second instance, overall rejection rates remained high. During my primary field research, when the asylum process corresponded to that outlined in Presidential Decree 61/1999, the opinions issued by the committee were advisory, not decisive. Each member would make a recommendation, but final plenary power was accorded to the minister; in a number of cases I read rejections that were issued despite positive recommendations by the majority of the appeals committee. However, ministerial decisions alone do not account for the high number of rejections. Committee recommendations were, by in large, stringent, reflecting also an entrenched culture of suspicion, doubt, and mistrust toward asylum seekers (Daniel and Knudson 1995; Fassin and Rechtman 2010). Following the various changes to the asylum law instantiated in 2008, 2009, and 2010, committee decisions became binding (see Presidential Decrees 90/2008, 81/2009, and 144/2010).

For refugee-related NGOs in Greece and elsewhere in the EU, the problems in the Greek asylum process have also made it a powerful advocacy tool. In language that invoked, almost uncannily, the logics of moral governance I have been outlining here, Stefan laughed: "We use and abuse Greece." He explained that by targeting the problems evident in Greece, asylum advocates can encourage broader changes in Europe, with more widespread effects. In contrast to the MSS judgment, which bears the disciplined language appropriate to a formal court decision, many NGO and media reports have characterized Greece as backward and disorganized, with corrupt, arcane bureaucracies and violent police. As a result of pan-European advocacy efforts, culminating in the MSS judgment, EU member states have suspended the return of asylum seekers to Greece demanded by the Dublin II Regulation. Partly in response to this growing culture of critique led by Greek and

European NGOs (as well as the, then pending, MSS decision), a presidential decree issued in 2010 (114/2010) established a variety of measures meant to make the Greek asylum procedure more efficient and transparent. In January 2011, the Greek government produced a new asylum law (law 3907/2011), which has initiated the process of radically revamping the asylum procedure. Though the law is currently still in the process of implementation, the changes taking place include the formation of a new, semi-independent authority for the processing of asylum claims (based in Athens) and regional offices for the acceptance of applications and the reception of claimants (currently operating in Alexandroupoli, Thessaloniki, and Oresteiada). The new asylum authority began processing applications as of June 2013.[9]

However well intended, successful, accurate, or inaccurate, the many critiques of Greece's "crisis" of asylum—many of which, significantly, come from outside Greece—also reinscribe Greece's position on the margins of Europe and the power asymmetries embedded in that relationship. The conservative Karamanlis government did not do much to shake this image, blaming a lack of infrastructure, organization, capital, and the intrinsic pressures of its geographical position for Greece's difficulty in managing its borders. Later, in the midst of the financial crisis, Papandreou advocated for increased transparency and oversight in Greece's asylum process, called for EU assistance in tightening its border enforcement regime, and promised a Greek political will to meet its responsibilities as an EU member state. Both diplomatic tactics, however, reified Greece's marginality, framing it as an impediment to rectifying the problems of the asylum process.

In addition to their marginalizing effects, the recent characterizations of the Greek asylum procedure as an area of crisis run the risk of mistaking immigration and refugees as entirely new phenomena in Greece. Despite new patterns of displacement and migration, Greece has long been entangled in Balkan, Mediterranean, and more global mobilities. Greece is known primarily as a country of emigration, with large diasporic communities throughout the U.S. (Laliotou 2004), Europe, and Australia, as well as other perhaps less obvious locations such as Sudan, Egypt, Denmark (Christou 2009), and Ethiopia. Greece has also functioned for years as a migration destination, with mass arrivals from the former Soviet bloc and the Middle East and Africa in the late eighties and early nineties. Greece only began offering protection to refugees within its own territory in 1991, with the issuance of Presidential Decree 1975/1991,[10] which formally established a foundational legal framework for multiple forms of migration to Greece, but it engaged in resettlement projects before that. In addition to large communities of Albanian migrants, there are also significant, and relatively established, communities of first- and second-generation migrants from countries such as Poland, Ukraine, Russia, Georgia, Bulgaria, Eritrea (Petronati 2000), Romania, and the Philippines.

The current terrain of refugee protection in Greece is also overlaid upon Greece's involvement in forced population movements in the early and mid-twentieth centuries. The Treaty of Lausanne and the 1923 "population exchange" following the dissolution of the Ottoman Empire, in which some two million ethnic Greeks and Turks were (in many cases, forcibly) relocated to their ancestral homelands as refugees, has been characterized as one of the first implementations of Modern European refugee law. In what is often denoted as the "Greek Catastrophe," ethnic Greeks were displaced from Asia Minor, particularly from areas near the eastern Aegean and Black Sea coasts, including Constantinople and Smyrna—the *khamenes* patridhes [χάμενες πατρίδες]) (lost homelands) (see Hirschon 2003, 1998; Papailias 2004). This territory was once the center of the Greco-Byzantine Empire, but long after it came under Ottoman, then Turkish, rule, it remained central to the imagined, irredentist vision of the Modern Greek nation state. While Lausanne initiated the first and perhaps most violent of these refugee movements, it was followed by various waves of "return" migrations of Black Sea Greeks from the former Soviet bloc (Ascherson 1995; Tsimouris 2001, 2007; Voutira 2003) and, just as controversially, a series of expulsions and eventual repatriations following the Greek Civil War (see Danforth and van Boeschoten 2011). These diverse groups of refugees, across disparate experiences of displacement and return, often found themselves at the social and economic margins of the Greek national body, thus challenging dominant notions of Greek identity (Christou 2006; Hirschon 1998; Karakasidou 1997). The figure of the "refugee" (*prosfighas* [πρόσφυγας]) has thus come to hold powerful and fraught connotations that are eminently and specifically Greek (Cowan 2008; Voutira 2003). Yet those now seeking refuge in Greece are perhaps even more marginalized, juxtaposed against the increasingly longstanding and accepted presence of refugees who lay claim to Greek heritage.

Since 2010 there have, according to many of my long-term interlocutors, been significant increases in efficiency and recognition rates at all stages of the procedure, thanks largely to personnel and procedural shifts. The Presidential Decree of 2010 (114/2010) introduced more systematic trainings for police officers examining asylum cases, as well as the possibility for representatives from the UNHCR or collaborating NGOs to take an advisory role in first instance decisions. Experts in refugee law were appointed to second-instance committees meant to deal with the backlog of cases, which led to a notable increase in positive decisions. Until recently (June 2013), new applications still fell under the purview of the Ministry of Public Order and Citizen Protection and, thus, the police, though this is changing, as the asylum authority in Athens recently opened its doors. The outcomes of the new asylum process are still to be seen. A former ARS lawyer, who now assists decision makers at the new asylum authority, highlighted that she was deeply impressed by the quality of the employees and of the work that they were doing. However, another former ARS lawyer expressed concern that these decision makers' lack of experience, and lack of familiarity with the problems embedded in the refugee status determination procedure, would translate to an overly stringent approach.

Despite skepticism about the new process among advocates, bureaucrats, and asylum seekers alike, I have also noticed a growing discourse among adjudicators and advocates regarding positive change, cooperation, and increased transparency. One UNHCR representative told me that the asylum process is "something in Greece that is actually improving," though she lamented that with the financial crisis, this does not hold much significance among a wider public. In 2011, I spoke with police and UNHCR representatives alike who praised a more structured interview process at first instance, a greater sense of competency and efficiency among adjudicators, and more effective collaborations between the Ministry, the UNHCR, and civil society organizations. I also interviewed one of the workers who assisted in the training of police adjudicators, and he underscored that a core element of his approach had been to "treat all parties with respect." He added that after the first day of training he had been thanked by a number of police officers, who explained that they had never received any formal education about asylum-related matters. Despite the evident disciplinary qualities and power asymmetries embedded in such rights-based trainings (Babül 2012), these reform measures seem to have provided substantive relief for those engaged in adjudication processes. The critiques and recent reforms surrounding the "crisis" of asylum are ultimately two-edged, vehicles for change as well as new forms of marginality.

Advocacy and the EU

As the oldest and largest asylum-related NGO in Greece, the Athens Refugee Service has participated in multiple phases of the establishment of the Greek asylum system and has witnessed the changing trends and demographics of asylum applications. This history can be traced through a cursory glance at old files in the storage room on the organization's sixth floor. Files from the early 1990s attest to the many applicants from the then just-dissolved, former Soviet bloc: most were from Poland and Albania, interspersed with applicants from Iraq, Iran, Turkey (primarily Kurds), Somalia, Syria, and Palestine. During the period of my fieldwork, there were few applicants from Eastern Europe and the Balkans, but large numbers from the Middle East and Africa, and many more Iraqis and Afghans. There were also many from Southeast Asia, in particular Pakistan and Bangladesh, who in 2006 accounted for approximately 50 percent of asylum applications.

The ARS was born as a collaborator of the UNHCR. This formal affiliation has since waned, but its traces continue to structure many elements of the ARS. These include the importance of English in many of the official forms and documents, and the interview procedures through which client eligibility is determined, modeled explicitly on UNHCR refugee status determination procedures (discussed in detail in Chapters 3 and 4). Before the 1991 establishment of a nationalized process for accepting refugees, the UNHCR adjudicated asylum applications in Greece, resettling those it recognized as refugees. The ARS assisted applicants with their claims, providing legal support and advice. As the Greek state itself began to process applications, the ARS maintained its role of providing legal support for asylum seekers. Now there is a social service department at the ARS and an entire floor devoted to educational materials, particularly for children. Yet with its strong tradition of providing legal support and casework, the ARS legal service (*nomiki* ipiresia [νομική υπηρεσία]) fills an important gap in the panorama of legal assistance available to asylum seekers.

While the ARS is devoted primarily to providing support for individual clients, it also engages in what might be called policy advocacy. It is a member of trans-European networks of asylum advocacy NGOs, and among its stated goals, it strives to share experience and know-how for the configuration of better policy internationally. The ARS has also historically tried to maintain a relatively cooperative relationship not just with the UNHCR but with the agencies of the Greek state that come into contact with asylum seekers (the Ministry of Public Order and Citizen Protection, the Athens police, and police in border areas). ARS workers have explained to me that this more cordial relationship with state agencies is necessary for furthering the cases they take on, but it can also translate directly to an engagement in policy making and implementation. Recently, ARS workers gave their input in the formation of the new asylum system, and former staff members have taking on important positions as overseers and asylum adjudicators, working for both the UNHCR and agencies of the state. This close entwinement of the ARS with more governmental roles, particularly through the social networks of current and former workers, is aptly illustrated through the fieldwork that I conducted in 2011 in the asylum department of the Athens police. I acquired access largely through the assistance of former ARS workers, who were employed by the UNHCR to provide advisory opinions at first-instance adjudications. Yet while formally positioned as advisors, this meant that they were ostensibly working alongside the police. My friends and acquaintances in these positions, most from NGO backgrounds, spoke of the new insight this gave into both the asylum process and the psyches of their former "enemies," so to speak (the police adjudicators). Yet as one of them explained, this "intimacy" can also be troubling, bespeaking a potential conflation of police, NGO, and international human rights interests through the socialities of everyday practice. This ambivalent relationship between NGO and state responsibilities appears throughout this book as a fundamental dilemma of work and life at the ARS.

In the past, I have heard Greek activists and members of migrant and refugee community groups in Athens describe the ARS as somewhat conservative, explicitly referencing the close relationship between the ARS and the state. Some advocates from other European NGOs described the ARS to me as not vocal, active, or activist enough. One advocate from northern Europe explained that he sometimes finds it hard to work with members of the ARS: "They have all of the cases, they know everything," but, he lamented, "they don't write about it." However, as the asylum process has become an object of active reform, the ARS has also become increasingly visible and vocal, collaborating with other Greek and European organizations in exposing and critiquing practices that continue to be problematic, such as the detention of children and poor reception conditions. With the increased incidences of race-related violence that have accompanied the financial crisis, which I address in Chapters 6 and 7, the ARS has also become more active in antiracism activities and actions.

Some ARS workers, however, have explained that they simply have too many cases to engage deeply in the more political work necessary for changing policy, which is such an important goal for many asylum related NGOs elsewhere in Europe. During an evening gathering at a 2008 NGO conference in Brussels, I asked Nikos, an ARS delegate, how he felt about the policy focus of many of the other NGOs and if he thought the ARS was engaged in "advocacy," which had been a buzzword at the conference. He paused for a minute as he thought, then answered rhetorically: "What is 'advocacy'? I don't think we do 'advocacy'" (Τι είναι advocacy [Δεν νομίζω ότι κάνουμε advocacy]).[11] As one of the more experienced lawyers, with fluent knowledge of English and French, Nikos often represented the ARS at such meetings, collaborating with other NGOs and the UNHCR to lobby government representatives in Greece and elsewhere in Europe. In his own commentary, however, he adamantly resisted the project of policy advocacy, despite his evident engagement in this area. Certainly, with the increasing involvement of the NGO sector in the current reform of the Greek asylum system, such attitudes may be changing. Yet Nikos's response attests to the central, even entrenched, role of individual casework at the ARS over and against policy advocacy.

At this same Brussels conference, a Dutch advocate, trained as a lawyer, commented astutely on the distinction between casework and policy advocacy: "There are two kinds of workers [in asylum-related NGOs] and they operate in two different time zones. You have policy advocates—lobbyists, but we don't use that word—who are always focused on the future, who are always trying to change policy. Then you have legal advisors, who are focused on the present, the way the law is now. And it is really hard for these to combine." Such differences between ARS workers and many of their European counterparts reflect fundamentally differing institutional ethics, varying individual approaches toward law and labor, as well as the specific *habitus* (Bourdieu 1977) in which this labor unfolds—the anxieties, passions, pressures, and routines that shape workers' everyday lives.

These disconnects can, however, also reproduce familiar patterns of marginalization. A European NGO conference was held in Greece (Delphi) in May 2007, marking the new centrality of Greece in pan-European asylum advocacy projects, I heard numerous delegates comment on the closed, disorganized nature of the ARS and how difficult they were to work with. "They are just different," explained one delegate; another commented that in a role-play meant to illustrate the distinctions between state and NGO interests, ARS staff seemed to have confused the two. Such comments echo the *moral* critiques often lodged at Greece on a European scale, depicting the ARS as backward, even alien, in cahoots (though perhaps unknowingly) with the very corrupt state it "should" be trying to challenge.

Despite its own marginalizing tendencies, however, the MSS decision itself speaks to the surprisingly effective, hybridized advocacy projects that can sometimes emerge across such differences of approach and power and, in particular, the merging of casework with lobbying efforts. The story told in the MSS decision is uncannily reminiscent of the accounts of numerous asylum seekers with whom I spoke during my ethnographic research at the ARS, some of whom appear in this book. Such stories accumulated both in my notes and in the file cabinets of the ARS, as aid candidates chronicled their entries into the EU/Greece and their (at times successful, but often unsuccessful) attempts to travel to other European member states. Many also spoke of their expulsions back to Greece, a country where most claimed never to have intended to stay. ARS lawyers rarely challenged the EU and Greek legislative frameworks that made such stories possible. Rather, lawyers focused on the myriad procedural tangles in each client's encounter with the Greek asylum system, whether this involved renewing a client's identity card, lodging an asylum application, preparing for an asylum hearing, writing an appeal, getting someone out of detention, or reorienting "Dublin Returnees."

MSS, however, was in touch with a savvy, highly motivated lawyer in Belgium, Zouhaier Chihaoui. Through contact initiated with the court even before MSS's deportation to Greece, he and his lawyer were able to formulate an effective critique not just of Greece's asylum procedure but also of EU legislation, in particular, the Dublin II Regulation. The decision also invokes various reports on asylum in Greece issued by EU governing bodies and NGOs (including both Stefan's NGO and the ARS), as well as the opinions of experts that included former and current ARS workers. However obliquely, the decision served partially as a vehicle of collaboration, which drew, in a patchwork way, on a variety of NGO, governmental, and individual voices to legitimate the judgment. In this sense, the decision also enabled those caseworkers at the ARS to bring their specific, practice-oriented knowledge to a European public. The decision attests not just to the power of the human rights court to influence asylum policy at both supranational and member state levels (Joppke 1998), but also to the important role of NGO collaborations in managing asylum in the EU (Menz 2009:5). The capacity of NGOs (whether case based, lobbying focused, or both) to affect the implementation of law and policy is easy to discount, owing to what Menz has described as their unstable institutional characteristics and "feeble or non-existent links" with government ministries. However, through the very looseness of the networks that they comprise, NGOs often have a surprising—and powerful—flexibility. Moreover, as we see at the ARS, links to government bodies, while often informal, are not always so feeble. European asylum-related NGOs of all stripes take part in both ad hoc and more long-term collaborations with each other across member states and often engage directly in working with both national and supranational governance bodies. Such collaborations, however, are uneasy and uneven (Tsing 2005), and rarely undermine or contest power asymmetries. Rather, *advocacy* itself unfolds through and often reproduces the multiple forms of marginality constitutive of European governance and geopolitics.

Conclusions

EU and international discourses around the problem of asylum in Greece highlight Greece's legal, bureaucratic, and moral failures in managing its borders in ways that fulfill EU prerogatives of security and humanitarianism. Yet such logics simultaneously elide and further perpetuate long-standing forms of marginality and asymmetry endemic to EU governance techniques. These moral geographies are instantiated across multiple scales of governance: national, regional, supranational, and international, and in various governmental venues, including legislative bodies and the courts. EU advocacy projects, themselves interlocking with more formal venues of governance, also reproduce these marginalizing tendencies, though often with surprisingly productive effects. The coupling of moral and geopolitical marginality in the management of EU borders is, in some ways, peculiar to the European context, but may also highlight the predicaments of border states more broadly (such as, for instance, in the case of Arizona). This is not to deny the many problems that have plagued the Greek asylum process; indeed, this book, in many respects, is a chronicle of these problems. I want to highlight at the outset of my analysis, however, that such failures are built into the framework of EU border management regimes: border states remain surrogates for systemic and structural problems, and meanwhile "crisis" persists on a European scale.

Chapter 2

Documenting Legal Limbo

Athens "Aliens Police," July 2009: Armed officers guard the entrance to the compound, a monumental building on a shade-less, fenced, concrete lot. Lawyers and social workers who visit the station regularly are waved through the gates with a smile and a bit of banter, but people with unknown faces must show their papers and explain their business. Those who have appointments at one of the departments, and those accompanied by a lawyer, are usually granted entry. But those who wish to make asylum applications must wait, among the long lines of others waiting, in enormous crowds that cluster in the streets behind the building, invisible to those entering through the main gateway. Presumably owing to the tight surveillance at the external gates, the doors to the building itself are largely free of controls. An x-ray screening system sits to the side of the entrance, dormant and unused, and no one monitors entries and exits—not even the sleeping stray dogs who cool themselves just inside the doorway in the summer heat. Haphazardly arranged photos of Greek tourist attractions, in dusty frames, decorate the walls of the main hall: Meteora, the Olympic complex, a charming island harbor. This high-ceilinged room is a space that people pass through on their ways to various offices and departments, but directly visible to the right as one enters is the crowded waiting area for those awaiting asylum interviews. There, having acquired an appointment to enter the building—after untold hours and even days of waiting in the lines outside—applicants must again wait until asylum officers and interpreters are available to interview them and process their applications.

At the far end of the waiting area is a door marked "interview room," and directly above the sign is a framed reproduction of an El Greco

> painting: against a deep blue stormy sky, a ghostly-pale woman looks to the heavens, her eyes rolling up in an expression that is difficult to interpret. I puzzle over this painting with Mariela and Gina, two young social workers who assist women who have been detained. When I suggest that the subject of the painting looks as though she is in pain, Mariela imitates the woman's rolling eyes and laughs that her expression mimics the boredom of those waiting. We agree that both boredom and pain are appropriate to the atmosphere of the Asylum Division at Allodhapon.

The Aliens and Immigration Directorate of Athens and the Attika Prefecture, on the Boulevard of Petrou Ralli on the outskirts of central Athens, is most often referred to simply as "Allodhapon" [Αλλοδαπών] (of/for aliens) or "Petrou Ralli" by asylum seekers and NGO workers. Allodhapon houses a detention center for undocumented migrants, but during the research for this book it was also the police station with the largest number of officers qualified to examine asylum cases. New applicants filed asylum claims at Allodhapon and police presented them with "pink cards," the identity documents to which asylum seekers were entitled as long as their claims remained in limbo.[1] Allodhapon was thus a central apparatus in the bureaucratic machinery of asylum in Greece; it was also the place where new applicants came face-to-face with the regulatory authority of the state through encounters with the police.

In this chapter I approach the *roz karta* [ρόζ κάρτα] (pink card) as an entry point into the multiple forms of limbo that characterize asylum seeking in Greece. I follow the pink card's "career" (Brenneis 2007) or life from its bureaucratic production at Allodhapon, through its circulation in the talk and everyday survival practices of asylum seekers, to its final disappearance at the end of the asylum process. Throughout, I consider how the document also acquired various "lives"—diverse meanings and uses—through the engagements of police, bureaucrats, and asylum seekers. Finally, I consider how the document as a thing-in-itself had an important role in governing both persons and regulatory technologies, and how its materiality enabled and foreclosed various legal, political, and social futures. The many lives of this document highlight the indeterminate relationship between bureaucracy, governance, and subjectivity in the assignment of limbo status.

The Governance of "Things"

Not unlike the U.S. "green card," the denotation of the pink card through its color was overtly straightforward and yet appropriate. Its pinkness first announced its presence, but you might also have noticed its fragility or makeshift quality. Some cards were wrinkled and torn at the edges; others had been laminated, covered with protective tape, or inserted in plastic sleeves. Cards displayed a photograph of the bearer and the written marks of rushed hands in blue, black, and red inks. Some asylum seekers kept their pink cards casually in their back pockets; others took them gingerly out of wallets or folders, where they had been carefully placed among other documents. Asylum applicants were required to have this document with them at all times, in the event that police stopped them and ask for *khartia* [χαρτιά] (papers), or *taftotita* [ταυτότητα] (identification). But unlike passports or credit cards, pink cards were not made to last. The traces of travels, labors, and bureaucracies were rendered tactile on this paper through smudges of dirt and moisture, in creases and folds and crinkled edges. Newly minted cards were sturdier and brighter, while those that had withstood multiple renewals were often wilted like fading roses, washed out through everyday handling by the bearer, police, and lawyers.

In this chapter, I show that through its association with the ambiguities of limbo, this document served to make asylum seekers illegible to both the state and themselves. Recent ethnographic scholarship has shown that "governmentality" (Foucault 2009 [2004]) and subjectivity are mutually and dialogically constituted (Coutin 2000; Coutin and Yngvesson 2006; Fassin and Rechtman 2010; Ong 1999). Despite the fluid interplay between governance and subject formation, however, documents are most often characterized as regulatory technologies that render both citizens and aliens visible or legible to state power (Scott 1998; see also Cohn 1987; Comaroff and Comaroff 1991; Dirks 2001; Mamdani 1996; Torpey 2000). The passport, for instance, brings citizens into the state's "embrace" (Torpey 2000) with accompanying rights and obligations. Legally present aliens may be marked as such through residence permits or visas, which inscribe a bureaucratic visibility that entails certain benefits as well as exclusions (Malkki 1995a). Those who are undocumented may be "non-existent" within the legal body of the nation-state (Coutin 2000) yet hypervisible (and vulnerable) to the state's regulatory gaze (Feldman 2011). While documents are, indeed, deeply enmeshed in these politics of legibility and visibility, the effects of such regulatory projects are unpredictable. I show that the pink card, as a technology of regulation, also facilitated highly variable reconfigurations of regulatory activities, as police, bureaucrats, and asylum seekers engaged with and made use of the document.

I also suggest that these many indeterminacies of documenting limbo in Greece expose holes integral to the process of governance itself. Foucault (1991: 93) characterizes the "art of governance" as "the right manner of disposing things so as to lead to an end which is 'convenient' to each of the things to be governed." Describing "things" as "men in their relations, their links" (93), he asserts that governance has multiple teleologies: "a plurality of specific aims . . . a whole series of specific finalities, then, which become the objective of government as such" (95). Foucault suggests that this plurality of relationships and "things," which elsewhere he defines as a *dispositif* (apparatus) (1980 [1977]), has gradually become incorporated into the political formation of the state and its "downward" (1991: 91) mechanisms of regulation. By considering how the pink card figured in a particular project of governance, and the nexus of relationships that in turn "governed" the document, I highlight multidirectional, indeterminate forms of governance that unfold within and alongside the regulatory work of the state.

Origin Stories

> The man tells me he was apprehended in Samos, when he came from Turkey in a small boat, and he was detained for three months. A UNHCR committee came a few times—people with lots of different nationalities. A lawyer also visited a few times . . . and asked if he had any particular requests or demands, and a guy from Algeria translated.
>
> I ask if he applied for asylum there.
>
> He answers that the lawyer had asked if anyone wanted to apply for asylum in Greece. But he did not understand what asylum was. Five men from Africa said they wanted to apply for asylum and they were taken away, but something must have gone wrong, because they were returned, and remained all together. When he was released he was given a deportation letter that was good for 30 days. He came to Athens. A lawyer helped him get "a paper valid for one month," and he paid 50 euros. Four days after the expiration of his deportation order, he was stopped by the police and detained again for three

months. He was then released with another deportation order. When he was released people he knew told him that he must go to "Allodhapon" to get a pink card.

How did he get the pink card, I ask.

He went to a private office near "Allodhapon" which helped him fill in the application. He waited in the queue. A translator asked him his name, and why he came to Greece. He explained that he came to find a job. They took his fingerprints. He got another appointment, and he went to collect his pink card. When the first card expired, he went to renew it, and they took it and gave him this paper (he shows me a rejection of his asylum claim). At that point he came to the ARS, where they helped him file an appeal, and he got his pink card back. (Cabot fieldnotes, March 7, 2008)

On a routine morning at the ARS, I met with a Syrian client, a middle-aged, wiry man with a trim gray mustache, whose direct delivery style sparked the interpreter, Omar, to describe him as a "very matter of fact man," which is evident in the no-frills summary of our meeting reproduced in my fieldnotes. (This was, of course, a few years before the refugee crisis in Syria incited in 2011.) Despite the significant time he had spent in detention, he recounted his experiences succinctly but in detail, and with a face seemingly clear of emotion. He had entered Greece at an Aegean island border, Samos, but he had received a pink card only many months later, when he came to Athens. His account underscores the circuitous, far-flung, and often shrouded bureaucratic web in which the pink card was entangled.

This loosely articulated web of bureaucracy and policing procedures is, in turn, enmeshed in broader maps of this man's movements in Greece, encompassing border and transit sites, detention facilities, and police stations. He acquired a pink card not upon his initial entry, but after multiple detentions, and after he had received a number of different documents. In his account, these bureaucratic processes are often obscured or mediated by the corollary presence of other state and nonstate actors: the "guy from Algeria," the lawyer on Samos, the lawyer in Athens, the "private office" near the police (also very likely a lawyer or notary), the ARS, and the police interpreter. The pink card is similarly mysterious and unpredictable: once he acquired the document, he did not retain it, but it was taken away, and he needed a lawyer's help to reclaim it.

The asylum application, the structuring event of the asylum process within the host country, implies intentionality and active diligence on the part of applicants. While the events that drive persons to flee, cross borders, and seek protection from persecution are framed in asylum legislation as forms of compulsion, one must, nonetheless, request asylum. The asylum claim thus has a strongly directional, intentional quality, and the pink card, as a documentation of this claim, implied specific pathways of law and bureaucracy, with predictable patterns of connection. Yet when I first started tracking the lives of the pink card through the accounts of asylum seekers, I had incredible difficulty identifying its trajectories. The origins of the document—how someone actually acquired it—were particularly confusing. I met many who spoke of acquiring the pink card only through active and extensive effort, but others seemed to have become asylum seekers almost accidentally, receiving a pink card without asking explicitly for asylum. "Asylum" does not play a significant role in this man's account, but rather, I myself asked him if he tried to apply for asylum on Samos, thus introducing the category into our conversation. He even went on to clarify that he did not know what asylum meant. When he finally acquired a pink card, it was not because he "applied for asylum," but because his acquaintances told him he needed a "pink card."

During the period of my primary fieldwork, asylum seekers could officially make asylum applications at any police authority at the border or within Greek territory, whether they had entered with or without documents. Further, police were formally obligated to accept asylum claims, regardless of the apparent credibility of the case, and issue pink cards upon receipt of the application. As we see in this man's account, however, the procedure rarely unfolded with such openness, and in fact, efforts to make an asylum application did not necessarily entail acquisition of a pink card. Only police officers trained to hear and examine asylum claims could issue pink cards, the vast majority stationed at Allodhapon in Athens. This meant that border sites were rarely locations where a pink card could be obtained, even though they are prime sites for asylum requests. To lodge an asylum claim on the border, a lawyer most often needed to intervene, as in the man's account of the five Africans on Samos; and even if one succeeded in making an asylum claim at the border, it was often accepted but not examined, owing again to a lack of competent officers.[2] This often necessitated that the applicant go to the central police station in Athens to complete the process. Just as one could acquire a pink card without actively asking for asylum, an active attempt to request asylum often did not result in the acquisition of a pink card.

Analytically, the card cannot be easily located in zones of legality or illegality, but rather, moves unpredictably through the shifting spectrum or "continuum" between illegal and legal status and practice (Calavita 2005; Cohen 1991; Coutin 2000). This Syrian asylum seeker repeatedly traveled in and out of partial il/legality, always positioned precariously in sites of limbo contingent on documents that he might, or might not, possess for long. In particular, his two deportation orders highlight the intimate entwinement of legality and illegality in the culture of documentation surrounding migration and asylum in Greece. Stapled to a memo that included the individual's photograph, name, and country of origin, the deportation order was often the very first document people received when they entered Greece and were released from detention. Issued to those who had entered Greece in a "clandestine" manner or whose legal permission to stay had expired or been revoked, deportation orders stated that the individual had to leave Greece voluntarily by a specific date, usually within one month.[3] Nevertheless, many new arrivals described the deportation paper not as an order to leave but as a permission to stay, or as in this man's account, a paper "good for one month."

With the increasing EU scrutiny of and involvement in Greece's migration management processes since 2010, deportation has become a more regular practice. During my primary fieldwork, however, deportations to home countries were rarely carried out, largely because of the expense involved (though migrants from Albania were often bused or carried in vans to the border, owing to the ease and low costs of transport). Others were expelled to Turkey, even if it was not their country of origin, thanks to the Turkey/Greece readmission agreement discussed in Chapter 1. I met many, however, who were never expelled, even though they had received multiple deportation orders and spent multiple periods in detention. Such protracted periods of limbo can heighten the ambiguities surrounding documentary practices. Farzan, an Afghan interpreter at the ARS, told me that many Afghans asked him how to *renew* their deportation order. He laughed at this absurdity, explaining that to "renew" it, one simply had to get arrested again, much as this man received a new paper each time he was detained. While the deportation document was formally aimed toward expulsion, it was also interpreted as a temporary permission to stay; arrest thus became a form of renewal.

In the documentary practices surrounding asylum in Greece, illegality and legality are closely entwined, easy directionalities explode, and instead we see reversals, transformations, and objects that—like the deportation order—become chimerical. Attending to the unpredictability, mysteriousness, and even chaos, of the pink card's bureaucratic movements is crucial, owing to the official and even moral force of the asylum claim, which can grant illusory predictability and solidity to asylum-related bureaucracies. These unpredictable, indeterminate qualities permeated every stage of the pink card's bureaucratic movements, evident also in how both police and asylum seekers engaged with the document.

Police

Allodhapon, July 2008

Accompanied by my partner Salvatore, I went to Allodhapon early in the morning to observe the lines of would-be asylum applicants waiting outside the gates behind the compound. We woke at 4:00 a.m., sweat already forming on our skin, and drove down the loud boulevard of Peiraios until we reached the cross street, Petrou Ralli. We parked near Peiraios, about half a kilometer away, then followed a group of men and a couple of solitary women across an adjacent vacant lot that opened onto a narrow street, Salaminas, fortified by high walls topped with wire. As we stepped out into the street I suddenly saw row on row of people on every available spot of sidewalk, some standing, some sitting, some asleep on cardboard boxes, some stretching and yawning. This scene was even stranger in that I had not heard the crowd; they were eerily quiet and subdued. Looking to my left, in the direction of the station itself, I saw a small cluster of women waiting together and identified what had made the crowd so quiet: a police car parked sideways in the middle of the street blocking further passage, and three visibly armed police officers, two men and one woman.

Allodhapon is a place where a certain invisibility is desirable for researchers. In 2008, heavy criticism by activists, journalists, and NGO workers regarding practices at Allodhapon had made police particularly suspicious; those who took pictures of the crowds were harassed, and an English journalist acquaintance of mine, who had been filming a report for the BBC, was interrogated and his tapes confiscated. As the only light-skinned woman in sight (among so few women in general), it was almost impossible for me to blend in, so Salvatore went to observe the front of the line, where his beard, dark hair, and gender might provide some protection. Meanwhile, I walked a few blocks to the back of the line.

I approached a number of people and asked in both English and Greek why they were waiting, in order to gain insight into how they themselves

Figure 2. At Allodhapon: the line of people waiting to apply for a pink card, July 2008. Photo credit Salvatore Poier.

described their activities. One man who told me that he was from Pakistan explained in English: "Here for paper. Political stay. UN. . . . Red card." Then, switching to Greek, he clarified that he had *khartia* (papers), and he took out his pink card to show me, but he had come with a friend who did not have papers. Without papers, he added, you cannot go openly in the street and cannot work regularly. Two other men approached us. Also from Pakistan, they greeted my conversation partner with familiarity. One of them, clutching an asylum application protected in a plastic sleeve, explained that he had been in Greece for six years, and I was surprised to learn that only now was he trying to obtain papers. His companion said that he too was here for papers, because without them he must always stay at home and cannot go out.

The bureaucratic pathways for acquiring the pink card positioned new asylum applicants directly outside the central structure of police power for "aliens" in Athens. While asylum seekers often traveled to the capital from border sites to initiate applications, the militarized waiting zone at Allodhapon remade the border within the city in a spatial and temporal enactment of limbo. Applicants had to wait to cross the threshold from illegality into limbo through the acquisition of papers, and, more directly, entry into the building itself. The pink card thus conveyed both protective attributes and the terror associated with the policing apparatus of the state, providing protection from the very authorities that distributed it. None of the men I spoke with mentioned applying for asylum as their primary rationale for being at the police station, though the first man, who spoke specifically about the "red card," demonstrated a clear acknowledgment that this paper was related to "political problems." Their aim, however, was papers, because without papers they moved in fear.

As we were speaking, we heard disturbances from the front of the line, and some of the men around us began to move toward the barricade; one of my companions explained that they were starting to "open the doors." The disturbances increased—men pressing into the crowd, some shouting, surging forward then back. Groups of young men began to run away from the barricade toward the back of the line, many of them laughing, shouting to each other the Greek expletive *Fiye re malaka* [Φύγε ρε μαλάκα] ("Go away, jerk-off") and *fighe, mavre* [φύγε μαύρε] ("Go away, black man")—a mimesis of a police officer's shout thus transformed into a source of both humor and challenge.

Meanwhile, Salvatore had made it all the way to the very front of the line and was present when the doors opened. He later gave me the following account, which I summarize here. The police controlled the crowd with gas, and one police officer, in particular, openly hit people with his hands and a stick. Once the crowd was quiet, an older man came out, with white hair and glasses, wearing no uniform but a simple white shirt: apparently a bureaucrat, not an active officer. As Salvatore explained to me later, the police officers attending this man made everyone sit on the street, and he then began "choosing" people by "looking at their papers [their asylum applications] and their faces." People held up their applications for him to see, and he began picking faces out of the crowd, announcing that they wanted people from Africa, and about 20 Africans came forward. The man admitted about 20 others, mostly from Afghanistan and Iraq. Then the choosing was over, and the doors were shut.

Alongside more spectacular forms of policing at Allodhapon, classification categories had a central role in the asylum process. The pink card itself was devoted to recording various categories of identification, including kinship, gender, and national origin. At Allodhapon, however, informal classification categories, which had yet to become official through bureaucratic

Figure 3. Asylum seekers waiting to be allowed to lodge an asylum application, July 2008. Photo credit Salvatore Poier.

authentication, both enabled and restricted access to the document. "Choosing" was carried out through a compound usage of papers (application forms) and faces, but the explicit call for Africans highlights also the role of race and the body in shaping these categories, which were only later codified in documentary form. These technologies of race and classification did not necessarily facilitate legibility, however, but were highly unpredictable. As I was speaking with the group of Pakistani men, a green-eyed, wiry man threw his arm around one of my companions, flashing a broad smile. He told me he was from Syria and stated, almost as a matter of pride: "I have been here for four months, every weekend [waiting]. . . . One time I came here with a friend of mine. [From the] same country, we look the same—but they took him and not me!" While the doors of Allodhapon opened selectively, one never knew who would be let in, or why. Uncertainty, however, did not defuse the power of policing practices or surveillance mechanisms but imbued them with an arbitrariness that engendered confusion, frustration, and anxiety.

This account of the pink card and its bureaucratic apparatuses reflects how, through the police, regulatory, "law-preserving" (Benjamin 1999) violence becomes entwined with the terror, unpredictability, and also indeterminacy of state power. The unpredictable, even nightmarish "magic" of the state (Das 2004; Hoag 2010; Taussig 1997) also vitalizes the instruments of regulatory authority with phantasmal dimensions (Nuijten 2003). While policing practices were formally aimed toward increasing control and legibility over asylum seekers, these activities themselves appeared anything but legible or rational (see Herzfeld 1992); the arbitrary, even mysterious qualities of procedures at Allodhapon increased the anxiety and fear among those waiting, who came back week after week in the hopes (but never the certainty) of acquiring the pink card.

Asylum Division, Allodhapon, July 2011

It is summer 2011, and I have returned to Athens for just ten days of follow up fieldwork, in order to examine the reforms currently being instituted in the asylum procedure. Through a kind of miracle, the person in charge of the asylum division at the Ministry of Public Order and Citizen Protection has granted me permission to spend three days with the police, observing first instance asylum applications. Those I tell about my lucky break describe it as a product of the new culture of openness and transparency surrounding the reform of asylum in Greece.

At around 6 a.m., I get a ride to Allodhapon with Dora and Elektra, two acquaintances who now work for the UNHCR overseeing first instance asylum interviews. Dora flashes her badge, and following a cordial nod by the officer outside, we pass through the gates, around to the back of the main building, and down a ramp to a basement garage for employees. After picking up three surprisingly decent espressos (which cost about 50 cents each) at a café above the garage, we enter the main building through a side door, and I find myself in the "interview room" of the asylum department. I note how the informality and ease of our entrance contrasts with my earlier experiences at Allodhapon.

In addition to my 2008 participation among those waiting in the lines outside, for years I have heard from ARS workers and asylum seekers about the disorganized, corrupt, and chaotic world of the asylum division, and its entrenched disregard for procedural matters. I have been told that interpreters, not asylum officers, conducted the interviews, flagrantly mischaracterizing their content. I have heard repeatedly of the notorious near-zero percent acceptance rate at the first instance of the asylum procedure. But this was before the new asylum law and the transitional measures that have been put in place at Allodhapon.

Dora and Elektra have both prepared me by asserting that the police are not as difficult as they expected, and some of them are in fact "very good." Though when they first took on their positions it was hard to establish trust, relationships are now generally very friendly. Indeed, an aura of vibrant, bustling sociability greets the beginning of the workday in the asylum division. Police officers, interpreters, and UNHCR representatives mill around, smoking, drinking coffee, chatting, and arranging files for the day's series of interviews. Since there is not a uniform in sight, it is sometimes difficult to distinguish the officers from the UNHCR employees. A few lawyers drop by to check on cases that are up for review today, including Fani, the wife of my longtime interlocutor Dimitris, a former ARS lawyer who now works as an adjudicator on the appeals board; Fani, with many years of experience in real estate law, is now representing asylum seekers. Many of the interpreters are dressed neatly in gray, collared t-shirts reading METAdrasi [METAδραση], a play on the Greek words for translation (*metafrasi* [μετάφραση]) and action (*drasi* [δράση]), an NGO that, among its activities, trains interpreters and contracts them out to the asylum division. Among them I recognize a young Afghan, a former ARS client whom I had last seen in 2008, and he greets me warmly. He too comments on how he has been surprised by his positive experience at the police: he used to hate them, but now that he has seen how some of them conduct their work he wants to say "thank you." I poke my head out into the main hallway at the waiting area immediately outside the interview hall, packed with those awaiting asylum interviews. I have been told that the lines outside the building have diminished, but that there are still people waiting.

Elektra and Dora suggest that I circulate among the different officers, as they do, to see the different interview styles of the various police. Generally, the UNHCR representatives try to keep moving so as not to get too tired (or bored or overwhelmed) and to distribute evenly the "good" and "bad" officers so no one gets stuck with one for too long. Among the more problematic officers, some representatives gossip, is one who uses the pink card as a kind of bargaining chip: when he interviews persons who he believes are not legitimate asylum seekers, he offers to give them additional time on their pink cards if they agree to say they are in Greece for "economic reasons." He offers even more time if they get their friends to do the same. For the UNHCR overseers, such practices serve as a reminder of the ad hoc and arbitrary police work they are trying to eradicate.

Elektra, however, sits in with one of the younger officers, who she emphasizes is "very good." I accompany her into an office cubicle, recently constructed to meet demands for privacy (before, all interviews were conducted in the same room). A young man in jeans and a t-shirt greets me warmly, gesturing to a chair; this is the asylum officer. Next to him behind a computer screen sits the "secretary," a muscled young man in a tight t-shirt—also a police officer—who takes down notes during the interview directly onto the computer. The asylum officer tells me he was recently hired through the transitional procedure, and has worked in the asylum division for just a few months. He has gone through the specialized training but has never worked in asylum related issues before. From the north of Greece, he applied for this job in Athens because it is compulsory that police officers spend time in the capital. But he claims to enjoy his work, in particular the contact with asylum seekers, though he finds it difficult at times. He agonizes over some of the cases, taking files home and working well into the night doing his own internet research. It turns out that there is no internet at Allodhapon, though the UNHCR reps have laptops and mobile internet devices which allow them to do on-the-spot research to assist the police.

During the interviews I observe, I am struck by this young officer's enthusiastic and crisp professionalism combined with an almost jovial warmth: well-placed jokes, which alleviate the tensions of the interview process and put the applicants at ease. The first interviewee, from Egypt, is currently in detention. At the end of the interview, the officer issues him a pink card, asking him whether he has ever had a pink card and, if so, where he received it. The interviewee answers that he received a pink card at a different location [from Allodhapon], but does not say where. The officer explains that with his new pink card no one will arrest him, but adds that it is good only for a few months, and in the meantime, his case will be under examination. Indeed, with the reform process, the six-month renewal process is no longer a given, since the decisions are now coming much faster. The asylum seeker asks the friendly officer if he can do anything about the pink card (issue it for longer), or if a lawyer can do anything. The officer is firm, however: he must await the decision on his claim.

Interestingly, this young officer is the one who will be issuing the decision, and it is he who decides the amount of time granted on the pink card.

Yet unlike his colleague, who apparently (if gossip serves) relies on ad hoc and arbitrary methods, this officer of the new generation invokes a hidden, impersonal bureaucratic apparatus that produces pink cards and decisions. After hours, he feels very personally the weight of the process, as he ponders and researches decisions. In his contact with asylum seekers, however, he distances himself from the process, presenting himself as a mediator between the bureaucracy and the interviewee. In the new spirit of openness, an ethos of bureaucratic accountability holds sway, which itself serves to shroud police plenary power.

Later, another interviewee—a woman from Georgia—references the violence outside Allodhapon.[4] She explains that a few months ago, she went to renew her pink card, but that she was not able to make an appointment; the police officers in charge kept saying *ela avrio, ela avrio* [έλα αύριο, έλα αύριο] ("come tomorrow, come tomorrow"). But she was afraid, particularly when she saw another woman stripped naked by the crowd after coming out of the building. The young officer shakes his head in disbelief and comments: "last year the situation was not controlled easily," and the interviewee interjects, explaining that now it is "fine." When I ask the officer later about the violence outside, he comments that he has heard and seen things, and particularly that the situation was very bad before he came. Yet overall, it strikes me that from his position inside, in the interview room, he does not involve himself in the enforcement measures outside.

These two accounts from Allodhapon point to very different formations of state regulatory power surrounding the pink card. Though the violence I witnessed earlier outside the building contrasts with the relatively warm atmosphere currently unfolding inside, it is not entirely erased. Discussions of the document as an instrument of both protection and enforcement give spectral testament to arbitrary forms of regulatory control and police violence, which persist in and through the reform process. The newer process emphasizes openness, oversight, and bureaucratic accountability, particularly through additions and shifts in personnel, including both UNHCR representatives and a number of newly trained police officers. For the young officer, who is in many ways a product of this new environment, documentary practices and decision making emerge as part of a bureaucratic process and procedure, while enforcement measures remain outside the purview of the asylum division, curtailed both spatially and temporally (outside, and in the past). The old-timers remain, however, attesting to the persistence of another culture of documentation and decision making that is more personalized, arbitrary, yet also flexible. The pink card can be used as a bargaining chip, which dilutes the image of bureaucratic distance and accountability that the young officer cultivates, indicating, for some of the UNHCR representatives, ongoing forms of corruption that undermine the reform process. But for asylum seekers, such as the young Egyptian man, such flexibilities may also enable more immediate goals. In the end, whether the asylum seeker is greeted with a depersonalized but accountable bureaucracy or a highly personalized (and seemingly arbitrary) ad hoc approach depends very much on which officer he or she encounters (see Ramji-Nogales et al.).

In her analysis of the limbo of indefinite detention, Judith Butler (2004) draws on Foucault's assertion that "governmentality" serves to *vitalize* the state, replacing traditional forms of sovereignty with diffuse formations of power that grant the state a powerful everyday life. When "petty sovereigns" (57) (in this case, police officers and bureaucrats) enact Greek and European territorial sovereignties through documentary practices, asylum seekers encounter a diffuse disciplinary power, which ultimately remains unpredictable even through emerging forms of bureaucratic accountability. Yet the pink card does not simply reinforce the power of the state; it reflects *both* police and asylum seekers' attempts to make this document and limbo meaningful. The very practices that vitalize state power also imbue the pink card with meanings and functions that reshape or even undermine state regulatory activities.

Narrating Limbo

In addition to the powerful physical-spatial dimensions of limbo enacted through policing practices at both Greek and EU scales of governance, limbo is implied in the juridical formulation of asylum seeking itself. Asylum applicants occupy positions precariously between undocumented, paperless illegality and "refugee" status. While recognition as a refugee conveys the right to protection in a host country, the category "asylum seeker" connotes a temporary relationship to a nation-state in which the right to stay is itself highly transitory (Coutin 2005). In seeking asylum, one has asked to be granted the status of refugee, but one has not been "recognized" as such. Asylum seekers thus occupy a neither fully legal nor illegal position of nonbelonging, suspended in limbo between multiple bureaucratic stages conveying possible acceptance, rejection, or appeal. If an asylum claim is approved, one is "recognized" as a refugee, but if the claim is rejected, temporary permission to stay is revoked and one is rendered, de facto, an "undocumented" migrant; in Greece, one must leave voluntarily, attempt to employ other methods of regularization, or risk arrest or deportation.

Amid the many ambiguities and instabilities of limbo, the pink card acquired vitality in the intimacies and informalities of daily life, as persons invoked the document through narrative attempts to make sense of their encounters with the asylum procedure. At times, these moments of discursive engagement highlighted the document's power to immobilize, imprison, or make one vulnerable. Yet individuals also infused the pink card with hopes for belonging, recognition, freedom, access to rights, and economic survival, thus reinterpreting both the pink card and the condition of limbo that it consigned.

In March 2003, with the U.S. invasion of Iraq, the Greek Ministry of Public Order effectively "froze" asylum applications from Iraqis, implicitly anticipating that the situation in Iraq might improve. Between 2003 and 2008, few Iraqi claims were approved or rejected, meaning that many Iraqi asylum seekers could renew their pink cards repeatedly but that their cases rarely progressed to a decision or even a second-instance interview. The extreme difficulty of obtaining an asylum decision made this limbo, for many Iraqis, particularly protracted, lasting months and even years.[5] Take, for example, the case of Kamir, an Iraqi Kurd. In an informal interview over coffee in January 2007, he explained that he had been in Greece since before the U.S. invasion of Iraq but that his asylum claim had been "frozen." He had initially "started out with a pink card," but after a few years of waiting while working and making a life in Greece, he quit the asylum process and initiated a new process of legalization as an economic migrant, successfully applying for the Greek equivalent of a "green card." Thanks to his excellent Greek, good education, and an employer who had hired him, this different legalization pathway was ultimately more convenient, and much faster, than the asylum process.[6] However, he explained that he was disappointed because he was a refugee and should have been recognized as such.

Kamir's commentary evoked an ambivalent relationship between the limbo to which he was consigned through the pink card and his own self-identification as a refugee. He suggested that refugee status would have signified the recognition of crucial elements of his experience, while the failure of his asylum claim implied a delegitimization of that history. He discursively associated the green card with this failure, as a document related to *economic* migration, which labeled him a migrant, not a refugee. A few months after our conversation, however, Kamir traveled back to Iraq to see his family, a trip that would not have been possible had he been an asylum seeker or even a recognized refugee, since the travel document issued to refugees expressly prohibits travel to the holder's country of origin. Thus, while the green card came to signify a lack of recognition, this document also provided a way out of limbo, with significant forms of mobility.

In addition to the overwhelming frustrations and delegitimizing effects of limbo, many asylum seekers characterized the card as a powerful indicator of physical immobility. Through a series of interviews in spring 2008, Asad, a young man from Somalia, told me how he had attempted a number of entries and undergone multiple expulsions in crossing the border into Greece. After being expelled twice from Greece, in Turkey he arranged for a false passport, and traveled directly from Istanbul to Britain, where his aunt lived. He applied for asylum there, and for a year lived in Manchester while he awaited a decision. The British authorities, however, discovered Asad's fingerprints registered in Eurodac (the EU biometric data system), revealing that he had first entered the EU via Greece, so they deported him to Athens under the auspices of Dublin II. When he asked for asylum upon arrival at the Athens airport, he was issued a pink card, and finally officially became an asylum seeker in Greece.

Asad narrated himself and his experiences clearly through the tropes of violence and persecution that international law associates with the figure of the refugee, even enlisting the language of the 1951 Geneva Convention: "I had a well-founded fear of persecution. I was tortured, harassed. If I had not left Somalia, I would have died." When I met him, he had been in Athens for just a few months, awaiting a decision on his claim, but he was already growing impatient: "Whatever they decide, I will accept. I just want to know. I want to know where my life will be. Here I have nothing, nothing. I just have this *pink card*. [He removed it from his pocket and showed it to me]. What is this? It is shit. With this card, I am supposed to be free. But I am in prison." The pink card did not just signify the temporal limbo of waiting, but through its coupling with biometric data, it enacted a form of physical imprisonment. The document was laden with the inescapable details of fingerprints (Cole 2001), through which Asad had repeatedly been caught, and so the pink card—which he imagined was supposed to make him "free"—brought disappointment, frustration, and imprisonment.

Despite its many frustrations, however, limbo can also be useful, as in the case of Roya, an asylum seeker from Iran. The first time I met her, in October

2006, Roya explained almost casually to me that she and her husband were "refugees," though, like Kamir, they had not received a final decision or even been called for an asylum hearing. She invited me to their home to eat: "You can come see a refugee house," she smiled. We convened on a Sunday in early spring, and I sat with her and her husband in their living room as they showed me pictures of their lives in Iran and their family. Leafing carefully through pictures of multiple shapes and sizes, they told me that many of the photos were from before the Revolution: wedding photos, and the two of them together wearing bellbottoms and fitted button-down shirts. "Can you imagine I went from this to having to wear a head scarf?" Roya laughed and shook her head. "For two years after the Revolution," she explained, "nothing really happened. But one day, it all changed—and I remember it, because it was the day my son was born. My mother came to the hospital with a scarf for me to wear." Roya went into the hospital with her hair free and came out wearing a headscarf, frightened by stories of noncompliant women having their faces burned and cut.

Roya and her husband had also suffered under the Dublin II system, undergoing a traumatic experience of expulsion within Europe. She told me that they had initially entered Greece with no intention to apply for asylum or stay; they came with passports, en route to Germany to visit relatives. While they were in Germany, however, "something happened" in Iran, making it dangerous for them to go home, so they applied for asylum in Germany. They remained there for almost a year, and Roya was already learning German, but one evening, when she was just putting the bread dough in the oven, German police arrived at their door. After a night in detention, which Roya described as one of the darkest nights of her life, they were sent "back" to Greece as "Dublin Returnees."

Roya explained that after this terrifying experience of expulsion, she was pleased that they had established a simple but legitimate life in Athens. She clarified that it was, in fact, better that they had not yet been called for an asylum hearing, because so many asylum claims are rejected, and she could not face another experience of deportation. She planned simply to complete all papers correctly and on time, and "let the lion sleep." The relative safety of limbo thus outweighed Roya's desire to receive a result on her asylum claim: no decision was better than a rejection.

Across these various accounts, the pink card is enmeshed in the pasts, presents, and potential futures through which these persons describe their experiences of flight, as well as projects of surveillance carried out by the

Greek state, international law, and European policy (see Feldman 2011). The document also figures centrally in how these individuals interpret limbo, reinforcing or contradicting their own self-identification as refugees. Roya's self-described "refugeeness" is not dependent on legal recognition but is, in fact, further substantiated by her experiences of limbo. Kamir, however, implies that documents are tied intimately to his own sense of self, describing the change in his papers from pink to green with frustration. For Asad, not knowing where his life will be is what makes limbo difficult, as he recounts his experiences with certainty that he fits the criteria for refugee status, whether or not he acquires formal recognition.

The divergent ways in which asylum seekers narrated the pink card and the experience of limbo also reflected asymmetrical access to legal knowledge and qualitatively different interpretations of asylum law. While, for the above individuals, the category of "refugee" played an important role in identity-making projects and in their interpretations of documentary forms, as I discuss next, I also met many asylum seekers who acknowledged neither the relationship between the pink card and the asylum system nor their own positions as applicants for protection.

A "Residence Permit"

In the winter of 2006–2007, many of those seeking legal assistance from the ARS were from Bangladesh; I would often help to register between 15 and 20 Bangladeshi visitors a day, sometimes less, often more. Most often, all but one or two would tell me explicitly that they had come to Greece for *kaz* and *taka*, which, from the few words of Bangla I had picked up, I recognized as "work" and "money;" many would also refer to *orthonotic shomasha* (economic problems) as their primary reasons for leaving Bangladesh. I was initially extremely surprised that so many people, all with pink cards and classified formally by the state as asylum seekers, explained their own migration so matter-of-factly in terms of work, money, and poverty. Many of these individuals described the pink card simply as a "stay permit" or "residence permit," with no reference to the asylum procedure. To my questions why and how they acquired the document, some explained that they acquired it because friends told them they needed it, and, in some cases, because the police had advised them to apply for it. A few implied that they had been issued a pink card on release from detention.

Despite the salience of poverty and labor in the accounts of these asylum seekers, this does not necessarily mean that they could not be considered refugees according to international law. Rather, in contrast to Asad, for instance, who fluently leveraged the language of rights in describing his past, asylum and refugeehood simply did not figure in how these claimants talked about their lives with NGO workers or with me. Like the Pakistani men I met outside Allodhapon, these individuals from Bangladesh framed the card itself, *not* asylum, as a primary object of desire. While limbo was certainly rife with anxieties and immobilities, it also enabled them to live and work in Greece, if only temporarily. I want to suggest that this widespread understanding of the pink card as a "residence permit" granted the document new meanings and effects, revealing often unacknowledged ways that both asylum seekers and the Greek state made use of this document, limbo, and the asylum process as well.

In March 2007, over coffee one Sunday afternoon at a café in Thisseio, a peaceful neighborhood in sight of the Acropolis where many Athenian residents come on the weekend to enjoy the view and the bright touches of green on the hillside, I spoke with Stavros about my encounters with these individuals. He smiled, nodding his head knowingly, and took out his Greek national identity card. He unfolded the blue laminated card and pointed to the various categories on its surface, some of them identical to those on the pink card: name, father's name, mother's name, date and place of birth. He explained that this was the state's *engrafo* [έγγραφο] (record) of him, and that the pink card was not any different. Stavros then reasoned that with so many people entering Greece, there was no way for the state to know who was in its territory, so the police had begun to use the pink card to document "economic" migrants. As far as the state was concerned, he went on, the Bangladeshi individuals I had spoken to were "not really asylum seekers," but were economic migrants, and the state "controlled them" through the pink card.

Stavros characterized identity documents as instruments through which the state controlled both citizens like him and "aliens" (migrants and asylum seekers). Much like policing practices at Allodhapon, however, this "control" was achieved not through transparency but through an unpredictable and seemingly arbitrary intermingling of formal and informal practices. In describing the pink card as enacting a kind of informal census of undocumented migrants in Greece, Stavros suggests that police and bureaucrats use formal documentary materials to accomplish unofficial ends, in order to deal with the allegedly unsolvable "problem" of illegal migration. In light of these asylum seekers' own descriptions of the pink card as a "residence permit," however, I want to highlight that the pink card also facilitated activities attached to so-called "economic" migration, which is formally elided in asylum legislation. In Stavros's assertion that (for the state) they are "not really asylum seekers," we can see also a profound limit to the state's capacity to "produce" these individuals as asylum seekers and render them "legally cognizable" (Coutin and Yngvesson 2006: 178) through documentary practices. Instead, these individuals themselves granted the document legibility as a "residence permit," shifting the meanings and uses of limbo and the asylum procedure itself.

State projects of "control" thus take on unpredictable effects that can undermine these very regulatory activities. This refashioning of the pink card as a residence permit could perhaps be described as a form of corporate agency (Hull 2003; Ortner 1984, 2006), which is not dependent on explicit forms of consciousness or resistance but instead involves what Susan Coutin (2000: 173) describes as "maneuvering within a particular set of conditions." Such "maneuvering" can have powerful consequences, creating a new set of conditions to which state agents must also adapt. Despite (and even thanks to) these Bangladeshi asylum seekers' apparent *lack* of formal knowledge regarding the law, the document, and their own status, they used the pink card to serve their own needs, thus reshaping its significances and effects.

The pink card could be framed as a kind of "boundary object" (Bowker and Star 1999), a bureaucratic artifact at the center of a complex network of relationships (Latour 2005; Riles 2001), differently salient for diverse individuals who redispose and refashion it in ways that are simultaneously contradictory yet "collaborative" (Riles 2007). Governance, thus, emerges as an evolving, unruly nexus of persons, practices, and things, constantly redirected toward variously overlapping, conflicting, or even unrelated ends.

Document, Limbo, and Rights

On the second floor of the ARS, new aid candidates arrive for the brief but crucial process of registration, in which longtime employees, Melike and Hadi, take down information to be entered into the database. They operate in a small, sunny office off the street-side end of the waiting room, their desks facing each other: Hadi over the street, Melike against the far wall. A coffee pot and tea and coffee accoutrements stand neatly on a cabinet behind the door.

Melike, herself a refugee from Turkey who has been in Greece since the 1980s, spearheads the registration process. A diminutive woman, with smiling eyes and a tinkling laugh, she readily speaks assertively to lawyers, interpreters, and clients alike. Having studied sociology in Greece, she also has a degree in chemistry from Turkey, a background that, one might argue, makes her overqualified for her current position in registration. She has worked for many years as a language instructor and interpreter at asylum hearings, and is the official coordinator for interpreters at the ARS, serving also as their representative to the NGO's Governing Board. As a single woman among the many foreign-born coworkers and clients who, like her, come from culturally Muslim backgrounds, she works doubly hard to command her office, the registration process, and interpreters' schedules. Yet with her territorial professionalism and firm, but good-natured, humor, she keeps things running smoothly.

In the winter of 2007, I spent a month assisting Melike with registration. When new aid candidates arrived, Melike would give them a registration number and an appointment with a lawyer and educate them about their pink cards. She followed a formulaic and complete script, which she most often delivered in perfect Greek, though sometimes, depending on the applicant's country of origin, in her native Turkish; if no interpreter was available, she could provide this information in English, Farsi, Arabic, and some Bangla: *With this paper you can get a work permit. If you get sick you can go to the hospital. And at the hospital, there is a pharmacy where you can get medicine for free, you do not have to pay.*

Although EU directives on reception conditions (Council Directive 2003/9/EC, January 27, 2003) and asylum procedures (Council Directive 2005/85/EC, December 1, 2005) outline minimum standards for the treatment of asylum seekers in member states, asylum seekers in Greece have limited, and highly unstable, access to basic social rights. The Greek state attempts (though not very effectively) (Lauth Bacas 2011; Papageorgiou and Dimitropoulou 2008) to provide housing to unaccompanied minors and other "vulnerable" categories of persons (families, "victims of trafficking," and victims of abuse and torture). Housing, subsistence, and legal representation are, however, left overwhelmingly to the nongovernmental sector. As Melike emphasized, bearers of the pink card were entitled to free healthcare and had permission to work, privileges that together constitute the primary state-sanctioned social support for asylum seekers in Greece. However, I found that asylum seekers demonstrated enormously varied knowledge of these "rights," and like the meaning of limbo itself, these rights were subject to highly varying interpretations by those who encountered the pink card. This interpretive work, in turn, facilitated or undermined asylum seekers' capacity to access or activate these rights.

Greece is somewhat unique among EU member states in granting asylum seekers permission to work immediately, but many applicants with whom I spoke appeared unaware of this right. Many stated that they did not have a work permit and others seemed downright puzzled when Melike mentioned *adhia ergasias* [άδεια εργασίας] (work permit). Yet most said that they were working in some capacity—likely without papers. This can perhaps be accounted for by the further bureaucratic hurdles necessary for a work permit, including multiple medical examinations, which can discourage asylum seekers, given their uneven understandings of the Greek language, law, and bureaucracy. Yet work permits also offer significant benefits, enabling asylum seekers to work officially and legally, and most often, with steadier, better wages (at least until the recent financial difficulties, which have made work for everyone more difficult, both Greeks and non-Greeks). Yet when I asked Rahman, the ARS's Bangladeshi interpreter, about why so few people had work permits, he explained, "most people don't care about that. They just want to make money quickly."

Asylum seekers work primarily as temporary laborers in construction or agriculture, or in the unofficial trades of street vending, thus working informally, for less profit, but indeed, often making money more quickly. Such informal labor has been widely tolerated and even encouraged through the temporary economies of day labor, the seasonal logics of agricultural work, and widespread consumption on the streets, given the demand for goods with lower prices, without the cost of VAT (value added tax). Greeks and tourists alike cluster around the blankets and flattened cardboard boxes, where foreign vendors display products for sale; many also buy from the peripatetic sellers who frequent cafés. In addition to the widespread demand for these informal economies of labor and trade, it is often more difficult for asylum seekers to find official employment. This is not just the case for asylum seekers and migrants. Many Greeks also complement one or two formal jobs with undocumented forms of employment to make meager incomes livable, though in the new post-crisis spirit of accountability, such practices have been discouraged. In the formal sector, employers must pay taxes that go toward state health insurance for registered workers from "IKA" (Ίδρυμα Κοινωνικών Ασφαλίσεων [the Social Insurance Institution]). Yet in industries that are difficult to regulate, such as domestic work or construction, many potential employers are unwilling to pay IKA. Some asylum seekers recounted that their employers gave them a choice: to make more money without social insurance, or work officially and lose some of their wages to the state.

For others, however, who work in more formal and regulated sectors, such as factories, work papers are a big concern, and citing advice from friends, many came to the ARS specifically requesting assistance with work permits or finding employment. For asylum seekers who have been advised by friends or lawyers, work papers are not just a ticket to steadier incomes but may also provide opportunities for regularization later on; according to the current legislation, evidence of formal, legal employment can furnish one of the prerequisites for a green card. Both the exercise and recognition of the right to work vary widely, depending on asylum seekers' knowledge and goals, sector of employment or labor, and employers' willingness to recognize it.

Access to healthcare, the other primary right encoded through the pink card, was similarly inconsistent. Officially, undocumented migrants in Greece have no access to healthcare except in cases of emergency, and even then, only until the patient is in stable condition (though these stipulations are interpreted in highly variable ways by healthcare providers). Many ARS clients expressed surprise and puzzlement when Melike explained that they could receive medical care with their pink card, and some did not even seem to acknowledge it. For those who encountered health problems, however, healthcare access became crucial. In March 2007, Amara, a young woman from Ethiopia, came to the ARS simply, she explained, on the advice of her friends to register in case she ever needed help; she was not seeking urgent assistance. Amara described herself as an economic migrant, saying that she was in Greece to "live and work." She told me that she came to Greece after her husband left her and both her parents died, making her the primary supporter of her younger brother and sister, still children, now living with their aunt. Asserting that she was "paid well" (seven hundred euros a month, which indeed was a relatively livable wage, even pre-crisis) she said that she "loved" the Greek family for whom she worked and the children she looked after. But she also said that she was very unhappy, "alone," and always worrying for her brother and sister: "I think about them not having food or underwear—and I can't sleep."

She had lived in Greece without any form of documentation for a year and a half, working as a house cleaner and nanny for the Greek family. When she injured her leg at her employer's house, however, she found her access to healthcare extremely limited, receiving just initial treatment and no follow-up care. Her Greek employer then did some research and suggested she apply for a pink card, helping her fill out the forms and file the application. Amara's relationship with her employer thus facilitated her acquisition of the pink card. Unlike the men I discussed earlier, fear of arrest was not a primary motivating factor for her acquisition of documents; Amara was already living and working without papers. Rather, she applied for the pink card explicitly to obtain access to health care. Jack Donnelly (2003: 9) writes of the "possession paradox" of rights, in which " 'having' a right is of most value precisely when one does not 'have' (the object of) the right." Only when she found herself without a right to healthcare did Amara take steps to acquire it through the document. The pink card thus emerged here as a vehicle that conferred this right, enabling treatment and access to care.

In their own work of providing advocacy and assistance, ARS staff also invoked the pink card's capacity to confer the right to medical care. In a particularly dramatic case, two recently arrived Iranians came to the ARS after having injured themselves when land mines exploded, as they walked ahead of their families to protect them while crossing the mine-riddled border with Turkey. One had shrapnel in his back, and the other had severe lacerations in his arm. Having somehow avoided detention, they arrived in Athens in particularly bad shape though with their families intact, yet neither received treatment at a state hospital until the lawyer Stavros helped them acquire pink cards.

Access to healthcare was, moreover, very much dependent on individual hospital employees' knowledge of this right and familiarity with the pink card itself. Certain hospitals in Athens are known to be more willing and accustomed to treat asylum seekers, and social workers at the ARS often form liaisons with these hospitals, even accompanying clients to ensure treatment and follow-up. Nevertheless, many asylum seekers still face difficulties in obtaining treatment. One client, who came to the ARS twice in one week asking to see a doctor, was sent by a social worker to Evangelismos, the large central Athens hospital. But he returned shortly to the ARS office, explaining that he had been turned away. After checking that his pink card was valid, the social worker explained that with a pink card, he had a "right" to go to the hospital. With an expression of surprise, he responded that he had shown his card to people at the hospital, but they seemed not to know what it was. While we cannot know why exactly this man was not treated, his account highlights the arbitrariness of the rights consigned through the document. While the pink card encoded a right to healthcare, recognition of that right depended on those who encountered the document, how they interpreted its significance, and whether they chose to acknowledge or disregard it at particular moments. How rights for asylum seekers become *active*, if they do at all, depends very much on the diverse knowledges, motivations, and circumstances that characterize cultures of documentation.

The pink card often became significant not for the rights that it conferred, but for those that it did not. Though many asylum seekers cited a place to live among their most urgent needs, the pink card encoded no right to housing or subsistence. On the contrary, the police authorities who processed initial applications required that applicants have an address as a prerequisite for filing an asylum application and obtaining a pink card: along with their application, asylum seekers had to present a lease agreement bearing their name. This was not specified in any law or presidential decree, but remained in the domain of police practice.[7] This requirement situated asylum seekers in a clear "catch-22": in order to lodge an asylum application, which would allow them to live and work legally and Greece, they had to achieve enough financial solvency to pay for an apartment. In 2006, I spoke with a man from Afghanistan who was waiting to meet with Stavros. He expressed utter defeat and exhaustion regarding his experience in Greece: "I have no one. I know no one. I need a job." When Stavros arrived, the man explained that he had been in Greece for a month and had been sleeping in the park; he emphasized repeatedly that he needed a job but that he wanted to work legally to avoid problems with police. Stavros explained that he would help him apply for both a pink card and work papers, but that he could not get a job legally without a house contract. In response, the client distilled perfectly the tension in which he found himself: how could he have a house without a job?

Not surprisingly, this practice frequently incited asylum seekers to seek informal work in order to obtain housing, though the requirement not just for an address but also for a house contract encouraged some simply to obtain such a paper, as opposed to finding actual accommodation. The widespread demand for house contracts sparked underground documentary economies spearheaded by "landlords" and housemates (often other asylum seekers) who provided house contracts for a fee; it was not rare to find several individuals listed at the same phantom address, or large groups living in derelict buildings that had, nonetheless, been rented according to a contract. While such strategies may have worked for the initial asylum application, asylum seekers ran into trouble if police went to their address on file and found it invalid, which could interrupt or invalidate their asylum claim. The pink card thus often came to signify not rights but their lack, and insidious forms of injustice and entrapment.

Brutal Materialities

In summer 2007, Dimitris, who at that time was a lawyer at the ARS, decided to support the case of Balram, a Hindu man who said he had been persecuted by the (then) conservative Muslim majority government in Bangladesh. When Balram went to renew his pink card, the document was taken away, and he received in its place a deportation order; his asylum claim had been rejected and he had become an "undocumented migrant." His only legal recourse for contesting this negative decision was to send an application or "writ of annulment" (*etisi akirosis* [αίτηση ακύρωσης]) to the Council of State, a time-consuming and expensive procedure. Just before the deadline, Dimitris filed an application to STE and obtained a receipt indicating that the case would be heard. When I gave Balram the positive news, however, his most pressing concern was his lack of a document: "Are you going to give me some piece of paper? What will I show the police?"

Although Balram's application had been filed, thus repositioning him in limbo, this did not necessarily mean he would receive a new pink card, even though claimants often waited years before receiving a decision from STE. The process for reclaiming a pink card, also done through the Council of State, involved a supplementary legal procedure grounded on "interim measures" involving an application for suspension or *anastoli* [αναστολή] of deportation. A suspension of deportation, when granted, affirmed the applicant's right to stay temporarily in Greece until the case was processed, and thus also required that the applicant be issued a new pink card. Dimitris filed this application, but because it required a few weeks to process, as a temporary solution he gave Balram notarized copies of both applications and instructed him to show these to the police if they stopped him. Attesting to both his conscientiousness as a client and his evident fear of arrest, Balram carried these bulky documents with him at all times. Nevertheless, two weeks later he called from detention with the news that he had been arrested.

On our way over to the station, Dimitris expressed confidence that he could persuade the police to release Balram. We found him in one of two temporary holding cells in a small police station in the neighborhood where he lived. There were just two officers there when we arrived, and both these women laughed at Dimitris's easy banter while we were signing in. But when we saw Balram in his cell, he was visibly afraid, dirty, his beard—like his clothes—a few days old. From the cell he shared with another man, also from Bangladesh, he pleaded in a combination of English and Greek for Dimitris to help him get out. Although Dimitris explained the situation in detail to the police officers, the captain, still smiling, said that she was very sorry but that she could do nothing without a pink card. Balram was only released three weeks later, when his pink card was reissued.

Like other bureaucratic objects (Bubant 2009; Hull 2003; Riles 2007; Veesman 2008), the pink card here has an indissoluble, brutal materiality (see Feldman 2008; Hull 2012). As the document becomes unmoored from the very bureaucratic processes that produced it, Balram's right to remain temporarily in Greece comes to depend on the material presence or absence of the paper itself, not the legal procedure or even his official position as an asylum seeker; indeed, here it appears as if "status inheres in papers, not persons" (Coutin 2000: 55). Some scholars have valuably suggested that the displacement of social processes, values, and norms onto documents makes papers, in many ways, fetish objects (Cohn 1987; Gordillo 2006; Pietz 1985). Yet here we see that the material fact of the document had a life beyond its political, legal, and social meanings, with significances and effects that exceeded the "governance" of any person or group. The pink card was not only a vehicle or vessel for the uses and meanings that police and asylum seekers granted it, but it had a material life and vitality all its own, which figured crucially in the everyday unfolding of the asylum process in Greece. Michael Taussig (2004: 25) shows how the material practicalities of making gold and coins displace the Marxian fetish quality of gold as money, taking on their own life, "their own poetry, vivid and shocking." Sometimes, as in Balram's case, we are just left with materialities: the brutal presence or absence of the thing itself.

Conclusions: The Ungovernable

Through the material lives of this particular document, we see how diverse actors and objects reinforce, undermine, and reconfigure regulatory power. Attending to the governance of "things"—this interconnected fabric of people, ideas, relationships, and objects—helps us nuance understandings of regulatory activities and the ways in which persons and things engage with them. "Governance" here entails not just how states and supranational bodies attempt to enact control over subjects and objects, but how persons and things themselves *govern* (that is, dispose, position, shape, and make meaningful) sociopolitical and legal life.

In a commentary on Foucault, Giorgio Agamben (2009: 23) writes that even as apparatuses of governance "pervade and disseminate their power in every field of life, the more government will find itself faced with an elusive element, which seems to escape its grasp the more it docilely submits to it." This elusiveness is, in part, a question of "agency": the maneuverings through which individuals attempt to make tolerable lives within sets of conditions and constraints, and the entailments of bureaucratic artifacts within social networks. Yet such indeterminacies are also, I suggest, embedded in the very process of governance, which itself persistently gives rise to what Agamben calls the "Ungovernable." Even as national and supranational institutions attempt to enact control over the lives and bodies of "alien" subjects, material techniques and tools of regulation persistently enter into new relationships and uses, open to various contradictory and collaborative ends. Things themselves, with their complex lives and indissoluble materialities, are central participants in the always indeterminate art of governance.

ACT II

Judgment

The outcome for both sides
To let them stay or to send them away
Contains helpless disaster.

—*The Eumenides*, 481–483

Chapter 3

Engaging Tragedy

In a spontaneous moment of reflection brought on by a particularly difficult day, this is how the lawyer Phoevi described her work at the ARS: "It's like you have been given a life raft. You can save some people, but just a few, and you can make space for them. But even though I can save some people, I also have to recognize that the others are going to drown."[1]

Phoevi's short statement—delivered between meetings with clients to an audience consisting of just one listening ethnographer—captures the morally and ethically fraught character of asylum related advocacy and support at the ARS. In his *Nicomachean Ethics,* Aristotle invokes a similar—though less powerful—image to describe decisions and actions that are somewhere between "voluntary" and "involuntary" (3). He writes of a ship's captain who throws goods overboard in a storm to save the lives of his crew. Aristotle suggests that in the end, this decision is *voluntary*, in that the captain himself must make a choice to "move his limbs" and initiate the action. Phoevi, however, raises the stakes, just as Martha Nussbaum (2001 [1986]: 27), in her engagement with Aristotle, also ups the ante: "things would look different if the only way to save his ship had been to throw his wife or child overboard." When people, not cargo, must be thrown "overboard," the dilemma becomes even more pronounced. Phoevi highlights the centrality of contingency, conflict, and disaster in the work of decision making and judgment: how people are always vulnerable to forces and outcomes beyond their control.

ARS work is characterized by what Nussbaum might describe as a kind of ethical "tragedy." While workers offer assistance to some, they turn others away, owing to limitations in labor power and resources, constraints of law and bureaucracy, and ARS institutional commitments. Even the process of granting services to clients is riddled with problems of mistranslation and disconnection, which may further thwart the provision of assistance. The decisions of ARS workers are rarely undergirded with the certainty of those who can know, judge possible outcomes, and choose appropriate actions based on that knowledge. Rather, according to Nussbaum, in the world of "tragedy," humans—even those who are deemed virtuous—must face the hazards of fortune and severe limitations in their capacities to know (Oedipus) and navigate conflicting gods, laws, and moral orders (Orestes); even "right" action can end in disaster and often death (Antigone).

This chapter explores how ARS workers and asylum seekers attempt to navigate and make sense of the tragic dilemmas that characterize Greek NGO cultures of assistance. Tragedy, I argue, does not simply produce constraints to which workers and asylum seekers must respond and adapt; it also incites engagements through which all parties manage the dilemmas of the asylum process, the work of service provision, and their encounters with each other. Tragedy thus provides the conditions of possibility for maneuverings (Coutin 2000), tactics, and, often, creative ways for dealing with moral-ethical quandaries. While these engagements may not provide ways out of tragedy, they produce a surplus of ethical and affective labor that opens up unpredictable possibilities for reflection, action, and sociality.

Crisis, Services, and Governance

At the ARS, tragedy reflects a deep structural ambivalence in Greece regarding state and NGO responsibilities to provide services to refugees and asylum seekers. Ilana Feldman (2008) shows that "crisis" services, meant to respond to temporary, extraordinary need, are "at the heart of government's relation with the population" (124)—in particular, marginal, potentially "dangerous" populations. Yet such services constantly threaten to exceed the purview of governmental responsibility, producing considerable anxiety among bureaucrats and service providers about getting "too involved" (124). Governance in sites and times of crisis thus entails the management of both services and need, and the constant recalibration of what is (or is not) appropriate to provide or request. Services for asylum seekers and refugees, in an important sense, always occupy zones of crisis. The status of "asylum seeker," like that of "refugee," is conceived as a temporary and anomalous legal category (Hathaway 1984), resulting from violence that disrupts the capacities of citizens to belong and claim rights in their countries of origin. Yet while they are indicative of "crisis" in the national politicolegal "order of things" (Danforth and van Boeschoten 2011; Malkki 1995a, b) these anomalous statuses often become protracted and even indefinite, forms of what Duffield (2007) has called "permanent emergency." The ongoing forms of crisis circumscribing the lives of asylum seekers and refugees in host countries further destabilize both the services offered and the capacity to claim them. When ascribed to the "nongovernmental" sector, as in Greece, services become even more limited, partial, and crisis-driven.

Without the legitimacy of state-based government, however, NGOs in Greece are caught in ambivalent positions with regard to the form and extent of their responsibilities. Feldman (2008) suggests that the temporary, ad hoc nature of "crisis services" puts in abeyance questions of governmental legitimacy and responsibility, allowing service provision to claim only a limited scope, remaining at the level of emergency and immediate need. At the ARS, however, questions of legitimacy and responsibility are never placed in abeyance, but remain fraught. Who is really responsible for granting services to these marginal(ized) populations? Who can legitimately claim these services, and how? In their engagements with tragedy, workers reflect on, analyze, and respond to these dilemmas in both explicit and implicit ways. Like Phoevi, some assert both a sense of responsibility and also a kind of helplessness. At other moments, they claim only limited responsibilities by asserting their distance from the state, yet the state-like, governmental qualities of the work they do are often undeniable. Workers may invoke other notions of responsibility and obligation with roots not in frameworks of governance, but with cultural, religious, and affective genealogies. These problems of responsibility and legitimacy are flexible, allowing workers to frame them differently depending on the interactional context, which itself further heightens the ad hoc character of service provision. Yet these dilemmas remain always on the table through the conflicted and unstable moral-ethical engagements of ARS work.

In addition to these dilemmas of responsibility and legitimacy are problems of capability and resources. In their classic analysis of decision making under conditions of duress and scarcity (1978), Calabresi and Bobbitt locate "tragedy" in the structural pressures that impinge on individual and state capacities to act. The dilemma that Phoevi describes emerges largely from the fact that, materially speaking, ARS workers cannot assist all those who come there seeking support. Greek NGOs, and certainly the ARS, are, in concrete and highly visible ways, frequently at the limits of capacity in terms of resources and labor power. However, an even more central (though closely related) dilemma is often one of power, *dhinami* [δύναμη]: what *can* an ARS worker do? Extensive discussions among workers about their limited resources and capabilities perpetuate an institutional ethos of lack and helplessness,[2] which, in part, Phoevi's anxieties also reflect. Thus, the further dilemma emerges: With only limited capacities and power at one's disposal, what responsibilities does one truly have? And further, if one can only offer less, should the recipient be satisfied with—or even grateful for—less?

Here I show how the moral-ethical engagements of ARS workers and asylum seekers articulate with patterns of governance enacted through the nongovernmental sector. In this sense, governance implies an "ethics" of care of both self and other (Foucault 1978), particular configurations of approved or acceptable comportment, which shape dispositions on all sides of the aid encounter, both recipient and service provider. Governance thus includes both the enactment of explicit forms of discipline and control, and the processes through which subjects cultivate dispositional norms appropriate within this particular culture of care and assistance. Yet in line with the argument of Chapter 2, governance necessarily entails indeterminacy, variation, and invention: persons do not simply strive to inhabit existing subject positions, but also shift and play on these normative frameworks of virtuous or "right" action.

The two sites of tragedy I consider in this chapter involve two different moments in the NGO encounter. First, I consider practices for determining client eligibility, through which workers identify certain persons as eligible for aid and turn others away. I explore how ARS workers manage their own sense of complicity in enacting exclusion through eligibility practices. Eligibility practices enact what Fassin describes as a "politics of life" (Fassin 2007, 2011), instantiating hierarchies, both explicit and implied, of lives characterized as more (or less) worthy of being saved. Yet I also show how engagements generated *through* tragedy can destabilize the exclusionary qualities of eligibility and its politics of life. The second site of tragedy that I consider is the ongoing work of service provision. Here, the question of eligibility is either suspended or already decided, and the task of assistance is at the forefront: what will be provided, claimed, received, and how? I consider the, often conflicting, notions of assistance that workers and clients entertain and the dispositional tactics that they invoke which, again, reflect dilemmas of responsibility and legitimacy. These conflicts and disconnections often generate debate and reflection, yet they also reconsolidate practices of (self-)

discipline, power asymmetries, and behavioral norms. Finally, I consider how engagements with tragedy often lead to new forms of sociality among workers and asylum seekers: moments of joy, humor, hope, attachment, and other intersubjective modes that spill over from the space of service provision, with equally unpredictable effects. These often mundane socialities produced *through* tragedy have a generative and even transformative role in the ethical lives of ARS workers and in ARS cultures of assistance.

Ethnographic Engagements with Ethics

I approach ethics as an emergent field of social engagement, involving both everyday practice and active reflection, constantly undergoing transformation and reconsolidation. Recent work on morality and ethics in anthropology, grounded largely in a Foucauldian perspective, explores how practices aimed toward "care of the self" cultivate particular moral-ethical dispositions (Davis 2011; Mahmood 2005; Paxson 2004). Other scholars focus less on ethics as a regime of (self-)control and highlight instead their entwinement with questions of knowledge and judgment: the processes through which persons undertake active reflection to engage dilemmas and arrive at particular decisions (Howell 1997; Laidlaw 2002; Redclift 2005; Robbins 2004). Jarett Zigon (2007, 2008, 2010) emphasizes the complementarities of these scholarly trends, asserting that they denote distinct components in a broader "ethical-moral assemblage" (Zigon 2010). He explores the embodied and dispositional factors cultivated through the *habitus* of everyday life, yet he emphasizes the ethnographic value of moments of "moral breakdown" (2007), when people encounter a rupture in the moral fabric of their world and engage consciously with this breakdown through ethical tactics. Similarly, Michael Lambek (2010: 43) distinguishes moments when ethics are "tacit" from other moments when ethics are explicitly performed. James Faubion (2011) likewise suggests that ethical life has diverse modalities. Yet rather than framing these modalities as distinct he highlights their entanglement, arguing that the "dynamic" elements of ethics are entwined with their "more homeostatic and reproductive components,"[3] consisting of normative standards of right action.

In my analysis, I show conscious reflection and the everyday practice of ethics to be mutually inclusive, both entailing elements of indeterminacy and normativity. On the one hand, ARS workers inhabit a context that is often explicitly ethically "marked" (Keane 2010), rife with moments of "moral breakdown," when decisions are undermined through conflict and uncertainty. Workers must consciously reevaluate decision making criteria, putting in question not only their individual commitments but also those enacted through institutional norms, law, and policy. Moreover, as in my conversation with Phoevi, such moments of explicit reflection are, themselves, encouraged through conversation with an ethnographer, which makes one's own commitments and dispositions—like one's "culture" (Rabinow 1977)—an object of reflection and analysis. These reflective moments, however, are themselves located within more tacit, embodied moral-ethical formations: ongoing institutional practices, macro and micro configurations of power, and dispositional norms. In engaging tragedy, ARS workers rely also on these structural, institutional, and dispositional factors, which are not simply reproduced but may also be finessed or transformed.

My analysis of tragedy is above all an exploration of what Faubion (2011) calls "ethical complexity": first how persons are simultaneously called upon to perform different and contradictory forms of "right" or appropriate action; and second, how persons encounter each other *across* ethical frameworks or fields, producing both a "middle ground" of shared meaning (R. White 1991) and forms of disconnection and mistranslation. In the anthropological study of moral-ethical life it easy to confuse the ethnographer's own analysis with that of his or her "informants." This also points to a productive slippage: the subjects of ethnographic work are also deeply engaged in making sense of ethical complexity. The engagements that I highlight in this chapter have both analytical and practical significances. In navigating tragedy, ARS workers and asylum seekers persistently offer meta-commentary regarding moral-ethical life, which itself serves to manage ethical dilemmas and also reflects norms related to Greek cultures of humanitarian assistance. They also take part—both tacitly and explicitly—in the very debates philosophers and anthropologists of ethics themselves are concerned with: how does one make decisions under conditions of duress, uncertainty, and conflict? When is one responsible? When do structure, power, and other forces outside one's control trump individual choice and responsibility?

In Phoevi's commentary, tragedy is not just expressed consciously but also conveys a deep sense of individual complicity. Such reflective expressions of individual responsibility are, however, juxtaposed against other moments when workers cite the constraints of law, the state, the government, bureaucracy, or even the NGO itself as playing a determining role in their decisions and actions. This latter tactic frames tragedy less as a problem of individual choice and more as a product of *structure*. Such appeals to structure entail a performance of fatalism that Michael Herzfeld (1992) identifies as key to the functioning of Greek bureaucracy, with the apparent "indifference" of its bureaucrats. As Herzfeld highlights, such appeals to fatalism should not be taken simply at face value; instead, they often create space for individual agency, allowing people to invoke and play on the system as well as manage failure retroactively or even preemptively. At the ARS such invocations of structure rarely include displays of indifference. Yet even when they express compassion or sympathy toward asylum seekers, workers may describe structural factors as limiting their capacity to provide assistance. Take, for instance, the phrases—often heard in encounters with aid applicants—"it's not in my hands" or "we *can't* help." Or that typical Greek performance of resignation, uttered with raised chin and hands, *ti na kanoume* [τι να κάνουμε] (what to do).

Invocations of individual choice on the one hand, and structure on the other, are both important methods of engaging tragedy, and they often work in tandem, as workers and asylum seekers navigate the dilemmas that permeate aid encounters. These tactics are, I would suggest, familiar to each worker whom I met, varying depending on the particular asylum case, rapport with the asylum seeker, and even simple (but crucial) factors like fatigue. Moreover, various moments of ARS work encourage different forms of engagement. "Moral breakdown" is a characteristic of eligibility determinations, which often demand conscious reflections from workers. In the ongoing task of service provision, however, workers and clients alike often rely on more tacit engagements that may appear to perpetuate or remake normative frameworks of value (even as they may, in some cases, innovate upon these norms). Both modes of engagement are important components in the lives of ARS workers and, more broadly, highlight the peculiar moral-ethical configurations that permeate Greek humanitarian cultures of care, aid, and assistance.

Eligibility, Moral Breakdown, and the Law

Practices for determining client eligibility were among the most ethically marked ARS institutional procedures I analyzed, presenting workers with explicit dilemmas of judgment: who will receive assistance, and who will be turned away. *Eligibility* conveys the framework, timeline, and possible future trajectories of assistance through which an individual's contact with the ARS will unfold. If found eligible, the aid applicant emerges as a beneficiary or *eksipiretoumenos* [εξυπηρετούμενος], which translates directly as "one who is served." Those deemed eligible are officially entitled to receive, pro bono, active NGO legal intervention at various stages of the asylum procedure. He or she may also be offered certain forms of social support, consisting of small stipends and assistance obtaining medical and psychiatric care and housing, whether from other NGOs, at one of the few government-affiliated camps, or in some cases, at the ARS's own small housing facility for mentally troubled clients. If found *in*eligible, he or she may still be offered free legal advice during the legal department's open office hours, known in NGO vernacular as "Duty." Depending on the attitudes and workloads of lawyers or social workers, the applicant may even receive assistance preparing documents and arranging appointments at hospitals and other institutions that provide care. However, such support for ineligible individuals, if offered at all, is informal, without any institutional commitment.

Official ARS parameters of eligibility mirror the pathways of legal protection that Greek, EU, and international law carve out. Eligibility is thus largely embedded in juridical potentialities: the cases that are possible, and the categories of protection that particular persons with particular cases could be said to fit. The ARS specializes in asylum law and is primarily devoted to serving individuals who meet the criteria for political refugee status according to Article 1A(2) of the 1951 Geneva Convention. During my stay at the ARS, workers also found individuals eligible based on "humanitarian" reasons and offered support to "vulnerable" categories of persons (children, unaccompanied minors, and victims of trafficking). Just as crucial for eligibility is the "credibility" of potential clients and their claims, though as I will show in the next chapter, this criterion has extremely complex and fluid grounds of assessment.

Almost all aid candidates I met at the ARS were in positions of politicolegal and social instability. Many had lodged asylum applications, while some still hoped or planned to do so; others may have made an application but then encountered problems with the asylum process. Some had acquired the appropriate documents (such as the pink card), while others were not so fortunate. For those who arrived at the office without any documents, or with only a deportation order, the challenge for lawyers was how to lodge or reactivate an asylum claim, and/or how to (re)acquire or renew documents. Even those with active asylum claims and suitable documents had to navigate constantly changing, and always cryptic, policies and practices, as procedures and deadlines were amended without notice or warning, and forms and appeals had to be prepared in Greek with, at the very least, basic knowledge of legalistic linguistic formulations. Keeping one's claim active and guiding it through various bureaucratic stages of the process were themselves extraordinarily difficult challenges. Finally, those with rejected asylum claims often needed help preparing an appeal to the second-instance asylum committee, or the protracted, labor-intensive, and expensive application to the Council of State. Finally, among these legal challenges were often much more urgent social needs: how to find housing, subsistence, medical care, and work.

While eligibility for ARS assistance does not guarantee the success of an asylum claim, the stakes of eligibility practices are high. "Eligible" clients have, at the very least, the promise of pro bono legal assistance in a country where the state provides next to none, and when money to pay for a private lawyer is hard to come by. Moreover, by taking on an asylum case, an ARS lawyer may grant it additional weight and legitimacy at the state level, given the well-known rigors of NGO eligibility determination processes. This is particularly owing to the many private lawyers now working in the field of asylum law who, in the eyes of state and NGO workers alike, may be of uneven credibility and quality.[4] A police officer in the asylum division at Allodhapon explained to me in summer 2011 that having a lawyer does not always strengthen someone's case, since (in his opinion) many lawyers will do almost anything for money; yet, he emphasized, an applicant supported by an *NGO* lawyer is most likely a refugee, since NGOs only take on the most "serious cases." Finally, the social assistance offered to eligible clients, while certainly limited, can make a material difference in their struggles to survive.

Given the high stakes of eligibility decisions, NGO workers often faced difficult dilemmas in choosing whom to support and whom to turn away. They often undertook active reflection regarding the material and institutional limitations in their capacities to provide assistance to all. However, the formalities of law and legal categories also produced dilemmas that lawyers finagled or undermined through their everyday practice. Eligibility decisions, ultimately, highlight the flexibility of law as a matrix for moral-ethical engagement.

"Results"

Two weeks into my fieldwork, Giannis, the Legal Department coordinator, gave me a task: he asked me to type up documents he referred to as *apotelesmata* [αποτελέσματα] (results), letters through which aid applicants are officially notified whether the ARS will support their cases. His assistant, Athanassia, directed me to a desk with a decent computer (a rare find) and a hefty pile of files. She opened the top file, leafing through photocopies of various documents until she arrived at the last page of the applicant interview form. There, under the final heading, *Decision* (in English), I read the statement, also in English: "Does not meet criteria so as to be recognized as a refugee. Ineligible." "Ineligible" was written on a separate line and underlined twice, followed by the signature and the handwritten name of a lawyer.

Athanassia instructed me simply to summarize these sections of the form, inserting the resulting paragraph into a standardized document, with ARS letterhead and Giannis's name signing off at the bottom of the page. She explained that I should not reproduce any rationales for eligible decisions, but for ineligible applicants I should type a brief paragraph with details supporting the negative decision. These "results" would later be printed out, signed in ink by Giannis, stamped with a *sfrayidha* [σφραγίδα] (the official seal of the organization), and given to applicants when they inquired about the status of their interviews.

Examining these interview forms and distilling them into the brief, letter-like format of "results" is how I first began to examine the logics of decision-making through which individual workers formally grant and withhold services. I thus first encountered eligibility practices quite literally through their "results," not the processes through which lawyers render decisions. The vast majority of results in this first group of files were rejections, and as I transformed them into brief and impersonal summaries, I found them unsatisfying and often troubling. Nonetheless, in their very brevity, they presented a broad panorama of the often surprisingly flexible logics through which eligibility is granted, denied, granted conditionally, and often nuanced.

Below I reproduce five examples from this first set of results, which comprise a range of categories through which ARS workers formally consign (in) eligibility. On the actual decision letter, the result carries personal information, such as name, nationality, gender, and file number. For persons deemed eligible, only the name and file information changes. Across the rejections, however, with their customized rationales, one can discern unique styles of phrasing or the written-English idiosyncrasies of the particular worker who interviewed the candidate. Yet despite their individualized qualities, rejections are often highly formulaic in the wording and stated logics of assessment.

> NATIONALITY: DR Congo
> It is hereby certified that the above-mentioned person has been considered to fulfill the criteria in order to benefit from free legal assistance by the Legal Assistance Unit for his recognition as a refugee under the 1951/1967 (Geneva/New York) Refugee Convention.
> NATIONALITY: Afghanistan
> It is hereby certified that the above-mentioned person has been considered to fulfill the criteria in order to benefit from free legal assistance as a humanitarian case by the ARS Legal Assistance Unit. He can benefit from full assistance by ARS, but not financial assistance.
> NATIONALITY: Bangladesh
> The applicant has not expressed any fear of persecution whatsoever and, according to his statements, he left his country of origin solely for economic reasons and to improve his living conditions. Therefore, the applicant cannot be considered as fulfilling the criteria of art. 1A2 of the 1951 Geneva Convention.
> NATIONALITY: Nigeria
> IC [the individual case] did not substantiate her claims of having faced problems because of her religious beliefs. It appears more possible that she and her boyfriend left for economic reasons, the possibility of trafficking not excluded. The IC does not fulfill the criteria so as to be recognized as a refugee.
> NATIONALITY: Somalia
> IC's credibility regarding her origin is reduced by the fact that she does not speak the Somali language and her knowledge of Somalia is inadequate. Furthermore, IC moved exclusively for economic considerations and for that reason her claim for international protection does not fulfill the criteria of article 1A2 of the Geneva Convention.

This brief sample provides a broad spectrum of both stated and implied eligibility criteria, with distinct possible trajectories of ARS assistance (or lack thereof). (In)eligibility entails not only the degree to which the "individual case" (IC) coheres with legal qualifications for refugee status or humanitarian protection, but also more nebulous factors, such as the possibility that trafficking has occurred and questions of credibility. I will address in detail the epistemic complexities embedded in both trafficking and notions of credibility in the following chapter. Here, I take "results" as a starting point from which to unpack processes of decision making that I observed around particular categories of (in)eligibility. Then I consider how workers reflect upon, contest, complicate, undermine, and finesse these formulaic notions of eligibility.

"Recognition as a Refugee" Versus the Problem of the "Economic"

Even if we consider the apparently "clear" results in this sample, very quickly this clarity begins to break down. The only eligible case is for a man from the Democratic Republic of Congo—one among just three eligible cases that I found in this group of sixty-nine files, with interviews dated between April and September of 2006. As stated formally in the result, this man's eligibility is grounded on the interviewer finding him to meet the criteria of Article 1A(2) of the 1951 Geneva Convention, indicating recognition as a refugee. From the result, we do not know the story he told or any other details. The practice to withhold details on positive results can, in part, be interpreted as an attempt by the ARS to keep such criteria hidden from aid applicants. A few members of the legal staff explained to me that an eligible person might show his or her result to others, who could then imitate the qualities that made the case successful (though applicants can—and do—conduct research on refugee criteria without such information, often through collaboration with one another). This bureaucratized mystification of positive eligibility criteria also achieves a kind of shrouding and sacralization of the elements through which eligible clients are identified. Further, these distilled and formalized positive decisions smooth over and elide the contradictions and processes of deliberation that may have gone into producing that "result."

As the antithesis to the client from Congo, the other apparently clear-cut result here concerns the individual from Bangladesh. Here, details are stated, very briefly, and the rejection is grounded on the assertion that the individual himself claimed to have come to Greece for "economic reasons." This result is, in fact, a typed reproduction of a formulaic rejection statement that the ARS Legal Unit produced in the form of a *sphrayidha* or stamp. This stamp was originally conceived as a timesaving method, allowing interviewers to reproduce rejections quickly, in series, rather than writing them out repeatedly by hand.[5] The stamp itself attests to the large numbers that NGO workers deemed to be "economic" migrants. Yet even without it, interviewers found ways of rejecting clients with "economic problems" using their own informal shorthand. One lawyer, for instance, consistently used the explanation that the person came to Greece to "ameliorate the conditions of his/her life." Another wrote that the applicant came here "solely for economic reasons and to improve his/her living conditions." Like the stamp, such phrases are not just formulaic; they also convey an ethos of clarity and confidence based on a fundamental assumption that an "economic" migrant can never be a "refugee."

Across these different formulas for conveying ineligibility based on economic reasons, we can observe what I came to identify early on in my research as the problem of "the economic:" that any mention of poverty, economic problems, or the need for work is the death knell for an asylum case, in the eyes of both ARS workers and the state. This problem can be summed up in a comment made by Stavros, who explained that when advising potential clients about asylum hearings, he always emphasized: "say anything at all—just don't say anything about economic problems." Or in the words of Dimitris: "'work' is the magic word that turns your case to shit." This incompatibility between "economic problems" and refugeeness, reproduced in NGO eligibility frameworks, invokes a fundamental binary division inscribed in asylum law. "Migrants" and "refugees" are, most often, legally and conceptually distinguished according to notions of "voluntary," economically driven migration versus "forced" displacement (Zolberg et al. 1989). This binary, in turn, invokes longstanding debates among human rights scholars and practitioners regarding the assumed distinction between political violence, which threatens civil and political rights, and poverty or deprivation, which undermine economic and social rights. ARS workers reinscribe this distinction repeatedly in characterizing eligible applicants in terms of their recognizability as refugees, and in the formulaic and seemingly confident codes of ineligibility applied to so-called "economic" cases.

Much like Phoevi's commentary, such binary distinctions between "refugees" and "immigrants" underline the tragic dilemmas embedded not just in eligibility decisions but, more broadly, in asylum law itself. Popular interpretations of the category of "refugee" rarely take seriously its role as an instrument of juridical inclusion and exclusion, a status that brings someone back into the framework of law and rights while casting others out. "The refugee" emerges precisely as one who can *be* saved through recognition as a subject entitled to protection. Certainly, frameworks of assessment mobilized through asylum procedures bring multiple forms of violence to bear on those recognized as refugees, who also suffer political and social exclusion. However, in a Europe that officially confines most immigration to zones of illegality, the *non*-refugees—the "economic" migrants, with "economic" problems—are framed as the lowest of the low. "Refugees" can be saved, while "migrants" may be left to drown.

Despite the ARS's institutional reassertion of the legitimacy (and assumed clarity) of this binary, in practice, positive results often took shape through protracted deliberation, which I will examine in detail in Chapter 5. Meanwhile, pronounced anxieties often accompanied the issuance of rejections. Workers frequently expressed frustration about rejecting individuals who spoke of poverty and economic problems, as well as evident discomfort with the assumptions on which these rejections were based. Most interviewers expressed distaste with using the stamp, though when workloads were particularly high I would sometimes see a few moving speedily through backlogged files with the repeated *thump* of the stamp hitting ink, then paper. Nikos reasoned that the result was the same either way—he might as well save time. Phoevi, however, took strong exception to the use of the stamp. Showing me an interview form that someone else had completed by using the stamp, she underscored that while she agreed that the applicant was ineligible, the stamp misrepresented the story and was inaccurate: "This is supposed to save time, but when you start to cut corners, this is a problem. When you start trying to fit people into something they are not, this is the beginning of discrimination." She added that it was particularly scary when she herself felt the need to cut corners, because she is now in a position of power. Phoevi thus identified the stamp itself as an ethically marked object, signifying the encroachment of bureaucratic expediencies into the moral-ethical imperative of accountability.

The stamp also was a source of dark humor, inciting illustrative (if backhanded) commentary, which highlighted the ambivalences surrounding the rejection process. At a group meeting of the legal unit, amid laughter all around, Dimitris—with his characteristic chuckle—presented the stamp ceremoniously to me in a mock rite of passage: inducting the *anthropologos*, with my evident interest in and sympathies for the rejectees, into the fraught world of NGO work. (The concrete point in presenting me with the stamp was that I should put myself to work and use it.) Even the Bangla interpreter, Rahman, participated enthusiastically in such acerbic forms of office humor. After an interview was complete and the applicant had left, he would often mime a stamping motion, hit the table in front of him, and wink at the interviewer; he was all too aware of the ineligible status of most of these cases. In other instances, however, lawyers expressed pronounced regret at these rejections and a marked ambivalence about their legitimacy. As Stavros explained, "I do accept that not everyone is a refugee. But what I do not accept is that it is morally wrong to want a better life for you and your family."

The problem of the "economic" is further compounded by the ways in which state and NGO bureaucracies came to associate "refugeeness" and "economic problems" with particular nationalities and countries of origin. Most eligible ARS clients came from countries of origin clearly denoted in UK Home Office and U.S. Department of State reports as "refugee producing countries," such as (at that time) Somalia and Sudan. Those from South Asia (primarily Bangladesh and Pakistan) were rejected almost across the board. As I discuss in detail in Chapter 5, in rare yet important instances lawyers supported individuals from these countries of origin, thus challenging the assumed illegitimacy of their cases. South Asian applicants became important topics of conversation at the ARS, sparking expressions of regret and bitter humor. I often heard statements capitalizing on the likability of these rejected applicants, as when Sophia, one of the more experienced lawyers, commented, shaking her head: "They are good guys—Pakistanis, Bangladeshis. If they could only stay legally for work—for just a little while."

The problem of the economic is a tragic dilemma inscribed in both asylum law and rights discourse more generally, the topic of ongoing debates among both practitioners and scholars. Individual ARS workers engaged this dilemma through both their talk and their practice, variously upholding the distinction between political and economic violence, contesting it, or finagling it. This division is a strong one. The "economic" remains the antithesis of a successful asylum claim, as well as the primary grounds for rejection by the ARS; no amount of finessing, however generous, can make "economic problems" grounds for recognition as a refugee. Yet the engagements that this distinction generates were also significant. As lawyers reflected on the exclusionary nature of this division and their own complicity in enacting it, they invoked and produced other forms of moral-ethical attachment. Whether through sympathy and regret directed toward "economic migrants," the penetrative insights of dark humor, stereotyped notions of South Asians as "good guys," or the recognition that wanting to work may be a legitimate goal in another moral universe, lawyers destabilized, undermined, and in some ways even moved beyond the tragic frameworks in which they operated.

"Humanitarian"

As one can see from the result for the applicant from Afghanistan (above), the ARS consigned a form of eligibility for "humanitarian reasons," which did not depend on the applicant's capacity for recognition as a refugee. "Humanitarian reasons," as defined by the ARS, mimicked the category of "humanitarian protection" then at use in Greek law and, in varying forms, throughout the European Union. Humanitarian protection was, at that time, grounded in Article 3 of the European Convention on Human Rights and Fundamental Freedoms, protecting against cruel, inhuman, and degrading treatment. European member states practice and apply this framework differently. Currently, as of 2013, following a number of changes in the legal apparatus, the Greek state grants humanitarian protection both to persons whose health and safety are in jeopardy owing to medical problems or particular vulnerability (such as families with young children), *and* to persons who can demonstrate stable and longstanding ties in Greece. This latter use is based on Article 8 of the European Convention, guaranteeing the right to respect for private and family life, home, and correspondence, without interference by state and public authorities except for reasons of national security or public safety. During much of my field research, however, the humanitarian category also functioned as a temporary "permission to remain" in Greece, conferred to rejected asylum seekers whose lives might be in danger if they returned home, even if they were not deemed at risk of personalized persecution according to Geneva Convention criteria. In 2008, with the issuance of Presidential Decrees 90/2008 and 96/2008, "subsidiary protection" emerged as the dominant category for conferring such temporary status, primarily to those from Iraq and Afghanistan, and now, Syria. In the ethnographic material presented here, however, ARS workers applied the humanitarian category *both* to those at risk of health related dangers and those facing generalized violence.

During the period of my primary fieldwork (2006–2008), the Greek state granted humanitarian status for one year, and this status could be extended annually on a discretionary basis. This temporary status could then be revoked when danger passed: when health improved or the situation in the home country became stable. Such forms of temporary protection have come under powerful criticism by scholars (Fassin 2005; Ticktin 2006) for their enactment of a kind of biopolitical sovereignty, framing persons in terms of their "bare" biological existence (Agamben 1998:131). Moreover, critics have shown that the proliferation of forms of temporary status (including "subsidiary protection" and, in the United States, "temporary protected status"[6]) dilutes claimants' entitlements to full and holistic protection measures and undermines the state's responsibility to uphold such rights (Soysal 1994). These are important critiques. At the ARS, however, I found that when invoked outside the official purview of state protection, the "humanitarian" category of eligibility also provided ways to finesse the tragic binaries implied in asylum law. For NGO workers, this category was highly flexible and could variously shift, dilute, or even strengthen available frameworks of eligibility.

Practically speaking, at the ARS there was little difference in the services consigned through the "eligible" category and the "humanitarian" assignation. A primary distinction was that "humanitarian" applicants did not receive the small stipends that the NGO granted to "eligible" individuals. Yet legal assistance was provided to both categories of applicant, and much of the support for "humanitarian" applicants centered on furthering their asylum claims through appeals or assisting them to reapply for refugee status. Among ARS workers, the humanitarian category thus provided a way of granting services to applicants who did not appear to have strong cases for asylum without the added pressure of having to legitimate their claims for refugee status.

Stavros, for instance, employed the humanitarian category liberally, explaining "let the Ministry decide" [whether he or she is a refugee]. He thus assigned humanitarian status as a way of taking on more cases, shifting the ultimate responsibility for decision making from himself to the state. A conversation with Sophia is particularly illustrative of the flexibility enabled through the "humanitarian" category. We were discussing an applicant from Nigeria who, from his interview, appeared to have a fairly clear-cut ineligible case. He had claimed "economic reasons" as his rationale for coming to Greece, but he and his wife had recently had a baby in Athens. Sophia was frustrated at the prospect of rejecting this family, but finally she shrugged her shoulders and smiled: *Tha valo ena 'humanitarian' yia to moro* [θα βάλω ένα "humanitarian" για το μωρό] (I will put a "humanitarian" for the baby). Even though the man appeared ineligible, she reasoned that to deport a family with such a young child back to Nigeria would put the baby's life in danger.

The "humanitarian" category enabled her not to reject the *moro* and also rendered the entire family eligible for legal aid services. This flexible label enabled Sophia to give this family more than she would have otherwise, finding a temporary pathway through restrictive frameworks of both legal protection and eligibility criteria. The humanitarian eligibility category thus provided ways simultaneously to assert and neutralize individual agency against a wider backdrop of what Herzfeld (1992: 143–44) describes as *efthinofovia*: the performance of being unwilling to take responsibility, particularly under anomalous circumstances. As Stavros shows, however, *efthinofovia*—such as his strategy of turning the responsibility back on the state—itself can provide space to maneuver, granting a default form of eligibility in the gap left by his own silence. Sophia, for example, deflects personal responsibility through her use of a category deemed bureaucratically acceptable, which masks the innovative character of her decision, even as she smilingly asserts it.

In other instances, however, the humanitarian category served as a way to grant minimum eligibility and thus less to persons who might otherwise be deemed to have legitimate claims for asylum. During the time when I was in the field, the ARS routinely granted Afghans and Iraqis eligibility based on humanitarian reasons, owing to the instabilities in both countries. Yet legal staff rarely suggested that these aid applicants could, in fact, be legitimate "refugees." Geneva Convention criteria demand that one demonstrate a vulnerability to personalized forms of persecution, not just generalized violence such as that predominant in both Iraq and Afghanistan. The irony, however, is that personalized persecution is often even more difficult to substantiate when violence is so widespread. For instance, the lawyer Costas explained to me that most Iraqis were "humanitarian" cases, but someone who had been a member of the Baathist government, for instance, might have a strong claim for asylum, owing to increased vulnerability after the U.S. invasion of Iraq in 2003.

This ARS practice was, however, challenged by a surprising source: the restrictive asylum committee of the Greek state. In the first few months of 2008, a few dozen Chaldean Christians from Iraq were granted political asylum in Greece on the grounds that their religious membership made them vulnerable to extra-state terror. As mentioned in Chapter 2, after the U.S. occupation of Iraq, many Iraqi cases were "frozen" by the Greek state, presumably in the hopes that the situation in Iraq would improve and many could return home. This made the sudden flood of positive decisions to these Chaldean Iraqis particularly noteworthy. Nikos, one of the more experienced and successful lawyers at the ARS, known among colleagues for his professionalism, attention to detail, and commitment to his work, accompanied a few of these individuals to their asylum hearings. The day when one of these clients received asylum, Nikos bustled about the office with a wide grin, and at a staff meeting there was a rare moment of celebration, as Giannis characterized the positive decisions as a huge success for the ARS. But Melike, the registrar, who on her own initiative keeps track of state asylum decisions in the margins of her large registration books, mentioned later to me that some of the Iraqis who had received asylum were initially found "ineligible" at the ARS.

I discovered the files of these Iraqi claimants in the locked storage room on the sixth floor, which the office manager Athanassia described to me as a place where files "go to die"—a clearinghouse for all older cases, regardless of their (in)eligibility. At the top of the very top staircase, unswept and littered with boxes and papers, this room is full of filing cabinets, stacked one atop the other. Files, many of them large, indicating significant or protracted legal and bureaucratic interventions, balance atop these cabinets and in piles on the floor. Luckily, the files I was searching for were easy to find, in a well-marked cabinet toward the back of the room near the window, which illuminated the dust in its glare. Most of these cases had been in process since before the war in Iraq, from 2000, 2001, even 1999, yet the files were surprisingly thin, particularly for persons who had ultimately received asylum, which indicated a lack of contact with the ARS. One lawyer, who had since left the ARS, had interviewed most of them, and just as Melike said he had rejected them all, with the rationale that their accounts did not amount to persecution in the sense of the Geneva Convention. However, this initial declaration of "ineligible" had been crossed out and changed to "humanitarian," Giannis's signature authorizing this change a number of years after their initial interviews.

This change in eligibility status was likely grounded on the political turmoil and increasing instability in Iraq owing to the U.S. invasion, which was particularly threatening for minorities. Yet both the original and amended ARS "results" were significantly more restrictive than the state's decision to recognize these applicants as refugees, despite the state's notoriously restrictive approach to awarding asylum. Most often, ARS eligibility criteria were far more open than the notoriously closed asylum system in Greece. Here, however, the flexibility of the "humanitarian" category diluted the forms of assistance offered to these aid candidates. While workers often used this label to provide more to those who might qualify for less, for Iraqis and Afghans who had been treated with a blanket "humanitarian" classification at the ARS, it functioned as a least common denominator. In addition to these aspects of classificatory flexibility, the humanitarian label saved time and energy. It was a "catch all" that allows lawyers to avoid the (often protracted) deliberative tasks entailed in more stringent eligibility determinations. On a busy day, Giannis interrupted a number of interviews with Afghan applicants, clapped his hands and shouted: "*Ela ela* (come on, come on). Simple simple! Afghan/ humanitarian. Chop-chop." Through this category, lawyers granted some candidates more stable forms of assistance, but some also ended up rendering decisions that were even more restrictive or diluted. The humanitarian category thus points to the unpredictable effects of moral-ethical engagements with the law.

Eligibility determination procedures, with their ethically marked character, often incited extensive reflective engagements from ARS workers through which they managed and, in some cases, destabilized (in)eligibility's tragic "politics of life." In practice, eligibility determinations thus were rarely as black and white as, for instance, Phoevi's commentary would suggest. While "results" may appear clear cut, the deliberations, reflections, and discussions that went into these decisions were dynamic, messy, and ultimately considerably grayer than their formal presentation on paper might convey. The final result certainly mattered, with its material capacities to effect hierarchy, inclusion, and exclusion. Yet the moral-ethical engagements generated through these decisions (before, during, and even after the issuance of the final result) were crucial components of ARS work, and in many cases, concretely shaped the lived effects of eligibility determinations.

Dispositional Tactics and Cultures of Assistance

On a busy afternoon, I met with a client the registration staff had warned was "difficult." Because all the other desks were taken, we met in a private corner office, which was empty as the regular occupant was away for the afternoon—an accidental privilege. When I greeted the client he answered with a wide smile that belied his "difficult" reputation: "You are very kind," he said in English. He had thick stubble and visible dust on his clothes, suggesting to me that perhaps he was homeless or without a stable living situation. I asked him for his pink card to photocopy it for the file, and he procured it with fingertips inscribed with dirt. The card was atypical—a light pink, which I recognized as the kind issued at the airport, unlike the bright pink cards issued at the Athens police station. Under the heading "nationality" the asylum officer had written "indeterminate" (*akathoristou*) [ακαθόριστου].

The interpreter Nasdar began the interview by stating that the man spoke perfect Farsi but that he wanted to do the interview in Arabic. Then the client explained, with the help of Nasdar, that although he is from Iran he is Arab, and that is why the police made a mistake on his card. From there, his story poured out. For years he had been an activist fighting for secession from Iran, but two people in his group were executed, so he and a few others fled to a neighboring country. There, some of his colleagues disappeared, and so he kept moving toward Europe, never feeling safe.

His movements in Europe were similarly complex. On his NGO registration form, his original port of entry into the EU was recorded as Greece, but he had been in Sweden for close to two years, and there he had even lodged an asylum claim. He had recently been sent back to Greece from Sweden under the auspices of Dublin II, but he insisted that he hated Greece and would never make an asylum claim there. He told me that after he had first crossed the northern land border between Greece and Turkey, Greek police arrested him and he asked—in Arabic, Farsi, and English—to apply for asylum. However, late one night the police took him and a few others back across the border to Turkey and left them. After making some money in Istanbul, he paid a smuggler to take him to Sweden, where, he explained, he was given a house, food, and money for a few months, until the Swedish authorities discovered his fingerprints in the Schengen Information System (SIS), documenting his stay in Greece. Thus, he was sent "back" to Greece, with no knowledge of the country or the language, and also with no house, no food, and no money. He was now homeless and without work. At this point in our discussion, he began to raise his voice, stabbing the air with his hands: "Why won't they let me go to Sweden? They need to give me my rights. If they won't give me my rights, they must let me go."

In subsequent meetings with ARS workers, he oscillated between similar expressions of anger, frustration, and pleas for help. In what became his final meeting at the ARS, he appealed to the lawyer Maria: "Why did they send me back here? Please help me: I need a house, I need food. Give me a paper to go to another country, or give me a house. I have no clean clothes, no food. Look at you—you are clean, you are full of food." Maria emphasized that because she does not work for the government, she could not give him a paper, but that meanwhile, social workers were trying to find him housing through other organizations, though it is often difficult to find housing for a single man, as families and unaccompanied minors are prioritized. The client then yelled, switching again to Arabic, which the interpreter translated: "Then give me a paper to go to another country. If Greece won't give me my rights, then I won't make my case here." Silence ensued, and after a few moments he walked out. Maria threw up her hands and raised her chin in a common Greek gesture of resignation: "What to do? Some people we simply cannot help."

This account illustrates another tragic dilemma that ARS workers often confront: the client whom one "simply can't help." He was most likely eligible; he requested assistance repeatedly and Maria wanted to support him, but she described herself as unable to offer services in a way that met his expectations, her own, and the institutional norms of the ARS. The tragic aspects of this dilemma were not just a result of simple scarcity in resources, though that certainly seems to have played a role. Rather, in this encounter, there was a profound disconnect between what this man asked for and expected, what Maria implicitly expected of him, and what she saw herself as responsible and able to provide. Through aid encounters, clients and workers meet each other across ethical fields that have taken shape in diverse worlds of practice, knowledge, and discourse (see Faubion 2011). Sometimes, these engagements produce points of shared meaning, but they also incite mistranslations and ruptures in communication, to which workers and clients must also adapt and respond.

Engaging the State

Maria's tactic for dealing with this client was resignation. Through such performances of resignation, workers invoke a "tragic sense of life" (Unamuno 1954) itself as a tactic for dealing with tragedy by gesturing to forces outside their control: structural pressures, limited resources, and the client's own agency. Maria's performance of resignation had an instrumental quality, serving to displace responsibility from herself, depersonalize her inability to meet the client's needs and, in a sense, legitimize the failure of her attempt to provide aid. Yet for the client this failure was evidently deeply personal: he refused to acknowledge Maria's reply as legitimate, and instead, through both his commentary and his affective response, he held her responsible. At the center of these disconnects is the figure of the state and the ARS's ambivalent position as a "nongovernmental" service provider.

The category of the *state* is an essential foil in the ethical engagements of ARS workers and also figures crucially in many clients' claims for assistance. At the inception of each meeting, lawyers and social workers insist on this boundary, mobilizing a kind of script that, while varying in its exact phrasing, contains the following statements: *this is a nongovernmental organization, which means we are not connected to the state; anything you tell me is confidential and will not be communicated to the state or to the police; we make no decision about your asylum claim.* This move has two primary impulses. By discursively distancing themselves from the state, NGO workers simultaneously cultivate potential closeness with clients (they "will not give information to the state"), but they also deflect certain responsibilities (while providing some forms of help, they also "make no decision about asylum claims"). Many clients, however, often interpret the ARS as a state office. A Somali client once explained to me that there was an "ARS" in Germany, an "ARS" in the Netherlands, and an "ARS" in Belgium (all places where he had spent time before being sent back to Greece under the auspices of Dublin II). When I asked him to clarify what he meant, he looked at me as if it was obvious: the "social service" office, he explained. I had similar conversations with clients from various countries of origin (see Cabot 2013a). The "nongovernmental" character of the ARS was never explicitly part of these discussions, but rather many clients framed "state" social service offices elsewhere in Europe as commensurable with the ARS. While for workers, the nongovernmental character of the ARS mattered deeply, constraining both their capacities and their responsibilities, for many clients this was irrelevant: it is a social service office like any other, and must provide assistance. Given this set of divergent expectations, many—like the Iranian client—expressed disappointment, resentment, and even outrage toward ARS workers.

The figure of the *European* state was thus also an important category in the moral-ethical terrains of ARS encounters. Countries in Europe's west and north—most often France, Germany, the United Kingdom, the Netherlands, and Sweden—emerged repeatedly as asylum seekers' stated "destinations." Even Italy was often framed as more desirable than Greece, not necessarily as a destination, but owing to its closer proximity to these other EU member states. These countries were, in part, deemed more desirable thanks to more established immigrant and refugee communities, where many asylum seekers had family and acquaintances. Many, however, also emphasized the *services* that they expected to find in the European north. For instance, a Kurdish man from Iraq told me that his life in Greece had been very difficult; "Greece is not vacationland," he said; "life in Greece is *askhimi* [άσχημη]" (ugly/bad). But he explained that he planned to go to Sweden, where he had friends who had told him that they had received housing, food, money each month, and even language lessons. The "bad" qualities often associated with Greece thus reflected qualitative differences in the assistance that many asylum seekers expected to find in different European destinations. Moreover, some ARS clients had extensive personal experiences with social service bureaucracies in other EU member states, despite the constraints that, until recently, the Dublin system placed on asylum seekers in Greece. Even for those who underwent multiple (re)deportations, shuttling between northern European sites and Greece, these experiences furnished frameworks of reference that mediated encounters with ARS workers.

Workers, meanwhile, entertained deeply ambivalent attitudes toward both the state and Europe, reflecting the ethical ambiguities of their own positions as NGO service providers. In early September 2007, the day after the wedding of one of the lawyers, and shortly after wildfires had devastated the hills of the Peloponnese, I sat at a beachside café in Kalamata with three ARS workers, all recognized refugees: Hadi from Afghanistan, Louis from the Democratic Republic of Congo, and Melike from Turkey. Often serving as intermediaries between workers and clients, they know intimately the extraordinary difficulties that asylum seekers and even recognized refugees face in Greece. Through their ties to particular migrant communities, they must navigate appeals by clients who invoke common origins and language as grounds for assistance. Nevertheless, they encounter the same tragic dilemmas as Greek workers regarding questions of responsibility, legitimacy, and capacity.

Our conversation frequently turned to the subject of work—mostly debriefing the wedding and office-related gossip. But during a lull in the conversation I asked the group a question I had been mulling over for a while: "What do you think is the most important work done at the ARS?" Hadi most often offered biting humor in response to my questions, but this time he turned serious. Rather than giving me a specific answer, he took this question as a provocation to elucidate the peculiar position in which ARS workers find themselves in relation to the state. He explained in Greek that Greece does not have social support or *pronia* [πρόνοια] for refugees and asylum seekers, unlike other countries in Europe, so the state gives this work to the ARS. He added that the Greek state receives money from the EU in order to provide services for refugees but, meanwhile, subcontracts this work out to the ARS and other NGOs. He recounted that both NGO workers and clients think that the state "keeps the money." Nevertheless, by contracting this work out to the ARS, the state does really have to do this work; meanwhile, "the ARS works for the state, but it does not seem like it." Louis nodded but then interjected insistently: "this work is not work for an NGO. It's work for the state." He then went on to explain that, in practice, the ARS is part of the state, but it does not have the money or the capabilities to do its work.

This conversation recasts the relationship between the state and the NGO in terms of mimesis and displaced responsibility. Hadi describes a conspiratorial, recursive cycle in which the state displaces services for refugees onto the ARS. Louis highlights the dilemmas of responsibility that this produces, yet his comment reorients this responsibility (though not the work itself) back toward the state. I turned to Melike, who had remained quiet throughout, and asked what she thought. When she replied, her voice was tight: "What is our work? It is *malakies* [masturbations].[7] If I could find other good work, where I could actually help people, I would not spend one more day at the ARS." For Melike, this mimetic project produces insufficiency and a kind of helplessness.

Among Greek ARS workers, I encountered similar commentary that grounded the tragic character of ARS work in the persistent blurring of boundaries between NGO and state responsibilities. Even while ARS employees distanced themselves from the responsibilities of government workers, they also emphasized the need to cooperate with the state; my very first day at the ARS, I was told by one of the lawyers that "we work *with* the Ministry." Yet ARS workers also insisted that their labor, and the organization itself, leaked into the territory of what *should* be state responsibility. Dimitris, who over time had cultivated cordial relationships with individual police officers, told me that it bothered him when one of his police or Ministry acquaintances claimed that they cannot do certain things because they work for the government. He explained that some members of the police claimed to feel strong sympathy for asylum seekers, but that they often called him for certain forms of assistance, under the assumption that he has more flexibility as an "NGO" worker: "They tell me, 'You should do that, you are an NGO.' I say, 'You are the police, why don't you do it?' " Such dilemmas regarding responsibility and legitimacy thus appear not to be entirely peculiar to NGO service providers, but at the ARS they had particularly powerful effects.

In ARS discourse, then, the state often came to represent structural limitations that impinged on workers' capacities to offer assistance. Yet their own ambivalent relationship with the state was also, for some, an uncomfortable signal that they themselves were complicit in (and thus responsible for) maintaining and even reinforcing such structural factors. In June 2008, Kyriaki, one of the younger lawyers, took on a supervisory role in the asylum division at Allodhapon, observing, on designated days, how police were undertaking first-instance asylum applications. She explained that she knew she should be critical of the police—and indeed she was. Yet when she looked around, the police station did not seem much different from the ARS: desks jammed up against one another, people shouting, no privacy, and no one really helping. "Chaos," she added.

Likewise, the many similarities between ARS eligibility processes and the state Refugee Status Determination Procedure (RSDP) were not lost on ARS workers. While most recognized eligibility determinations as a necessity, for some it emerged as frustrating and even ironic that, as advocates, they spent so much of their time turning asylum seekers away. A year after she left the ARS to work with the UNHCR overseeing the Refugee Status Determination Procedure (RSDP) at the Athens police, I interviewed Danaë about her time at the ARS. I asked about the similarities and differences between the state interview and the ARS eligibility procedure, commenting how it seemed, to me, to "mimic" the state process. She answered matter-of-factly: "it doesn't mimic anything—it's exactly the same." The ARS, she added, is *ena kratos mesa tou kratous* [ένα κράτος μέσα του κράτους] ("a state within the state").

Despite their evident discomfort with being associated with the state, workers persistently highlighted the entanglement of the ARS within state infrastructures, and the various ways in which the ARS mimics or even replicates state practices. Through such commentary, workers manage, give voice to, and make sense of the ways in which structural factors shape their own capacities and responsibilities to act and choose. While these engagements may not carry the urgency of Phoevi's emphasis on individual choice, they have similarly powerful affective dimensions, manifesting in a pervasive climate of helplessness and often cynicism. One lawyer summed up this sense of helplessness by painting it, much like Melike's description of *malakies*, as a kind of absurdity, which ends in exhaustive yet wasted effort on the part of both applicants and workers: "They come again and again, and we see them, and we do this and we do that. But we don't do anything."

These ambivalent and even conflicting interpretations regarding the relationship between NGO and state services both reflect and amplify the tragic nature of ARS work. These dilemmas speak to fundamentally ambiguous questions of responsibility and legitimacy in the task of service provision, and they generate further disconnects and mistranslations that complicate the already difficult tasks of asking for and granting assistance. Yet these moments of conflict also produce new tactics and modalities for ethical engagement, generating important forms of affective and emotional work and ongoing debates about what constitutes assistance, and where it can—and should—be found.

Rights and Hospitality

I have shown that the figure of *Europe*—in particular, a robust European welfare state—is a primary category over and against which some clients frame Greece (and the ARS) as insufficient with regard to service provision. Significantly, however, many Greeks also describe the notion of a strong welfare state, which recognizes the rights of both citizens and noncitizens to access services, as distinctly European and not Greek. This image of a generous, paternalistic "European" state contrasts starkly with popular *Greek* characterizations of their own state in terms of entrenched bureaucratic corruption (Herzfeld 1992) and traditions of violence (Panourgia 2009), which have only been heightened during the financial turmoil currently wracking Greece.[8] Amid such highly ambivalent attitudes toward their own state, for many Greek citizens the state is not a primary site to seek assistance or services.

The *ethnos* [έθνος] (nation), with its lines of familial intimacy, as opposed to the *kratos* [κράτος] (the institutional state) (Herzfeld 1985), is a dominant framework through which many Greeks seek support and assistance. Kinship and community ties in the European south have been shown to operate alongside (and perhaps instead of) formal state mechanisms of support and assistance (Zinn 2001). Ethnographers have long attested to the importance of kinship ties in diverse Greek experiences of belonging and subsistence (Campbell 1964; Dubisch 1986, 1993; Just 2000; Loizos and Papataxiarchis 1991; Panourgia 1995; Paxson 2004; Placas 2009), and Herzfeld's work (1992, 1997) suggests that "kinship" in Greece can be understood more broadly as a citizenship figured in terms of nationalized "metaphors" of descent and blood. This assistance offered through kinship ties (whether on the level of the family or the nation) is, however, not easily applicable when it comes to those identified as *kseni* [ξένοι] (foreigners). While asylum seekers certainly forge close networks of assistance within their own communities, they most often do not have access to stable networks of affiliation within the "insides" of the Greek nation. Their position at the margins of the Greek sociopolitical body necessitates that asylum seekers develop other tactics for claiming assistance, which are available and appropriate to "foreigners."

Asylum seekers thus must achieve a *good enough* fluency in this broader culture of assistance, cultivating dispositional capacities that can be deemed "virtuous" within an ethics of care embedded in Greek cultural norms. Many ARS clients, as might be expected, make claims to assistance through the language of rights, which may appear to cohere with the ARS's own values as a rights-based NGO. Indeed, the Iranian client asks Maria for assistance by asserting: "Give me my rights, or I won't stay in Greece." This tactic solicits the recognition of a shared humanness that makes one *entitled* to assistance, despite a lack of legal recognition, and regardless of individual networks and connections (or lack thereof). Yet Maria's response is telling. While she does not outright reject the client's rights-based claim, she explains that her own limited power as an NGO (not government) worker makes it impossible for her to honor his request. Rather, if he is to become a client whom she *can* help, he will accept and even be grateful for the limited assistance she offers him. To acquire assistance at the ARS he must, in an important sense, suspend his claim to entitlement.

The dispositional tactics that Maria invokes in her encounter with this man have roots in Greek cultural norms of *filoksenia* [φιλοξενία] "love of the stranger." *Filoksenia*, most often translated as "hospitality," is a long-standing vernacular framework through which "strangers" or "foreigners" are not incorporated but welcomed; yet in being welcomed as guests, strangers are further marked as outsiders in a territory or home (see Candea 2012). While *filoksenia* is generally invoked to describe relationships between hosts and guests in a household, Herzfeld (1987b) has persuasively shown that this concept acts as a "shifter" (Jakobson 1990 [1957]) that can denote the insides/outsides of social relationships on multiple scales: the house, the village, the island, the region, and the nation (Dubisch 1993). *Filoksenia* thus also serves as a broader "matrix" (Papataxiarchis 2006) that allows Greeks to manage and domesticate potentially dangerous foreigners (see also Zarkia 1996). Particularly in the context of immigration, *filoksenia* carries with it certain asymmetrical expectations of reciprocity and obligation (Campbell 1964), implying the imagined, eventual capacity of the guest to reciprocate the host's kindness (Papataxiarchis 2006). Likewise, the asylum seeker's or refugee's capacity to behave well, cooperate, and demonstrate indebtedness to the "host" nation (Greece) is crucial to being identified as a "good" guest (and eventually, a good "host") (Rozakou 2006, 2012).

Yet aid candidates at the ARS often ask for assistance through rights-based language, and human rights and *filoksenia* are grounded in fundamentally conflicting ethics of care (Cabot 2013a). Entitlement is crucial to the logic of human rights (Donnelly 2003), and further, rights are based on a presumption of symmetry—that all human beings have rights.[9] *Filoksenia*, however, does not bear that feature of entitlement distinctive to rights but invokes obligation and, necessarily, asymmetry (Campbell 1964), as well as much more arbitrary notions of *kindness*. In a discussion regarding this very chapter, then in process, a Greek immigration scholar highlighted this distinction between entitlement and kindness, explaining ironically: "You don't get anything in Greece because you are entitled to it, but because Greeks are 'kind,' and they give it to you." *Filoksenia*'s genealogies lie outside rights-based frameworks or institutional law. In a conversation with the lawyer Dimitris and his wife, Fani, also an asylum lawyer, they emphasized that *filoksenia* is not based on *dhikeomata* [δικαιόματα] (entitlements or rights) but is a matter of *ipokhreosi* [υποχρέωση] (obligation)—"the law of god, not the law of the state." Through *filoksenia*, asylum seekers are not *entitled* to assistance, but rather, it must be given—not by the state, but by individual Greeks.

I found that when ARS clients asserted rights-based claims combined with displays of anger, many workers invoked elements of *filoksenia* as a dispositional tactic, which both deflected clients' claims to entitlement and enabled them to offer limited forms of assistance. Most ARS workers are paid, though there are also a number of volunteers, and lack of funding often results in consecutive months of no pay for all employees. NGO workers often emphasized the voluntary nature of their work, highlighting their individual desires to help despite their inability to offer material forms of assistance. As one lawyer explained in English to a disappointed client: "I don't want anyone to be unhappy, I don't want anyone to be hungry. But it is not in my hands." Workers thus often characterized the assistance that they provided as intensely individual and unofficial, grounded in personal offers of kindness rather than in institutional, material forms of support.

Fourteen months into my fieldwork, I conducted an interview with Costas, a lawyer who had worked at the ARS for a number of years. He responded immediately to a question that, on his request, I had sent him beforehand, which I had also asked Hadi, Melike, and Louis. "What is the most important work done at the ARS?" He explained that he had thought about this question for a long time, and he had decided that generally ARS workers "cannot really help." But, he explained, they do offer "someone to yell at, someone to complain to, someone who listens." I asked about the legal aid work he does, and in particular, the assistance he provides with papers and legal processes. He shook his head. Costas thus insisted that the most important work he did at the ARS was grounded not on material assistance but on interpersonal encounters with clients. It is important to take this claim seriously, and I will return to it later. Yet as Costas implies here, *filoksenia* further limits the scope of already limited services, diluting their legitimacy and, likewise, the responsibilities of workers. Facing clients who implicated them as responsible, ARS workers rely even more heavily on the dispositional tactics of voluntarism and kindness, presenting their labor as invisible and *affective* (see Muehlebach 2007), rather than as material and effective. As one lawyer explained to a frustrated client, "You cannot always see the ways that we help you, but that does not mean that we are not trying."

Hierarchies of Clients

The dispositional tactics of workers positioned particular clients as more (or less) capable of exhibiting particular capacities. A particularly rich vignette, which I have discussed elsewhere for how it illustrates the relationship between social support and geographical imaginaries (Cabot 2013a), highlights how the dispositional tactics of workers produce hierarchies among clients. Kyriaki often provided nuanced commentary on the dilemmas she and other ARS workers faced in encounters with clients. She told me she had taken the job at the ARS specifically to have the opportunity to help refugees, but she was deeply frustrated with her work, particularly regarding how clients responded to her. After a particularly difficult morning, she explained to me that some asylum seekers "make a decision that their lives will never get any better here, and they do what they can to survive, but others keep trying to change their situation—they shout and complain." On another day, in meetings with two different clients, she pointed to a similar taxonomy of client behavior, which highlights how *filoksenia*, as a dispositional tactic, presupposes certain norms of right or appropriate action on the part of clients.

The first client was a striking young woman from Ethiopia, who said she was nineteen, and was dressed casually in jeans, sneakers, and a button-down shirt. While she sat close to Kyriaki's desk, she began her interview with downcast eyes, fidgeting and looking at her hands. She explained that she had been working in the house of a Greek family, though she had left her position recently and was now jobless. On repeated questioning by Kyriaki as to why she had left her job, she explained quietly that her employer (a woman) had beaten her and accused her of stealing. She did not offer this information openly, but rather, Kyriaki prodded her carefully, brought her water, leaned in, made small jokes, and smiled pleasantly. Gradually, the woman began to laugh and make eye contact, and finally, talked about her abuse by her employer. At the end of the meeting, Kyriaki reviewed the options for legal action against the employer and she gave the woman her card, asking her to call if she ever needed help. While the young woman explained that she did not want to pursue legal action, she smiled and thanked Kyriaki profusely before she left.

About fifteen minutes later a woman from Nigeria came in, carrying a newborn baby boy. The woman sat down, evidently exhausted, while Kyriaki and other members of the legal team admired the child. The baby cried persistently and during the meeting the woman was distracted repeatedly by trying to calm him. When Kyriaki asked about the child's father, the woman said that he was living in France, and went on to explain that she had also lived in France and the child had, in fact, been born there, but she and the baby had been deported back to Greece. She did not cite any particular difficulties in Greece, but emphasized that in France she had received food and money for herself and the child. Kyriaki told the woman that she would try to give her something immediately—not much but something. She called a social worker, who arrived a few minutes later with a bag of baby formula and diapers, offering to schedule an appointment to discuss other kinds of help. The client unsmilingly inspected the white parcel and asked, evidently nonplussed, "Is this everything?" She added that she did not need to make another appointment if this is all they would give her. When the woman left, Kyriaki commented: "So you see the difference between two women. One knows she is in a bad position and asks for your help. The other, maybe because she has been in France, expects more than you can give."

Kyriaki's interpretations of these clients' responses do not necessarily accurately reflect these clients' actual experiences. Indeed, the Nigerian woman's deportation back to Greece, her legally tenuous position, her separation from her partner, and evident exhaustion amid the pressures of caring for a young child were all most likely crucial factors in her response. Nonetheless, in suggesting that these clients must *ask* for help and be satisfied with—even grateful for—less, Kyriaki highlights the pronounced hierarchies embedded in *filoksenia*. The dispositional tactics of workers positioned clients as subjects who were more (or less) capable of exhibiting particular dispositional capacities. Aid candidates who responded to *filoksenia* in a way that complemented workers' own approaches often were framed as more worthy or deserving of assistance. Others, who presented claims of entitlement, were often characterized as more "difficult" or problematic. When communication broke down through these conflicting dispositional norms, across divergent fields of ethical engagement, assistance became even more subject to tragic limitations.

Anger and Resignation

In November 2006, Omar, the ARS Arabic interpreter, brought me to eat at an unlicensed Sudanese/Somali "community center" or "restaurant" on a crowded side street off Omonia Square, which has since been closed in the recent rash of policing. A social nexus for both of these communities, this restaurant was a place where new arrivals could find advice and assistance from compatriots who had faced common predicaments in Greece. Except for the few women working behind the bar serving tea and coffee, the regulars were almost all men, persons who moved in both "legal" and "illegal" spheres, in both the kinds of status they had and the work they did. Community organizers negotiated with smugglers to assist new arrivals in leaving Greece undetected, facilitating movement to the north of Europe, and construction workers supplemented poor salaries by selling a variety of other items on the side.

Omar is an elderly Sudanese gentleman who, at that time, was working occasionally as an interpreter at the ARS. With his dignified dress and perfect, British accented English, his Greek colleagues always addressed him as Kyrie or "Mr.," without the irony that sometimes accompanies such formal kinds of address. In another life, he used to wear a suit to work in an air-conditioned office and order coffee from an assistant, but after six years in Greece as a legally recognized refugee he still did not have a steady place to live. Despite his education, language capabilities, and "white collar" work experience, he had worked mostly odd jobs since arriving in Greece—a fish farm in Crete, picking fruit in the Peloponnese. Despite his job as an interpreter, he was unable to afford rent on his meager salary and was always on the lookout for other work. He was also an ARS client, but the assistance he received there also did not suffice: he had also been sleeping on the sofa at the community center, which had helped him through a few periods of homelessness. While in our many conversations he expressed frustration with his life in Greece, he was careful to display acceptance and calm resignation. "It would drive me crazy," he explained, to always be angry—"It doesn't help. It's like banging your head against a wall." So he frequently would laugh and recite a Greek phrase of cultivated resignation and helplessness: "*Ti na kanoume* [What to do]? This is Greece."

During our trip to the community center, Omar introduced me to acquaintances, both Sudanese and Somali, who were willing or interested to talk to me about my work. On the way out, I met a young Somali man, who introduced himself as Mohammed. The three of us walked toward the metro together, navigating pedestrians, mopeds, and potholes, as Mohammed explained that over the space of two years he had lived in a number of countries in the European north—Sweden, Denmark, and the Netherlands—and had been sent back to Greece twice under the auspices of Dublin II; in total, he had lived in Greece for only a few months. He then asked for more details about my research, and when I told him that I was doing research at the ARS, he interrupted sharply: "Crap organization. Crap. I have been there many times. I know some of the lawyers. When I was being sent back here from other countries, people at the social service offices [in other countries] said that if I went to the ARS they would help me. But nothing, nothing." Citing his experience with "social service" offices elsewhere in the EU, where he received contact information for the ARS, Mohammed thus marked the ARS as a site where he was *entitled* to help.

It is important to note that before asylum seekers like Mohammed were returned to Greece, NGOs in other member states often gave them information that, while likely intended to empower, was often highly simplified and only partially correct or even wholly inaccurate in practice. For instance, an information packet distributed at a UK airport specifies: "No financial assistance is granted to asylum seekers by the Greek state. However, [the ARS] provides free legal assistance to asylum seekers during all stages of the determination procedure. Applicants are also entitled to receive legal counseling at any stage of the claim's procedure by [a variety of NGOs, including the ARS]." No mention is made of the screening process or the NGO's own limited resources. Having evidently received similar information, Mohammed's frustration is not surprising, highlighting the fact that the ARS refused to recognize his entitlements as legitimate in the way that he had (perhaps quite reasonably) expected.

While Mohammed was explaining his frustrations with the ARS, Omar interjected: "I know, they don't give me anything either." Mohammed cut him off. "I'm going away now. OK? We are done." He left without turning around. Omar turned to me and explained, quietly: "He wasn't mad at you—he is mad at the organization. People think that they should be able to give them anything, but you and I know that this is not true."

Despite similar experiences with an insufficiency of services at the ARS, Mohammed and Omar illustrated diametrically divergent modes of responding to and managing this insufficiency: entitlement and anger on the one hand, and resignation on the other. Although Omar was in many ways an ARS insider, in the face of Mohammed's anger he invoked his common experience as a poorly served client, legitimating Mohammed's frustrations. Yet once Mohammed left, Omar repositioned himself as privy to the way the NGO "really works," suggesting that Mohammed's assertions of entitlement and anger are inappropriate and, at the very least, ineffective. Instead, when he himself is faced with disappointment, rather than "banging his head against a wall" Omar is careful to display resignation, a dispositional tactic coherent with *filoksenia* and the tactics displayed by workers themselves. Clients undertake diverse ethical engagements to deal with both conflicts with workers and the material insufficiencies in the assistance they receive. Some may cultivate dispositional capacities that cohere with long-standing "Greek" cultures of care and assistance, such as *filoksenia*; others (whether owing to a lack of familiarity or willingness, or differences in class, knowledge, and cultural background) may draw on dispositional tactics that undermine or bump up against those of workers. These diverse modes of comportment matter deeply not just in aid encounters, as we saw in the meeting between Maria and the Iranian client, but also, as here, emerge in encounters between migrants and asylum seekers themselves, creating further hierarchies and power asymmetries.

Tragedy is not just a series of constraints, but also generative, producing multilayered and dialogical ethical engagements between workers and clients. Despite the conscious reflective work that eligibility practices incite, they also reinforce an exclusionary politics of life which prioritizes certain categories of persons over others as more worthy or deserving of assistance. The dialogical interplay of dispositional tactics within a broader culture of care and assistance in Greece reproduces norms of behavior, comportment, and right action as well as further hierarchies. Yet as workers and clients engage tragedy, they also destabilize or exceed the hierarchies inscribed through law, governance, and dominant dispositional norms. Their engagements also generate new socialities between workers and asylum seekers. These socialities are often mundane, taking place at the margins of ARS work, yet they also entail modes of attachment and emotional commitments which have important and lasting effects in NGO cultures of assistance.

Socialities: "First Contact" and "Acting Well"

Anna and Danaë are friends. Having met when working at the ARS, they have both since gone on to work as UNHCR representatives at the Athens police. In July 2011, during a heat wave in Athens, Danaë and I met in a cozy bar at the edges of Exarcheia. I found her on a small sofa at the back, taking advantage of the *air condition*, and we both ordered tall cool beers. She explained that the bar was her "home," equidistant from her apartment south of the city center and the police department on the other side of the city; she often came there to rest. Two years earlier, when we had last spoken in person, she had expressed frustration and exhaustion about her work at the ARS, so when we turned to the topic of her new UNHCR position, I was surprised when she mused: "I miss the ARS. *Fayame tosa skata mazi* [φάγαμε τόσα σκατά μαζί] (We ate so much shit together)—we became a family." We both laughed.

Then she elaborated: she missed the "counseling," advising and talking to asylum seekers. She had come to understand that for many who arrived at the ARS, she was the *proti epafi* [πρώτη επαφή] (first contact) in Greece: "Someone finds him/herself before you who has not yet met any police officer." She went on to explain that as the "first contact," she had not only a chance to provide legal advice but also the opportunity to encounter persons coming from worlds radically different from hers. In her new role overseeing the police, she still had contact with asylum seekers, but no longer in the role of "counsel": instead, she sat alongside the officers, in the process of adjudication. At the ARS, "first contact" appeared to have been an intimate, even sacred, moment.

A few days later, I met Anna at her house, and, like Danaë, she expressed nostalgia for her life at the ARS. I asked her if there were any cases or clients that she remembered in particular. She thought for a moment, then laughed and told me about an Iranian client, whom she used to run into often in the metro and they would talk: "I met him by chance . . . I was going home and I was meeting him in the metro. We just would stop and talk, and he was very good . . . he was just really good personally . . . telling me how he was trying to survive in Greece." She went on to comment on the therapeutic quality of these kinds of interactions and conversations, both in and outside the office: "[If you have suffered and been discriminated against] even the smallest thing when you come to Greece or a European country you appreciate . . . when a person listens to you and acts well with you . . . I think for many of them [clients] it's really important that we listen."

Both these reminiscences point to the significance of quotidian socialities generated through ARS engagements. For Danaë, it is the contact she had with persons often new to Greece and to Europe; for Anna, it is listening, chatting in the metro, and encountering someone who—quite simply—was "really good personally." Anna's emphasis on the importance of listening is reminiscent of Costas's commentary on "the most important work at the ARS." Yet while for him this highlights the limitations of his work, for Anna it emerges as a crucial moment of intersubjective engagement that also furnishes a kind of ethical orientation: an emergent standard of right action that forms a new ground of intelligibility, across the diverse experiences of workers and clients.

The generative nature of tragedy lies not just in how it produces new forms of moral-ethical engagement. I would also suggest that it has the potential to incite, in a nascent way, what Gramsci (1992) denotes as "critical consciousness." Gramsci describes how consciousness of one's own position in the strata of social and class relationships, with its attendant responsibilities, emerges first in the sphere of "ethical life." He explains that in order to enter the field of the "political," such consciousness must be articulated, simplified, and reiterated for multiple audiences. Yet I believe we see it emerging here in the socialities of ARS work—though perhaps not always in the ways one might expect. Importantly, such fleeting socialities may not have an end outside themselves or any material effect on an asylum case, yet they can take on their own lives, leaking outside the space of the office figuratively and even literally. These commentaries certainly reference dispositional qualities related to the self-presentations of these asylum seekers, with accompanying forms of hierarchy and relations of power. Yet they also point to something that exceeds that: the mundane but ethically inflected pleasures of "acting well" with others whose experiences and positions are radically different from one's own.

Conclusions

I began this chapter with Phoevi's commentary on both her own agency and the inescapable limitations she must face in navigating tragic dilemmas. I want to close by suggesting that such fraught moral-ethical engagements speak to forms of subjectivity and modes of agency that may be peculiar to Greek cultures of humanitarian aid. Thomas Laqueur (1989: 177–78) argues that "the humanitarian narrative" is grounded on the presumed entwinement of agency and causality, through which "ameliorative action is portrayed as possible, effective, and morally imperative"; he contrasts this to tragedy, where the suffering of the protagonist is compelling precisely because it is *beyond* help. Similarly, David Chandler (2001) argues that the narrative tropes underlying humanitarian aid serve to *compel* action and intervention, whereas tragedy highlights the failure and impossibility of effective action. These theorizations of humanitarianism's ethical terrains, however, elide the specific textures and valences through which global discourses of humanitarianism emerge in the realm of praxis. Tragedy—as both a dramatic form and an ethical configuration—is at the heart of a particular Greek humanitarian practice, as it unfolds in the frequent struggles and rare but important pleasures of daily life at the ARS. The ethical orientations of ARS workers, as they engage tragedy, highlight the fraught yet surprisingly flexible configurations of subjectivity that permeate particular humanitarian projects. The tragic ethos of humanitarian aid in Athens points to a precarious, contradictory, yet canny subject, whose hands are tied even she acts; who finds ways to innovate even by reasserting the status quo; and who may speak through resignation and silence. Aid workers simultaneously assert and undermine their roles as agentive actors, in the face of ineluctable structural, institutional, and ethical conflict.

Chapter 4

Images of Vulnerability

In spring 2008, I sat chatting with the gruff, chain-smoking lawyer Dimitris as the afternoon light filtered through the city smog and the dusty windows of his office. The ARS was quiet, having closed for the day, and we were discussing the determination of client eligibility. I asked Dimitris what he considered most important in making eligibility decisions, and he pulled out some paper and compiled a list. Some factors were relatively concrete and empirical, including the applicant's country of origin, Dimitris's research and notes from meetings with the applicant, and advice of his coworkers. Yet the list overwhelmingly reflected much more nebulous elements: the applicant's effort to communicate, to gain trust, to express his or her situation, and to be sincere; the applicant's display of the appropriate degree of emotion; and both Dimitris's and the interpreter's opinions and emotions. Finally, however, Dimitris emphasized that eligibility depended primarily on the *sinoliki ikona* [συνολική εικόνα] (whole picture) of the case, comprising, in his words, both subjective and objective elements.

Taking Dimitris's commentary as a provocation, this chapter considers how *pictures* of cases are produced and how they render persons (in)eligible for ARS services. Dimitris's notion of a "whole picture," which takes shape through the shared efforts of both lawyers and aid candidates, highlights how eligibility determinations are supremely composite and dialogical, grounded not so much in formal articulations of law as in the sociabilities and sensibilities of NGO encounters. Eligibility decisions emerge through dialogical forms of "mutual co-authorship" (Brenneis and Duranti 1986) between workers and aid applicants. Brenneis (1987) coins the term "social aesthetics" to indicate the informal, often implicit conventions through which performer/audience interactions unfold (see also Cavanaugh 2009). Traversing linguistic, performance-based, textual, and visual genres, such conventions guide performers and audiences in execution and interpretation, comprising also the fluid frameworks through which a performance is judged (in)coherent or (un)successful. In the theater of the law, such conventions have a powerful role. Diverse participants act—often simultaneously—as performers and audiences, seeking to interpret, play on, anticipate, analyze, shape, or conform to the expectations of others. The "social aesthetics" of eligibility decisions, then, comprise the forms and conventions through which workers and aid applicants together produce a "whole picture" of a case.

My analysis here expands the framing of social aesthetics to explore its role in knowledge practices. As Kant outlined long ago in his *Critique of Judgment*, the Greek root of "aesthetics" refers not simply to visuality but to the broader domains of feeling or sense and their role in knowledge and judgment. This more holistic notion of aesthetics is often eclipsed in its English variant (which tends to refer to the arrangement of visual terrains) but is very much present in contemporary Greek. As Nadia Seremetakis (1996: 5) writes, the Greek verb *aesthanomai* [αισθάνομαι] means—often simultaneously—"I feel or sense, I understand, grasp, learn or receive information" and "judge correctly." The mutual performances entailed in aid encounters draw on a panorama of sensorial and stylistic cues in the formation of knowledge and judgment. Moreover, as Herzfeld (1997) highlights through his discussion of "social poetics" (a not dissimilar model of dialogical social performance), sensorial dimensions are never unmediated but are themselves saturated with essentialisms, stereotypes, and other normative qualities that participants also regularly invoke. As Herzfeld (1997) shows, such stereotypes are not simply normative but also create space for modes of agency that are strategic and even ironic in character. At the ARS, stereotypes around gender, race, class, and country of origin do not simply furnish forms of constraint but also provide tools for the "tactical deployment of ideal types" (47).

Dimitris's "whole picture" serves as a kind of template that designates particular applicants as (in)eligible. Didier Fassin argues that practices of aid distribution produce a "figure" (Fassin 2007: 512) of the deserving aid recipient, framing him or her as a victim in need of being protected or saved (see also Ong 2003; Ticktin 2006). He suggests that successful aid candidates "willingly submit to the category assigned to them: they understand the logic of the construction, and they anticipate its potential benefits" (Fassin 2007: 512). By attending to the social aesthetics of vulnerability, however, I seek to complexify and deepen ethnographic understandings of aid distribution.

First, I show that, rather than seeking to "fit" existing templates of victimhood and vulnerability, aid candidates actively participate in producing and even reshaping the pictures through which their eligibility is assessed. Second, I demonstrate how they engage in refusal as well as submission, as they—knowingly or not—(mis)read and (re)interpret the expectations of audiences, consisting variously of lawyers, medical assessors, peers, journalists, asylum adjudicators, and even ethnographers (Cabot 2013b).

Aid candidates and service providers thus together shape, refigure, and even resist dominant images of deservingness, victimhood, and vulnerability from within systems of aid distribution. Recent literature locates the agency of migrants and asylum seekers largely in the realm of political action, platforms where "alien" subjects make claims to civil entitlements (Alexandrakis 2013) outside infrastructures of support and care (see Feldman and Ticktin 2011). Miriam Ticktin (2011: 19) distinguishes "political" action, aimed toward radical change that disrupts the status quo, from the "antipolitics" of humanitarianism (see also Ferguson 1994; Fisher 1997). She argues, following Giorgio Agamben (1998) that, in claiming to stand outside politics through the moral imperative to offer care and support, humanitarian organizations often reproduce structures of power and violence; the migrants, asylum seekers, and refugees they serve often remain caught in these dynamics of exclusion. Therefore, she argues compellingly, rather than enabling radical change, aid organizations often reinforce the "established order."

The establishment and perpetuation of order is, however, inextricably wedded to indeterminacy. Sally Falk Moore (1978: 39) writes that "cultural, contractual, and technical imperatives always leave gaps" requiring adjustments and reinterpretations, which are themselves full of ambiguities, inconsistencies, and often contradictions" (see also Friedrich 1986). Here I track the indeterminate effects and potentialities of encounters in sites of "antipolitics." I argue that even as they reinforce frameworks of exclusion, aid encounters give rise to a circumscribed agency. These modes of agency may not be intentional, proactive, or revolutionary in the sense of "political" action. Indeed, they may be better described as a kind of tactical maneuvering (see also Ahearn 2001; Coutin 2000; Mountz et al. 2002; Ortner 2006). De Certeau writes of "indeterminate trajectories," "sentences that remain unpredictable within the space ordered by the organizing techniques of system" (De Certeau 1984: 34). Here I examine maneuverings that make use of gaps in ordering practices—and the gaps generated *through* ordering practices—with unpredictable but sometimes powerful effects.

The dialogical qualities of eligibility practices and the maneuverings they entail do not, however, imply a symmetrical relationship between aid applicant and aid worker. While the picture of a case is always coproduced, it emerges across axes of radical inequality based on gender, race, class, country of origin, and other less obvious forms of exclusion. At the ARS, gaps in power also reflect gaps in knowledge. Some aid candidates display only partial awareness of lawyers' expectations, while others may have more sophisticated or reliable knowledge acquired through social networks, literacy, or exposure to refugee regimes in countries of origin and transit. Workers and aid applicants meet across spatial, temporal, and evidentiary gaps entailing profound epistemological lacunae. Applications for assistance are grounded on events that happened in the past, in another country, which may or may not be substantiated by documentary evidence (Bohmer and Shuman 2008). Others, for whom assistance would mean recognition as victims of trafficking or torture, may have cases that NGO workers find suspicious, risky, or dangerous, owing to the illegalities associated with their claims. Eligibility practices are persistently haunted by "epistemic anxiety" (Stoler 2008; see also Bubant 2009): pervasive uncertainties that manifest in an endemic climate of mistrust and which, for workers, reflect the epistemological problem of how to know, really, about those whom they must judge.

At the ARS, aid candidates who appeared to be "vulnerable" in the eyes of the law—*trafficking victims* and *unaccompanied minors*—were particularly prone to generating epistemic anxieties among workers. In rights-based discourse, "vulnerability" is often a floating signifier, denoting individuals who are particularly "at risk" of having their rights violated, or for whom the stakes of rights violations are particularly high. Not based on the framework of asylum law, eligibility for vulnerable individuals at the ARS is grounded on two legislative apparatuses with international, EU, and Greek levels of application: the rights of the child and anti-trafficking measures. Largely through the illegality, danger, and fear associated with these claims, and the extraordinary power asymmetries that shaped these candidates' encounters with workers, those thought to be trafficking victims and minors often eluded the efforts of workers to know and understand their cases and render reliable judgments. While social aesthetics were important in ARS eligibility practices more broadly, they had a particularly crucial role in the assessment of vulnerability, as "vulnerable" cases persistently exposed the limitations of formal, bureaucratic modes of assessment. As workers sought to piece together pictures of "vulnerable" persons, however, these pictures often took on a life of their own, becoming phantasmagorical. Thus, knowledge of the other became even more indeterminate, comprised of shadows and projected images that may, or may not, reflect the real.

My analysis ethnographically tracks the dialogical production of "pictures" of trafficking victims and unaccompanied minors. First, I discuss the narrative and performative dimensions of the interview process and the role of social aesthetics in eligibility determinations. Then I turn to a case involving Dimitris and an applicant named Sarah, whom he initially identified as a possible trafficking victim but later considered to have a possible case for asylum, though ultimately her eligibility remained unresolved. Finally, through a consideration of ARS encounters with unaccompanied minors, I examine how pictures can take on a life of their own through rumor, fantasy, and nightmare. I show that social aesthetics, and the unstable, indeterminate forms of knowledge that they produce, have a crucial role in eligibility assessments, reflecting the epistemic anxiety endemic to vulnerability claims and asylum-related adjudication practices. Pictures of aid candidates ultimately emerge as blurry or unclear, evading visibility and knowability, yet they also highlight the importance of indeterminate forms of agency, through which aid workers and "vulnerable victims" may undermine systems of exclusion from within.

Storytelling and Information

ARS work entailed a strong reliance on bureaucratic practices in order to rectify epistemic anxieties by generating information about aid candidates. A *sinendefksi* [συνέντευξη] (interview) between applicants and workers (most often lawyers) was the primary event in eligibility determinations. Guided by a series of questions on an interview form, the interviewer, the applicant, and in many cases also an interpreter together coauthored a life history. Serving a crucial role in the assessment of asylum claims at both state and nongovernmental institutions, life history interviews can be highly consequential elements of intense scrutiny (Good 2011), with extraordinarily asymmetrical (Blommaert 2001), even "coercive" qualities (McKinley 1997). Through the interview process, however, the bureaucratic penchant for producing and assessing information became tightly entwined with the "art" of storytelling. Benjamin (2002: 144) writes that storytelling, grounded on "experience that passed from mouth to mouth," carries authority over radical difference and distance. "Information," in contrast, lays claim to "prompt verifiability"; it must "sound plausible," appearing "understandable in itself" (147). However, in both the eligibility assessments that I describe here and, more broadly, in state adjudications of asylum claims, a hybrid form emerges: the story itself serves both to produce and to substantiate information about the candidate.

In asylum claims, life histories may or may not be supported by documents or verifiable by country of origin reports (though such external indicators of legitimacy certainly have an important role). ARS workers proceeded under the assumption that an applicant may not be able to produce reliable documents, and thus the *story*—as both performance and textual, narrative artifact—became the primary object through which a person was deemed (in)eligible. As the "picture" of the case emerged, questions of form, plausibility, performance, and the applicant's comportment—in short, the social aesthetics through which the story unfolded—took center stage. Social aesthetics thus generated new ways of knowing—or, as it were, *ways of seeing*—when bureaucratic forms of knowledge production failed. The social aesthetics of eligibility are, in this sense, inextricable from what Annelise Riles (2001: 19) calls the "aesthetics of failure": the ways in which "bureaucratic practices point again and again toward their own incompleteness." When the interview process generateed further epistemic gaps, social aesthetics came to furnish primary ways of knowing and judging.

While social aesthetics allowed NGO decision makers to "fill in" epistemic gaps, they also generated new forms of uncertainty. Research on the role of narrative and performance in legal settings highlights how the aesthetic dimensions of speech often encode and reproduce normative frameworks of knowledge, interaction, and judgment (Conley and O'Barr 1998; Matoesian 1993, 2001, 1997). However, as Hirsch (1998) and, more recently, Richland (2010) have shown, normative elements of speech, performance, and interpretation can also enable flexibilities. Even when social aesthetics drew on normative, even stereotyped, notions of race, class, and gender and moralized conceptions of truth, deservingness, and credibility, those on all sides of the aid encounter finessed or adjusted dominant conventions and the power relationships that they evoked.

The social aesthetics of eligibility were intimately tied to the design aesthetics of documentary and bureaucratic forms (Riles 2001, 2007). Modeled on a format designed by the UNHCR, the ARS interview form—printed in English—asks for detailed family and kinship data; religious, ethnic, and linguistic background; work history in Greece and before arrival; routes of travel to and entry into Greece; reasons for leaving one's country; and, finally, the question, "What do you think would be the consequences of your return to your country-of-origin at this time?" At the very end of the form is the heading "assessment" and, under it, space to record comments addressing (1) main elements of asylum seeker's claim; (2) general credibility; (3) contradictions; (4) officer's thoughts on asylum seeker's claim/other points; and, finally, (5) decision.

Life histories, as narratives and, indeed, as lives of particular people, take shape within existing, though always dynamic, webs of human relationships (Arendt 1998 [1958]; Greenhouse 1996). Likewise, despite the bureaucratic, informational thrust of eligibility interviews, applicants' life histories emerged through the active work of all parties involved (see Coutin 2003: 87): interviewers, interviewees, and often interpreters as well. Although these life histories frame the aid applicant as both the subject of the story and the storyteller, the social aesthetics of the interview process render questions of authorship and agency dynamic and unclear.

When called on to perform their life histories, many asylum seekers actively attempt to conform to the expectations of their audiences. In the next chapter, I write in detail about Mahmud, an elderly man from Sudan who explained to me, in our own ethnographic interview, that in his asylum hearing he had been "a very good actor." He then reproduced a performance asking the state asylum committee to allow him to stay in Greece—a simple old man wanting to live in peace. With a chuckle, he indicated the single tear he had mustered during his asylum interview. To the adjudicators he presented himself as a vulnerable person in need of protection; to me he highlighted his canniness, fluency regarding asylum law and its adjudicative demands, and capacity to play with or even "game" the system. This does not make Mahmud any less a "real refugee," but rather underscores the intensive work applicants put into becoming recognizable as such and how they shift and adapt their own self-presentations depending on the interactional context. Ethnographic knowledge, like legal knowledge, also takes shape through the dialogisms of social aesthetics.

The same is true with the narrative dimensions of life histories. Through observations of eligibility interviews and ethnographic interviews that I conducted both inside and outside the ARS, I noticed that, over time, many asylum seekers incorporated particular narrative elements into their life histories. These included emotionally charged tropes of flight and violence, which often figure centrally in how displaced people narrate their lives

(Améry 1980; Ballinger 2003; Danforth and van Boeschoten 2011; Malkki 1995a). Of course, such narratives often reflect broadly shared experiences, yet asylum seekers must also *learn* to present such experiences in a manner compelling for particular audiences. Some life histories produced in eligibility interviews emerged as "refugee stories," with recognizable arcs that traversed a format of flight and arrival: a particular "problem" in a home country, an escape followed by a protracted period of travel, and finally arrival in Greece. More experienced asylum seekers and recognized refugees often told more polished stories, most likely having told them many times before, to both NGO workers and representatives of the state. These more polished ways of narrating and performing also leaked into ethnographic interviews with me, as I too was interpreted as an audience seeking a "refugee story."

Many of the life histories that unfolded in eligibility interviews were, however, messy, vague, scattered, demanding that lawyers actively re-narrate the accounts of claimants as they emerged both orally and on the interview form. Applicants' diverse ways of remembering and narrating were, in turn, inflected through interpreters' diverse styles of translation. The interview form, with its formulaic questions, thus produced highly variable responses, which rarely fit neatly into the arc of flight, travel, and arrival. By rephrasing questions, changing interview prompts, and giving examples, interviewers struggled to tame narratives so that they could locate them in space, situate them chronologically, and contain them on the form itself. Yet disciplining these life stories was difficult, as they persistently fell outside the form, often literally, in the scribbles, crossed-out sentences, and margin notes of interviewers. Practice and repetition helped not just applicants but also interviewers refine interview styles, producing cleaner, more logically progressive, and visually pleasing texts on the interview form.

The vast majority of ARS aid applicants were, however, found to be *in*eligible. ARS institutional norms often streamlined eligibility assessments, making rejections appear simpler, self-evident, *matters of fact*. Rejections were often grounded on the content and structure of the narrative, the performance, or a dissonance between the two. In July 2005, I observed an interview between a Bangladeshi man and a lawyer named Effie. The applicant spoke at times on his own in English and at other moments with the assistance of the interpreter. To her question why he came to Greece he cited "economic problems"—"don't get a job." At the end of his interview, Effie asked him if he wanted to add anything and he stated in English: "I am a refugee. Economic refugee." For Effie, the decision was obvious: ineligible, on the grounds that the law does not recognize "*economic* refugees"; instead, this man was a migrant. His ineligibility thus depended on the poor correlation between his story and narrative tropes that would have been more appropriate to his claim, as his insistence on economic problems rendered his application, for Effie, manifestly invalid. In his final statement, he leveraged a partial discourse of refugeeness by invoking a widely circulating phrase, "economic refugee," which is, nonetheless, woefully inadequate for his purposes here, suggesting also a lack of knowledge regarding the formal definition of the term "refugee." He was not able to interpret accurately his audience's expectations, and presented ineffective narrative material as a result.

Lawyers found other cases to be ineligible on questions of character or "general credibility," and stereotypes around country of origin mattered deeply in these assessments. For instance, NGO workers sometimes described West African applicants as engaging storytellers who are also utterly untrustworthy. Stories often referenced popular culture notions of a wild, strange, "primitive" "Africa," yet to lawyers they often appeared *too* fantastical, particularly when combined with performances that (for lawyers) may not have presented the appropriate emotional valence. Take, for example, the woman from Nigeria who—with wide eyes, big gestures, and loud voice—told the interviewer that her father had tried to sacrifice her. Or the Ghanaian man who asserted in an even tone that he came to Greece because the villagers in his town were going to cut off his head and bury him with the tribal leader. Such stories not only bore content and narrative structures that, for workers, skirted the edges of the possible, but they also suffered from performances that may have appeared too dramatic, not dramatic enough, or overall poorly rehearsed.

While this chapter focuses on adjudicative practices at the ARS, the importance of social aesthetics is by no means restricted to the NGO sector. In July 2011, I spoke with two state asylum officers who, in different ways, underscored the crucial role of aesthetic factors in their assignation of refugee status. One officer explained that in order for him to tell whether someone "really had a problem," he had to rely on *zondani epafi* [ζωντανή επαφή] (live contact): "It is not something that you can learn from papers . . . files." Another officer highlighted that while *andifasis* [αντιφάσεις] (contradictions) in a story were officially important criteria, for him, *andidhrasis* [αντιδράσεις] (reactions) had even more significance. He went on to explain that if someone carried him- or herself confidently and casually he may not take that person seriously [he slumped and pretended to be listening to ear phones in a kind of pantomime]; whereas if someone appeared to be afraid of him [he drew his shoulders up and glanced around warily], he sometimes granted their case greater merit. These commentaries underscore the centrality of social aesthetics in state adjudication procedures as well.

Bureaucratic practices and forms often enabled ARS workers to streamline and reinforce eligibility decisions, particularly when the performance or narrative of the interview deviated strongly from workers' own sensibilities. Many cases, however, were borderline, with some elements that were compelling and others that did not quite work; both the applicant's account and the worker's expectations then had to be adjusted in order to produce a decision. These applicants often had to re-perform their stories, while NGO workers actively elicited and re-crafted these narratives before issuing an eligibility determination. James Clifford (1988) highlights how borderline cases render "powerful ways of looking" problematic; from one side, the case may appear one way, while from the other side it may look like its opposite. Much like moments of "moral breakdown" (Zigon 2007) discussed in the last chapter, borderline cases incite forms of epistemic crisis, rupturing routinized, bureaucratic habits of seeing and judging, making the structures and assumptions that undergird the eligibility process "present-at-hand" (Heidegger 1962): objects of reflection and debate.

Borderline cases, particularly when combined with tropes of vulnerability, are important vehicles for rending and reconstituting habits of seeing and the "pictures" that they generate. I now turn to the borderline case of Sarah and the multiple encounters through which her eligibility was assessed. Dimitris and I sought to piece together a picture of Sarah and her case, as she told and retold her "story" to acquire legal assistance that she urgently needed: at times, she looked like a trafficking victim, and at other moments, like an asylum seeker, yet throughout, vulnerability and victimhood remained at the aesthetic core of her case. Dimitris's assessments of Sarah's case not only reflected on its workability but indicated profound dilemmas of epistemology and judgment: How to know, *really*, the truth of her account? And how to render a decision based on unreliable knowledge?

Sarah

It was a warm afternoon in April 2008, and most of the ARS lawyers were absent owing to work commitments outside the office. Louis, the Congolese gentleman who manages the waiting room, asked if I could help him find someone to do an interview with a woman from Ghana. I mentioned her to a couple of lawyers who were still in the office, but they were engaged in other meetings. A little while later, I spoke with Louis again; it was almost 3 p.m. (the ARS closes to the public at 3:30), and he explained that she had been waiting all day. I told him that because no one else was available, I would meet with her myself.

After a few minutes, she arrived at the upstairs office where I was sitting. I was struck immediately by her pleasant smile, but when she introduced herself as Sarah I understood why Louis was concerned about her; her hands trembled slightly and her voice shook. She sat down, saying that she had been ill, that the day was very warm and her head was hurting. When I asked to see her appointment card, she told me that she did not have an appointment, but that she had come to see "Mr. Dimitris." She took out a piece of paper: a deportation order, stating that she must leave Greece voluntarily on May 17, in approximately a month. This meant that her asylum claim had been rejected, and her only option was to apply to the Council of State to ask for her case to be reexamined, an expensive and labor-intensive procedure.

She did not know her ARS registration number, so I plugged her name into the database but found no trace of her file. She said that she had done an interview at the ARS months ago and had even gone to the hospital for an examination, because "Mr. Dimitris" had insisted. Improvising, I decided to collect some information to give Dimitris when I next saw him, and taking out an interview form, I asked her to tell me briefly what she had told Dimitris (while Sarah remembered him, he may not have remembered her). Without hesitation, she explained that she left Ghana with the help of a man who promised to arrange a job for her to "work in a house" in Europe. He told her to call a number when she arrived, and when she got off the boat—at a place she did not know—she called the number, and a man came and met her; he took her to a house with other African women, where he told her, "There is no house work for you." She concluded, again without hesitation: "They wanted to send me into prostitution. I tell them that I will not do that kind of work—women from Ghana don't. He beat me. I escaped."

I was startled by Sarah's brief but shocking story, delivered with such directness. This appeared to be an unambiguous description of sex trafficking, which would make her immediately eligible for ARS assistance. I took her phone number, put copies of her documents in a folder, and told her that I would call her once I had more information. I tried unsuccessfully to reach

Dimitris on his mobile to discuss Sarah's case, but the office manager explained that he was up in northern Greece for a big trafficking hearing. The office was closing and would not open again until Monday, but I thought about Sarah throughout the weekend.

Possible Victims

Sarah's direct and unselfconscious description of an experience related to trafficking was incongruous with the ARS's dominant institutional assumptions regarding trafficking victims. In coherence with EU law, the legal protection provided to trafficking victims in Greece is contingent, first, on their admission or confession to being a victim, and second, on their willingness to testify against their traffickers. On numerous occasions, ARS workers explained to me that owing to fear of traffickers, representatives of the state, and NGO workers themselves, victims rarely tell the truth in eligibility interviews, making a moment of confession very rare. Such assumptions frame possible trafficking cases as intrinsically problematic, based on the "double bind" (Bateson 1972; Fortun 2001) of a *true* victim with a credible case who does not speak the truth. This dilemma heightened the epistemic anxieties of eligibility determinations, making the identification of victims a kind of guesswork.

Owing to the (presumed or actual) rarity of direct confessions, applicants deemed eligible through the ARS trafficking program were usually characterized as those whom workers suspected of having been exploited. Employees who carried out client registration—Louis, Melike, and Hadi—screened for such possible victims according to gender and country of origin. Generally, they identified most women from Nigeria and some women from Ethiopia, Ghana, and elsewhere in Africa as possible victims, even before they were interviewed. Women from Balkan and former Eastern Bloc countries were also marked according to trafficking criteria. Yet, with the exception of Georgians, who lodged significant numbers of asylum applications during the period of my research, most women from non-EU European countries did not apply for asylum, but rather followed pathways of economic migration; many African women, however, did apply for asylum and were frequent visitors to the ARS. These screening criteria reflected informal guidelines that had emerged through conversations among ARS workers and administrators, as the organization sought to focus on groups deemed particularly at risk for trafficking.

Country of origin and gender were concrete, if extraordinarily stereotyped, elements in initial screening, yet lawyers described their methods for identifying possible victims largely in terms of feelings, impressions, narrative cues, and visual tropes—social aesthetics through which trafficking was signaled but rarely confirmed. When discussing a woman from Nigeria with whom he had just done an interview, Dimitris explained that she was likely a trafficking victim, though she had not said anything directly. When I asked why he thought so, he explained that her Nigerian origin was a signal but so was how she was dressed—she wore tight pants and a revealing shirt and had long nails and carefully braided hair. Similarly, Nikos, another lawyer, observed with evident embarrassment, "Some of these women take such good care of themselves." A pronounced or "exotic" (and deeply racialized) beauty thus came to signal possible victimhood.[1]

Indications of possible victimhood also acquired narrative shape through mundane sections of the interview form (the question why someone came to Greece was not particularly useful in trafficking cases, as victims were assumed not to speak the truth). Dimitris alluded to vague details regarding transit to Greece and spoke of "women coming here who have no idea where they were, no idea about the names of the streets in places where they have stayed, or even here [in Greece]." Another lawyer, Kyriaki, referred to the work history portion of the interview, explaining that women who say that they work in nightclubs or "do hair" are often victims. She also explained that some trafficking victims say that they are living with friends they met when they arrived in Greece. Interviewees' stories, and their details or lack thereof, were thus crucial identifying criteria.

The gendered and racialized social aesthetics associated with trafficking cases reflected political and moral economies embedded in Europeanization and international human rights, including a general increase in EU funds addressing trafficking as an area of urgent concern. In September 2006, when I began my primary fieldwork, the ARS board of directors had recently hired three lawyers to form a "team" on trafficking, consisting of Dimitris, Kyriaki, and Phoevi. While they did fundamentally the same work as other ARS lawyers, their hiring was initially supplemented through an EU counter-trafficking program. At an organization that consistently has difficulties paying its staff, this award was significant, making trafficking a central theme in meetings, divisions of labor, and of course, eligibility determinations. One of the directors of the ARS reportedly commented on more than one occasion that trafficking would provide the "future" of the organization.

At this time, Greece was at the center of European anxieties about trafficking, as it was one of the few EU countries that the U.S. State Department had identified as a "tier 2" country with regard to its counter-trafficking measures.[2] In fall 2006, I attended a conference in Athens on the challenges of trafficking. The conference was funded by the Council of Europe, and the opulence of the event attested to the significance of these funds and the importance of trafficking in negotiations of Europeanness. At a luxurious hotel near the city center, speakers from throughout the EU, both practitioners and scholars, spoke on trafficking and its challenges for civil society, EU member states, and governing bodies. As interpreters translated these talks into Greek and English, I heard the repeated sentiment that there is no place for trafficking in a "civilized" Europe. EU legislation identifies two general types of trafficking: labor trafficking and sex trafficking (also a form of labor). Frequently, however, "trafficking" is conflated with "*sex* trafficking," making *sex* a discursive and imaginative sphere in which the theme of "trafficking" often circulates. This is particularly evident in the video that played in the hotel lobby throughout the conference. Opening with a shot of a white thigh against a black backdrop, the camera pulled back to display bodies moving in shadow on a bed. Then the video cut to a lithe woman crouched in a dark room, her face buried in her hands, her legs and arms posed to cover her naked body. This incongruously sexy, tightly produced clip was later to be played on televisions all over Europe to encourage people to say "No" to trafficking.

Trafficking and its tropes of vulnerability and victimhood evoke the contradictory aesthetics of pleasure/pain, danger/enticement, and darkness/nakedness (Vance 1992), which, in turn, are entangled in desires for mobility and consumption (Agustín 2007; Rofel 2007; Tadiar 2005), patterns of migration and labor (Agathangelou 2004), and notions of civility, wealth, and Europeanness. Indeed, with its program on trafficking, the ARS itself engaged in an important form of consumption, tapping into funds coined in the halls of Brussels for protecting the civility of Europe. Trafficking, however, also evokes the tantalizing attraction of what is hidden, imagined, and unknown, reflecting the mystery attached to zones of criminality but also an epistemological umbra: trafficking is relegated to the shadows of the law, widely discussed but rarely observed directly, and victims are characterized as silent, ashamed, or afraid to speak the truth. Social aesthetics surrounding the identification of "trafficking victims" thus intersected with broader aesthetic constellations, as lawyers sought to perform a kind of epistemological unveiling: to find victims, expose traffickers, and, in a sense, render naked these shadowy economies. As the trajectory of Sarah's case makes evident, the methods through which lawyers identify, assess, and assist "victims" often invoke broader relationships of power (McKinley 2009), yet the social aesthetics of eligibility may simultaneously destabilize these frameworks of exclusion and violence.

"What if there were a different story?"

When Dimitris returned almost a week after my meeting with Sarah, he explained that he had initially taken her on as a possible trafficking victim, but her case "was not going anywhere." She had given him very vague information, which was a problem, because the police want names, locations—details she had claimed not to know or remember. He also presented me with her file. There were few details on Sarah's original interview form—not much more than the brief account she had given to me—but the file included photocopies of her identity card, the rejection of her asylum claim, and notes from various medical examiners. The latter attested to respiratory problems, mental anguish (anxiety and inability to sleep), and back and knee irritation that may have been caused by trauma. Citing his familiarity with such reports, Dimitris emphasized that the medical examiner's language framed her injuries as rather minor; indeed, while medical examiners are not officially entitled to rule on a claimant's credibility, their certificates often render implicit judgments (see Fassin and d'Halluin 2005; Fassin and Rechtman 2010). Dimitris explained, however, that the biggest problem was that he had scheduled Sarah for an appointment with the police committee that handles trafficking, but she had not appeared. This had undermined her credibility with the police and put his in jeopardy. Given the urgency of her situation, however, Dimitris agreed to reconsider her case, because, he explained, he still had the feeling that she did, indeed, have a "real problem." He asked me to reinterview her.

A few days later, Sarah returned to the ARS, and I initiated a formal interview, asking her to tell me in detail why she had left Ghana. I advised her not to leave anything out, even if she had already told Dimitris. Our discussion lasted nearly two hours. Below I outline in broad strokes the narrative that emerged.

Sarah left Ghana because of a problem with her husband, whom her father had forced her to marry because her family was very poor and her husband wealthy. "I didn't like him. He would beat me in order to be with me."

Her husband was a businessman, and every day he went to work, sometimes going on long trips. She started selling vegetables because she did not want to ask her husband for anything, not even money, but he did not like her selling vegetables and would sometimes come to the market and beat her, just like he beat her at home. When I asked if anyone else knew that this was going on, she answered that her father knew, but he was not willing to help, and her brothers are younger and unable to help. But one day, when her son was sick, she took him to see a doctor and, by chance, she met a man at the hospital who seemed to offer a solution. She was crying, and he talked to her, telling her that he helps women go to Europe "to work in the house." She decided to go, paying him $1,000, which she had saved from selling vegetables and hidden away. She left her son with her cousin in Accra and departed on a ship that later arrived in Greece.

She then repeated her account of what happened on arrival, but with a few more details. When she arrived, she did not know where she was. She called the number the man in Ghana had given her, and an English-speaking West African man met her (she thought he was Nigerian). He took her to a house with other African women, who she thought were also from Nigeria. There, "they told me I would have to prostitute myself, and I said no. He beat me." That night, she pretended she was sleeping, and when everyone else was asleep, she opened the door—the key was on the inside—and ran away. She got on a bus, where she met "a black woman," who told her where to find other Ghanaian people. She then met a man and his wife from Ghana, who gave her a place to stay, and "everything, everything."

She spoke with the directness I had noted in our first meeting, in a voice that was clear though often shaky, without changing her pleasant expression, though at times she raised her voice in a way that appeared to indicate heightened emotion. Sarah thus convinced me that I could provide Dimitris with what he needed to help her. When I later presented him with the interview form and the summary I had typed up, he examined it for just a few minutes, frowning in concentration. Then he stated simply, "I don't believe her." This, he explained, was owing to a contradiction in her story: "Would her husband, who tries to control her, who knows that she does not like him and beats her, let her go to work? And if he did let her work, wouldn't he watch her money very closely?" Dimitris wanted to know where she had saved the money and how had she hidden it. He concluded, "I do not think that this story works."

But after a brief pause, he suggested, "What if there were a different story? Let's say her husband has more than one wife. Sarah falls into disfavor. Her husband is not pleased with her any more. To take care of her child, and herself, she goes to work in the market and gives her husband the money. Until one day she decides to leave." That, he asserted, was a story that could work and would explain why her husband allowed her to sell vegetables. This was not a trafficking case but an asylum case, he emphasized: "A special social group—women. Husband forces her to be a slave!" When I asked Dimitris how he had thought of such a story, he told me that he had done extensive research on gender mainstreaming and had read about similar, successful cases of women from Ghana. The task, then, was to get Sarah to tell the "truth"; Dimitris told me to invite her back and we would both interview her.

Credibility, Trust, and Truth

In our exchange, Dimitris expressed doubt about Sarah's *aksiopistia* [αξιοπιστία] (credibility, which translates directly as "deserving of faith"), questioning her trustworthiness and cooperativeness, and the truth of her story. In his assessment, she had not provided details to assist the police and her story was not adequately consistent—factors with significant repercussions for the workability of her case. Moreover, her trustworthiness (or lack thereof) had important implications for his own credibility. Nonetheless, he also cited an overarching impression that she had a "real problem," suggesting that she might indeed have a credible case. The contradictions thus provided a way for him to imagine a different, "true story," which would allow him to find her eligible.

In our many conversations, and during the many times I watched him work, Dimitris advocated an approach to eligibility that was practical and strategic. I never heard him comment on the "character" of a potential client, as some other lawyers did, and seemingly outlandish stories did not appear to try his patience; rather, he often treated them as sources of humor amid otherwise joyless work. At times, I even saw him push the boundaries of eligibility, taking on a number of cases other lawyers had dismissed on grounds of credibility and feasibility. When it came to trafficking cases, however, Dimitris's criteria appeared to me to become notably more restrictive, perhaps reflecting the particular challenges of the criminal trials they entail. Unlike an asylum applicant, who is interviewed at a closed meeting by a committee of adjudicators, a trafficking victim must appear as a plaintiff or witness in criminal court; trafficking cases, therefore, proceed not unlike rape trials in the United States, in which the "victim" must undergo rigorous (often demeaning) questioning (see Matoesian 1993). These cases, arguably, demand especially thorough preparation by the lawyer and the plaintiff; Dimitris explained that he had once prepped a client for 24 hours before a hearing. Dimitris, moreover, had a reputation to protect. In just a short time, he had attained remarkable success in bringing criminal cases against traffickers and acquiring legal protection for victims. As the victim's capacity to perform in these trials matters deeply, client credibility and cooperativeness themselves become issues of legal pragmatism, directly related to the potential success of the case in court.

At the ARS, concerns about trust/mistrust, credibility, and truth (or lack thereof) unfolded through dialogical forms of sociality between lawyers and aid applicants. J. K. Campbell (1964) shows that trust (*embistosini*) and faith (*pisti*) (along with their opposites ill-faith, doubt, and suspicion) circulate within a constellation of values that govern relationships between kin and non-kin, insiders and outsiders, natives and foreigners. For Campbell, trust encompasses the "values and attitudes that make possible communion among kinsmen" (95), whereas suspicion and doubt form the dispositional ground on which relations with outsiders unfold. While Campbell's field context (rural Sarakatsani sheep thieves) is wholly different from the urban NGO where Sarah's case was negotiated, his analysis points to the difficulties underlying the establishment of something like trust among Greeks and foreigners, particularly amid radical inequalities and in a cultural and institutional context where the "stranger" is so often a target of suspicion.

Yet Campbell's analysis also suggests that despite their exclusionary character, suspicion, doubt, and mistrust also enable important forms of sociality across difference. In her ethnography of patients and therapists in Thracian psychiatric clinics, Elizabeth Davis (2010) shows that suspicions of deceit often foster socialities and even "intimacy" (131). Likewise, at the ARS, lawyers generated circumscribed forms of intimacy with aid candidates: somehow, they had to encourage potential clients to tell them the "whole story," a workable story, or the "truth." This, however, required that lawyers convincingly perform their own credibility to aid candidates and thus attempt to gain their trust. Lawyers often cited lack of trust on the part of applicants or, more strongly, fear or anger, as reasons behind an incomplete or apparently false story; this was particularly pronounced with regard to suspected trafficking victims, given the fear and mistrust ascribed to them. In Sarah's case, not just her own credibility and the truth of her story were at stake, but Dimitris implies that her own mistrust, shame, and fear of him (of us) may be a root cause of her contradictory story.

"Credibility," however, also depends on whether applicants are able or willing to meet decision makers' expectations regarding how they should behave and the story they should tell. As I have noted, candidates for legal aid are best served when their comportment and self-presentation fall in a particular range of aesthetic conventions corresponding to notions of gender, country of origin, and phenotype and race; when interviewees diverge from this spectrum, problems often result. In Sarah's case, this is markedly evident, owing to the extraordinarily gendered context in which her "picture" emerged. While Dimitris did not say so directly, another contributing factor in her lack of credibility may have been the unselfconscious, direct way in which she "confessed" to having been trafficked, which diverged dramatically from the expected shame and silence of trafficking victims. The "other story" that Dimitris suggested, in fact, refashioned the "picture" of Sarah in a way more appropriate to ARS institutional conventions: not as a trafficking victim but a victim of persecution, who was, nonetheless, a spurned and abused woman ashamed to speak the truth. The conventions that would augment Sarah's credibility remained entangled in a social aesthetics of shame and fear tied to her exploitation as a woman.

"I have told you all that I know"

Dimitris's goal for our next meeting was to convince Sarah to trust him and tell the "truth," to garner a confession he could use to find her eligible as a victim of persecution. She came in the following Monday, and she and I went together to the office across the hall from Dimitris. He arrived a few moments later, greeting her warmly and offering her his hand, then took a seat next to her, his elbows on his knees in a gesture of informality and intimacy, while I sat at the table across from her. Then, speaking softly, he asserted, "Sarah, I don't believe that you are telling us the whole truth."

I recognized this as a tactic Dimitris employed to encourage trafficking victims to confess. In an earlier conversation with me, he explained that, by telling a victim he does not believe her, he attempts to push her to an emotional catharsis wherein she admits she needs help and provides him with information he can use to help her. He credited this tactic for his impressive success in trafficking cases, but it was controversial among some of the women lawyers. Kyriaki stressed that she never forced anyone to admit victimization or stated directly when she suspected exploitation. Instead, she emphasized rapport building, vagueness, and indirection in establishing trust and eliciting the "truth." Phoevi told me that she admired the effectiveness of Dimitris's paternalistic approach but that it would never work for her, explaining that he could get away with it because "he is a man and he is kind." Dimitris himself emphasized that his approach was based on gender stereotypes and the violence they entail, explaining that many exploited women have learned to respond best to fear; moreover, he added ironically, "I look like a pimp," suggesting that this form of performance was especially suited to his comportment and appearance. For Dimitris, however, the crucial issue was that an urgent problem required urgent action: "This is your one chance to help this woman. When she leaves, she will never come back. What are you going to do?"

Such tactics were not just based on the "pictures" of victims that lawyers entertained. They also reflected lawyers' attempts to understand their own image in the other's eyes and the power relationships—gendered, raced, classed—that shaped how aid applicants interpreted lawyers' own performances. The performative work through which ARS lawyers approached aid candidates reflects deeply gendered norms of behavior amid the complexity of Greek gender politics (Dubisch 1986; Loizos and Papataxiarchis 1991; Paxson 2004; Placas 2009). While Phoevi and Kyriaki invoked a sense of intimacy grounded on gender symmetries in their encounters with potential victims, Dimitris performed a gruff, confident, even paternalistic Greek masculinity (a disposition that he often presented to me, the *Amerikana*, as well). Through the social aesthetics of aid encounters, amid gendered and culturally inflected behavioral norms, lawyers strive to imagine clients' subjectivities and the most effective way to approach them. However, although Dimitris responded to his own picture of Sarah, his tactic for engaging her implied a fairly narrow range of acceptable responses. He asked Sarah, in a sense, to take her cue: to perform the very catharsis and confession he sought to elicit.

Sarah, however, did not respond. Dimitris proceeded by speaking clearly and sternly, asking, "Did your husband have more than one wife?" Sarah's jaw hardened, and when she answered, she looked at me, not him: "I don't know." Dimitris then continued, in a coaxing voice, "Sarah, a woman knows if her husband has found another." She remained silent. Finally, after continued unsuccessful attempts to elicit information more in line with the alternate scenario that he had imagined, Dimitris grew somber.

> Dimitris: Sarah you are not helping us.
> Sarah: I have told you all that I know.
> D: You have to trust us, but you do not. Heath wants to help you. I want to. But for me, we will not support you. You are not telling us everything.
> S (finally): But I don't want to lie. I have told you all that I know.

In the end, Dimitris told her that he could not support her with the story she had given us. He told her pointedly to go home and see if she could remember more, and if she did, she should come back the following week at the latest. If not, she would have to find a private lawyer.

The lawyer Effie commented early in my fieldwork that "it takes a while to convince someone they are a victim." In our final encounter with Sarah, Dimitris, unable to elicit the performance and story he seeks, was ultimately unsuccessful at this task. Sarah continued to claim a charged and problematic category of protection ("trafficking victim") and refused to adapt her performance and story in a way that might make her eligible as an "asylum seeker," the category Dimitris has, in a sense, offered her. In so doing, she both fails and refuses to become a victim.

Despite her multiple previous visits, Sarah never did come back to the ARS. We do not know if this was because she would not tell Dimitris the "true" story (owing to shame, fear, or mistrust), she missed her cue, so to speak, or she simply did not have an acceptable story to tell. Sarah's choice not to perform the role that Dimitris has asked her to undermines the efficacy of her request for legal aid and his attempt to find her eligible. Yet her refusal also destabilizes the very notion of victimhood, exposing the complicity of practices of aid distribution in buoying up that category. She explains that to perform the role that Dimitris asks her to, she would have to tell a lie; this "lie" might not simply have factual grounds but, perhaps more crucially, would entail a simplification and reiteration of her life history, experience, and subjectivity in a manner to which she, as she makes very clear, does not want to submit. Her refusal grants us a window into unpredictable, circumscribed forms of agency through which aid candidates push back against dominant images of deservingness and vulnerability.

Minors

When I first met Angeliki in September 2006, I was struck by her gracious and spontaneous smile and laugh. We were the same age (then twenty-eight), and at that time she was completing a "practical" at the ARS, an unpaid internship that would make it possible for her to practice formally as a lawyer. We discussed her work in depth, and when I asked for her thoughts on client eligibility, she answered that for her it was about helping people who "really have need": not just "refugees," but also women who were trafficking victims, humanitarian cases, and, most important, unaccompanied minors, precisely because they are so "difficult to protect." "Many of the children become lost," she added. When I asked her to clarify, she explained that minors often "disappear" from housing facilities or simply do not return to the ARS. She told me that no one was sure how they disappear exactly, but that some are taken by traffickers, while others simply leave Greece.

Social aesthetics not only were crucial in eligibility determinations, but also had an ongoing role in mediating encounters between workers and "vulnerable" clients." Some workers deemed unaccompanied minors the most vulnerable of victims, but with their tendency to disappear, minors were also seen to be "difficult to protect," manage, and discipline. The ARS had a blanket policy of treating minors as eligible, but social aesthetics came into play in determining who was or was not "really" a minor. Moreover, for those who appeared to meet these qualifications, the problem for workers was how to keep them from disappearing: how to gain their trust and convince them to accept help from the ARS. Just as Dimitris attempted to gain Sarah's trust and convince her to help him help her, workers strove to communicate to minors their good intentions. Minors, however, persistently demonstrated forms of agency that were inappropriate or problematic to workers, appearing as precocious or difficult "children" who persistently undermined attempts to protect them.

Since 2008, there has been a proliferation of both Greek and pan-European exposés and critiques regarding reception of unaccompanied minors in Greece.[3] According to these critiques, the widespread practice of detaining minors in locked facilities along with adults not only flagrantly disregards the requirements of international law and "rights of the child" legislation, but, according to advocates, makes minors vulnerable to further forms of exploitation (physical, sexual, and otherwise). In particular, a highly publicized report by the UN High Commissioner for Refugees in Greece in 2008 (Papageorgiou and Dimitropoulou 2008) centered largely on the many young Afghans who arrived on islands in the Aegean. In summer 2008, these mounting concerns culminated in the opening of a *kendro filoksenias* [κέντρο φιλοξενίας] (hospitality center) for minors on Lesbos, in the town of Agiassos, with 90 beds, where residents could enter and exit freely; this center was closed in July 2011, owing to lack of funds. As recent reports attest, the treatment of minors in Greece remains a point of critique and concern, despite the reform measures currently underway in the Greek asylum adjudication and reception processes.

In addition to these anxieties among policy makers and advocates about the inhumane reception of unaccompanied minors in Greece, ARS workers were extremely concerned about what happened to them once they were released from detention. Occasionally ARS lawyers had the opportunity to meet with detainees thought to be minors, particularly when they conducted "missions" to border sites to notify detainees of their rights (including the right to apply for asylum) and review their options for legal assistance. On these missions, lawyers strongly encouraged those who appeared to be minors to come to the ARS on release, with promises to look into possibilities for housing, education, and other services. When minors did visit the ARS after being released, or in cases when they avoided apprehension altogether and were directed to the ARS by acquaintances, workers tried to provide not just legal help but also assistance in finding safe places to stay in one of the few state-run centers or at facilities managed by other NGOs.

Like discourses around trafficking, the social aesthetics that shaped ARS encounters with minors were steeped in stereotypes around gender and race. While trafficking is powerfully feminized, discussions about minors both at the ARS and in Greece more broadly most often focused on boys. This is, in some ways, a case of numbers, as many more "boys" or young men were detained than young women or "girls." However, this emphasis on alleviating conditions for boys in Greece also translated to a lack of infrastructure for housing girls. Whereas boys could be housed all together, the lack of gender-specific facilities for girls made young women appear to be a kind of *problem*: not just vulnerable, but also potential sources of temptation for boys and men. Such gendered qualities intersected with notions of race and country of origin. Many of the young girls who visited the ARS were Muslims from Somalia, and their swathed bodies and dark faces became powerful tropes of vulnerability for workers, who often identified them at the entryway or in the waiting room through mere appearance. Boys were mostly Hazara Afghan, and their smooth faces and strong features served to further infantalize them through widespread stereotypes regarding the youthful appearance of Asians. Finally, ARS methods for dealing with minors also intersected with anxieties regarding trafficking since, as Angeliki notes, minors (both boys and girls) were often thought to fall victim to labor and sex traffickers. Through ethnographic material relevant to these deeply gendered and racialized categories of minors, Afghan boys and Somali girls, I consider how social aesthetics served to mediate but also generate further epistemic anxieties among workers, while minors themselves often borrowed and played on the expectations and assumptions of workers.

Disappearances

The primary theory among ARS workers regarding the widespread "disappearances" of Afghan boys was that they usually left Greece and went elsewhere in Europe. A number of workers told me that young Afghans left to find better job opportunities, since their primary reason for being in Europe was to support their families through sending remittances home. In some cases, "home" was Afghanistan, but many had families living in diaspora in Iran and Pakistan. Indeed, many young Afghans expressed these sentiments explicitly in their meetings with workers, highlighting their need to find work, though they also frequently cited a desire to study, learn English, and travel. Nikos explained to me that in his meetings with young Afghans, they appeared always to be extremely *piesmeni* [πιεσμένοι], "under pressure," owing to this burden of providing for their families. ARS lawyers thus often depicted young Afghans as recalcitrant and difficult to pin down but also, in many cases, as worthy of respect: as intrepid, enterprising, and Europe-bound, with their quick command of Greek learned in the detention center or housing facility. Effie emphasized the toughness and flexibility of Afghan boys, explaining their resistance to NGO interventions in terms of contrasting conceptions of what a "child" is, and survival strategies developed through years of living independently. She highlighted that these "boys" were really men: "they prefer to circulate and make connections. They will find a way somehow."

As workers sought actively to imagine the experiences and sentiments of these disappearing Afghan minors, however, the "pictures" they assembled often took on nightmarish qualities, tinged with workers' own anxieties. ARS workers referenced reports that these boys engaged in sex work to acquire funds for the clandestine passage to other parts of Europe, from Patras to Italy, then to France, and perhaps eventually to England. These accounts were widespread even outside the ARS, likely attesting to a certain substance underlying them. An Afghan asylum seeker who worked for another NGO, explained to me in a low voice that I "wouldn't believe the kinds of things people asked Afghan boys do for money"—women and men, he explained, young and old—"all of them Greek." The sexual lives of Afghan boys thus became charged, if dangerous, topics of conversation, gossip, and rumor.

Irrespective of the substance of these rumors, they reflected the anxieties of NGO workers themselves and their fears that when Afghan boys chose to travel and work, they were also exploited and victimized. These rumors provided workers with a kind of knowledge about these young men, but they also reinforced and legitimized NGO practices that, in turn, drove these clients even further away. Such stories constructed these young people as vulnerable victims in *need* of being cared for and closely watched. Moreover, this meant that workers often did not take seriously the stated goals of many of these young men, which emphasized the need to work and stay mobile. Thus, the "pictures" through which workers approached these clients in many cases perpetuated a cycle: as workers sought to protect young people by increasing the surveillance around them, "minors" themselves often resisted coming to the ARS, expressed fear and mistrust of offers to find them housing, and frequently "disappeared."

In spring 2008, in a highly publicized event, a boat carrying over 200 persons, most of them Afghan and many of them very young, arrived on the Aegean island of Leros. As Leros, at that time, was unaccustomed to such arrivals, Angeliki went as a representative of the ARS to aid in the reception process. After she returned, we met in a large group for dinner, with a couple of fellow workers and some of her friends, including a young American man visiting Athens for the first time (hence, our conversation was in English). They had all just gone to see the *Kite Runner*, and they were discussing how beautiful Afghanistan must be (though the movie had been shot in Kashgar, a dramatically mountainous region of China). One of the other lawyers commented how the Hazara boy who was raped in the film resembled many of the boys who come to the ARS.

Over dinner, Angeliki discussed Leros, and she described the experience as "shocking": "I have never seen so many minors." She went on: "Imagine the situation in Afghanistan. It must be so bad that the impossibility of food and money must make it necessary to send your children to Europe alone."

She explained that all the "minors" had said they wanted to go to London: "I asked them: you want to go to England? No, London [they answered]." She laughed, and then mused that this was probably what they had been told to say by smugglers who arranged their passage. Finally, she explained that less than half of them agreed to apply for asylum in Greece; the others wanted to leave, to go elsewhere in Europe. As she went on, discussing the dangers of their leaving for other places in Europe, I again recalled her comment from the year before, about those minors who are "lost": "Do you know how much a 'ticket' to Italy costs? 3000 euros. No one ever speaks. But I don't want to know how they get the money. And what they do to pay it. Some of them probably work for life for the traffickers. It sometimes happens."

She shook her head with apparent disbelief, and her voice held a faint note of panic. She went on: "My dream for all these children, my dream is just that they could go to school, not just work, even though they are here for work. But they need somewhere to live. And they are not here with their parents. They are all in some way victims."

Angeliki's commentary highlights these young people's apparent vulnerability, past experiences of violence, the adult-like duties with which they have been charged (i.e., to work and support their families), and their persistent tendency to be "lost" to fates which she does not even want to imagine. A key point here is that "no one ever speaks," which highlights the climate of silence, mistrust, and epistemic anxiety that is so powerful at the ARS. Lacking forms of direct or reliable knowledge, Angeliki assembles "pictures" of these Afghan boys and the dangers that they face. But these images emerge as ghostly, nightmarish, without solidity or certainty, colored with her own anxieties, fears, and desires. Her assertion that she wants them to be able to go to school, not to work, conveys a desire for them to be *children*. Yet her insistence on their victimhood contrasts with many of these young Afghans' own scrappy attempts to find work, make better futures, and support their families by leaving Greece—in short, to disappear or become "lost" by remaining undetected and unseen by both authorities and NGO workers.

In encounters between ARS workers and Afghan boys, social aesthetics and the "pictures" that they generate were often expressed through rumor, which served as a kind of folk psychology, a method of rendering the other knowable. Like ARS institutional knowledge around trafficking, these rumors regarding the lives of minors may have had some substance, yet they were also laden with fantasies, nightmares, and anxieties that threw the "vulnerability" of minors into sharp relief. Rumor, however, should not be seen as irrational and wild; instead, it accomplishes important epistemological work and provides forms of social—and in this case, institutional—commentary. Luise White (2000: 58) writes that rumor "is not events misinterpreted and deformed, but rather events analyzed and commented upon." Rumors regarding minors provided an important, if unofficial, repertoire of institutional knowledge-making tools. Yet these rumors perhaps said less about minors themselves and more about workers' own sense of vulnerability in attempting to provide assistance across gaps of power, knowledge, and trust.

Interestingly, the "pictures" through which NGO workers sought to make sense of "minors" were often strategically invoked by these young men themselves, attesting, again, to the dialogical qualities of social aesthetics. While many of the young Afghans identified as "minors" resisted this categorization, others actively sought to acquire some of the benefits it was said to provide. A number of the young Afghans I met in Greece told me that when they were first detained on entering the country, they claimed to be younger than they really were. This appeared to be a fairly widespread practice, which in a number of European countries has led to the use of medical age assessment tests, making age itself a question of credibility. A young Afghan housed in a camp outside Athens told me that he was "really twenty-one," but he and everyone else he knew there had said they were under eighteen, because when he arrived in Greece acquaintances had told him to do so. He explained that it was not difficult to be believed, because with their Asian features or—as he put it—with faces that are "Chinese," people tended to think they are younger anyway. While some young Afghans refused the pictures that made them visible as victims, others drew cannily on gendered, racialized aesthetic norms to present themselves as compellingly vulnerable. We must remember, however, that social aesthetics are always flexible, playing on audience and performer expectations: his account may also have been a way to appear older and more grown-up to *me.*

There were other moments when performances of vulnerability failed, yet such disconnections and misreadings can also challenge and rupture aesthetic norms. The strategy of understating one's age, in particular, sometimes took a comical turn, as when I watched two Afghan men recently arrived in Mytilene, with visibly gray hair and beards, present themselves as seventeen-year-olds to an ARS lawyer who was interviewing them in the courtyard of the infamous Pagani detention center. The ad hoc interpreter, a detainee who had volunteered to assist with his limited English, was himself a very youthful-looking person who explained that he was thirteen (a claim the lawyers believed without question, owing likely to his small stature and beardless face). When the interpreter asserted, gesturing to the men, "They are both seventeen," the lawyer laughed in spite of himself. The interpreter himself began to laugh, but then added with a smile and a shrug, "Why not?" Certainly, these men had produced an ineffective (if entertaining) performance, without the appropriate aesthetic qualities. The interpreter's question, however, underscores the arbitrariness underlying the "pictures" of vulnerability entertained by both asylum seekers and ARS workers. Young Afghans persistently resisted, played upon, and reconfigured the pictures through which workers attempted to make them knowable.

Smira

On a blustery Wednesday afternoon in November 2006, I met with my friend and colleague Maria, an American Fulbright fellow conducting research on access to healthcare for migrants in Greece. Maria worked twice a week at the Athens office of Yiatri tou Kosmou (Médecins du Monde), which had an office about ten minutes by foot from the ARS. Over tea and *metaxa*, Maria told me that she had made an appointment at the ARS for a young Somali woman whom she had met at work that day. The appointment was scheduled for Friday, and Maria asked me to keep an eye out for her and make sure she was seen by someone; I would recognize her, she explained, because she wore two jewels in one of her front teeth. Maria emphasized that the girl was fourteen or fifteen—a minor—and that she would really like to hear the outcome of the appointment.

Friday morning, I peered into the waiting room to find Omar, the Arabic interpreter, chatting with a striking, robust-looking young woman, with two jewels in her left front big tooth. She wore a head scarf and a black wrap, but with a long jean skirt peeking through, and she was standing with a similarly attired woman who appeared to be older. I smiled and introduced myself, and she told me her name was Smira. In surprisingly good English she confirmed that, yes, an American girl had helped her [at Yiatri tou Kosmou]. Omar, meanwhile, gestured for my attention and whispered meaningfully in my ear: "she is a minor."

As we were talking, Eleni, one of the social workers, came into the waiting room and asked to speak to me privately. She asked: "Do you know these ladies?" and I explained to her about my conversation with Maria. Eleni then asked Smira if she might meet with her in a few minutes, and Smira assented.

Eleni invited me to come to her office while she prepared for the meeting, musing quietly to me that the girl seemed surprisingly open and smiling—and that this was rare since minors often do not trust the ARS. She explained that finding safe accommodation for Smira was a priority, but it is difficult to house young women: most unaccompanied minors are male, and women cannot stay with them, but it would also be problematic for her to live with a family, since the other women might be jealous and men could see her as a temptation. Eleni called a refugee camp in Thessaloniki to find Smira a bed, and as expected, the camp administrator said no, they were full. But in an unexpected stroke of luck, he called back a few minutes later and said they would make space for Smira.

Smira, with her long black attire, was recognizable to both Omar and Eleni as a particularly rare, even sacred category of minor: a young Somali woman. She represented "someone in need" who had come to the ARS before "becoming lost," and thus she could perhaps be protected or even saved. Yet the possibility of protecting her was doubly complicated by the infrastructural challenges of housing young women, and more broadly, by the deeply sexualized accounts of these challenges, as their bodies (and gender) are seen to make them even more vulnerable. In this first meeting, however, things went surprisingly well. Smira conveyed a sense of trust toward ARS workers. With the positive response from the camp in Thessaloniki, the primary task for Eleni was to convince Smira to accept her help.

Eleni, the lawyer Stavros, and I then met privately with Smira to conduct an interview, as her companion waited outside. Smira described the older woman as someone staying in the same place with her, a "Somali hotel." While the typical interview form was used, the purpose of this meeting was not to assess eligibility, since, as a minor, Smira was already eligible. Rather, the goal was to acquire the details of her case and find out more about her situation in Greece. Eleni began by saying that they were going to interview her to see what kind of help we could give her, but Smira interrupted: "I do not want to live alone. I lost my sister when we came to Greece. We were arrested, and when we got out, I couldn't find her. I am living with good people now. I want to go to England or America where I have family. If you can't help me with that, I don't want your help."

Eleni responded by giving her a tissue and telling her more about the camp, describing it as a nice, comfortable place, where she would have food and be able to go to school. But Smira remained silent, looking at her with a hard expression. When Eleni emphasized that we could not and would not make her go to the camp, Smira appeared to relax, and she explained she was living in a community of Somali people who are Muslim. She added that "women and men were sleeping separately—about 40 people total." She liked it there. Eleni asked her just to think about the camp. In a manner similar to young Afghans, Smira thus also asserted her desire to remain mobile, but in her case it seemed to be less an issue of work than of family; having lost contact with her sister, she did not want to be alone. The camp—where she knew no one, and where she would be without country-people or family—clearly appeared as a place where she would be "alone," and she preferred an unofficial hotel with other Somalis.

Stavros asked her for details about her family in England, and she explained that she had an aunt and brother there; her parents had died when she was seven. He promised to look into possibilities for family reunification and made an appointment for her to come back to the ARS on Monday. Eleni, meanwhile, asked her again to think about the camp. For both ARS workers, it was particularly crucial for Smira to return to the ARS since, among the few papers she presented during her interview, they found a record of her being hospitalized at the border, near Alexandroupoli. She had been diagnosed with tuberculosis. Follow-up care would be crucial.

On Monday, however, when Smira did not arrive at the agreed-on time, Eleni expressed both disappointment and worry, though not surprise. "We lost a minor," she sighed. She went on to say that in her work, people are like *fantasmata* [φαντάσματα], "ghosts" or "phantoms"; they disappear, but sometimes on the street she sees people and thinks she recognizes them. When I spoke with Omar, however, he explained he was not worried—that Smira probably just did not want to come back; she wanted to go to England, and Somalis, he explained, have extremely organized smuggling networks to facilitate the movement of compatriots. He offered to bring me with him that afternoon to see if we could find some information; he knew a couple of "Somali hotels" we could check.

After he finished work at 3: 30, we walked about ten minutes to a small street near Omonia Square, which he described as the "worst street in Athens," and stopped in front of a dilapidated building. A few men were hovering outside the entrance smoking, and Omar greeted them in Arabic. He motioned toward me, and I, taking my cue, introduced myself to the men, one of whom took us inside. The building was carpeted, and fairly bright, and struck me as, indeed, surprisingly pleasant for an unlicensed hotel. Omar spoke with a few of the residents and explained that we were looking for a girl named Smira who had jewels in her teeth. They talked among themselves for a minute but appeared to reach the consensus that they did not know her. We left, and Omar promised to follow up more on his own, but for now, the search was over.

The next morning at the ARS, I spoke about Smira's case with two of the lawyers. I passed on Eleni's comment that we had "lost" this minor. One lawyer, however, who has an impressive penchant for combining cynicism with levity, answered: *Ela* (come on). "For every one you lose there are ten more." This comment, while clearly ironic, also reflected the very real anxiety that we had indeed "lost" Smira, a minor we had had the chance to protect, and that in losing her we had left her vulnerable to other fates. Yet Omar's insistence that she was likely fine, that she (quite understandably) trusted people she knew more than the NGO, serves as a reminder that protection often runs counter to these young people's goals. Smira flatly refused "help" that did not meet her terms, and when Stavros and Eleni were unable to convince her to return, she "disappeared."

Such "disappearances" were persistently linked to the powerful forms of agency that unaccompanied minors asserted in choosing whom to trust and where to go, which, for many ARS workers, were incompatible with images of victimhood, vulnerability, and childhood. Yet Omar's account highlights how "disappearance" can simply mean a different trajectory, another life, into which ARS workers—and ethnographers who work with them—can only acquire glimpses. However, a crucial factor in aid encounters, and also for an ethnographer working on questions of asylum, is that no knowledge of the other is reliable. Even in piecing together information and knowledge from a variety of sources, the image we assemble remains indeterminate and unclear, which I learned in a profound and painful way a few months after my encounter with Smira.

It was early March 2007, and I was in the neighborhood where Omar and I had gone to look for Smira back in November. Rahman, the Bangla interpreter, had taken me to meet the head of a Bangladeshi migrant organization in Athens. As we walked, he described to me with dismissive irony the primary work of the organization: "They drink coffee and discuss. And when someone dies they arrange to have the body sent back to Bangladesh or buried in a Muslim way." As we walked and talked, a young man passing us grabbed my arm, and I recognized him as a man Omar and I had met at the Somali hotel months before. He began speaking to me agitatedly, in very broken but nonetheless intelligible English. It took me a while to make out what he was saying, but when I did, the meaning was crystal clear: "That girl, that girl you look. She die." He told me that someone had been trying to raise the money to give her a proper Muslim burial in Greece. Immediately, however—before I had fully registered what he said—he began to explain that he had questions about his papers and wanted my help.

I called Omar as soon as I could. He initially dismissed the information, explaining that he thought this young man was trying to find a way to establish a kind of connection or intimacy with me, for his own interest—or perhaps it was someone else who died. But over the next few days Omar spoke to his many contacts in the Somali community, and he learned that indeed a girl of a similar description, with jewels in her teeth, had died of tuberculosis. The Somali community was trying to bury her. Smira, for me, remains a ghost.

Images and Indeterminacy

The cases of Sarah and Smira, like those of "disappearing" Afghan boys, highlight how so-called vulnerable persons persistently exceed the ways in which law, humanitarian aid, and ethnographic practice seek to assess and codify, even under inexorable conditions of inequality and violence (Biehl and Locke 2010). Social aesthetics both reproduce and undermine dominant frameworks of knowledge-making and judgment, often at the very same time. Minors' persistent tendency to get lost and disappear, like Sarah's own disappearance, highlights how knowledge and "live contact" are persistently thwarted through the very methods that service providers and adjudicators use to render the other knowable. This is a form of tragedy: a failure of knowledge, law, sociability, and labor. Yet the fraught and circumscribed forms of agency that emerge within systems of aid distribution may also destabilize normative frameworks of assessment from within.

I too cannot know, *really*, what happened to Smira and Sarah. Problems of language, mistrust, power, and violence on all sides also thwart ethnographic knowledge. They are "ghosts" for me, yet in their ghostliness they also speak to a radical indeterminacy entailing both violence and agency. The cases of Smira and Sarah undermine not just notions of victimhood but also the image of an idealized liberal subject, who is able to choose, and in choosing, seek freedom. Their refusals to return to the ARS and submit to the category of vulnerability, with the protection it conveys, are indeed choices; yet their intentionality remains—and must remain—outside the picture. The futures they have chosen may include suffering, loss, what some might call "exploitation," and even death.

Slavoj Žižek (2000) describes how the image of the other always remains fuzzy when looked at straight on. Rather, such images become clear only when looked at "awry," distorted by one's own desire and perception; in the image of the other, the subject always "sees itself seeing" (10). Through the social aesthetics of eligibility, those on both sides of the encounter respond to pictures in which they are both seen and seeing. Yet trouble cases like these leave us with images that are blurry, indeterminate, unclear.[4] These pictures index a failure of knowledge, humanitarian aid, and rights-based protection, but they are also sites of opening: into indeterminate trajectories through which "victims" (knowingly or not) undermine the structures of power and violence in which they have been caught.

Chapter 5

Recognizing the Real Refugee

On an uncommonly warm early May weekend in 2007, I joined a group of lawyers and advocates from Greece and throughout the EU at the biennial meeting of a network of asylum advocacy NGOs. We traveled in buses from Athens, across the flat territory near Thebes, then up through the mists of Mount Parnassos. There, in an airy conference center near the small town of Delphi and the archaeological site, this international group outlined the advocacy agenda for the following six months through working groups and meetings and over dinners, lunches, coffees, and cocktails.

At a closing dinner on the last night of the conference, at the overly bright Omphalos Taverna, I sat at a table of delegates over a glass of wine, watching the presentation of toasts and awards after a heavy, too-oily meal of tourist-friendly Greek fare. The finale of the evening was a campy performance involving togas and singing, in which members from various NGOs honored a longtime colleague whose retirement was imminent. On requests for a speech, this man himself took the floor, and expressions suddenly became serious. He was an older man with white hair and spectacles, but tall and hale. He began by mentioning his years in the asylum advocacy field—the successes and satisfactions, but also the ongoing frustrations, of his work. Then he turned somber, explaining that he wanted to recount a meeting with a particular refugee that had remained important for him throughout his career. And so he began a striking narrative.

Shortly after starting to work at an advocacy NGO in London, he went to the home of a Somali woman, who was in need of assistance for herself and her children. Winding his way through a London slum, he arrived at a dank apartment building. He knocked, and a voice invited him inside, but when he entered, he did not see anyone. A voice then called to him from another room. There in the dark, he found a woman sitting on a bed cross-legged, erect, but with her back to him, long braids trailing over her shoulders, and without showing her face, she told him how she had fled Somalia. He did not discuss the details of her story, but rather, left the audience to fill in those details with accounts of violence that they had heard in their own work. But he explained that whenever he gets frustrated and cynical, he remembers this refugee, and that there are many more refugees out there who need help.

Intrigued by this man's account, as well as his oratory, I looked around to see a room full of somber faces, some contracted with emotion—one woman with wet cheeks. The speaker's description of his meeting with this Somali woman had clearly struck a powerful chord with the audience, perhaps sparking others in the room to remember similarly significant encounters.

His narrative then switched gears, as he described the genesis of his own career as a refugee advocate. As a young man, he had been an anti-apartheid activist in Cape Town and had gotten into trouble with the authorities there, so he boarded a flight with a ticket given to him by his girlfriend's parents, arriving in London with just the money he had in his pocket. He had no idea where to go or what to do, but some helpful people directed him to the NGO where he later worked. Employees there provided him with legal assistance and everything else he needed. As he explained, he went to this organization initially for assistance, in need. But, he added, they gave him a job shortly after he was awarded asylum.

As I looked around the room again, I saw some nodding with knowing expressions, suggesting that they had heard this story before. But on other faces, I saw surprise and then recognition. The figure of the refugee, whom the speaker had conjured out of the past in his account of a faceless Somali woman in a dank London tenement, had suddenly appeared here—a white man, a colleague.

The "refugee" is often framed as a rare, even sacred, figure, who persistently eludes those who work in the field of asylum advocacy; as the lawyer Nikos explained, "there are thousands of people for one real refugee." Yet the "refugee"—the "*real* refugee"—also emerges as a kind of guiding light that motivates this work. With its broadly resonant imaginative and emotional power, this category is not reducible to legal frameworks, though these have important roles in shaping and reflecting the parameters of whom states do—and do not—grant refugee status. Rather, the refugee is a figure whom multiple actors and audiences make *real* through dialogical, performative processes of recognition. This chapter explores the everyday politics of refugee recognition as they unfolded at the ARS, and the ways in which they served to make the refugee "real."

There are two specific moments in the narrative above that I want to highlight for the way they speak to broader themes in this chapter: first, the speaker's account of the Somali woman's engagement with him, and second, his own self-unmasking as a refugee. The woman, while she has her back to him, his audience, and us, conveys a certain recognizable typology of refugeeness. She certainly has unique qualities, and indeed, the speaker emphasizes how the *particular* power of his meeting with her served to inspire his ongoing work in the advocacy field. However, in his invocation of her, she in her facelessness also calls forth a series of actual or imagined refugees who also serve to guide him—and the audience as well. The dark room, her long black braids, the shrouded mysteriousness of their encounter, her Somali origin, her unspoken story of violence and loss—these factors simultaneously weave together and call forth a type, which is well known and also precious to many others in the room. The racialized connotations of his depiction also serve to typologize that figure as necessarily "other" than the audience (entirely white European except for a few attendees who came specifically as representatives of "refugee voices"). Thus, the first segment of the narrative conjures and reveals a type and an attendant series of possible encounters with refugees who, like this Somali woman, are out there, somewhere, in need of being helped.

The second segment of the speaker's narrative, however, achieves not just a moment of revelation but a reversal in the Aristotelian sense, enacting a switch in the expectations that the former narrative has set up. Through his rather mundane description of his own experience of flight and his application for political asylum in England, the speaker again calls forth a *refugee*. However, the refugee is no longer an imagined figure or type but now stands before the audience, in the body and person of the speaker. This moment does not unravel the former type, but rather, makes it simultaneously present and transcendent: present, in that the refugee becomes suddenly manifest; transcendent in that this figure exceeds both the body of the speaker and the typologies that were implied earlier. This tall, white-haired, pale-skinned, refugee advocate is no more and no less a refugee than the woman he remembers. But his narrative highlights how the category of refugee can be *recognized*—revealed, embodied, individuated, and made real—in multiple sites and forms. The refugee is no longer dark, vulnerable, with a dramatic history of violence and flight. Rather, the speaker reminds the audience of how the category of "refugee" was (perhaps) once envisaged to be, and as it is certainly often characterized: as a universal form of protection against forms of violence and displacement that could happen to anyone—including even "us."

In legal discourse, the term "recognition" describes the process through which a person or group is granted a particular status through the confirmation that they, in effect, were entitled to that status all along. Recognition is an important logic in indigenous politics and in discussions of minority rights, but it also describes the adjudication procedure through which asylum applicants are awarded protection in a particular nation state. Asylum seekers become refugees by being "recognized" as such by the state and the law. Among refugee advocates, however, the crucial question is also whether they themselves recognize someone as a refugee, regardless of what the state may ultimately decide about a case. Such everyday politics of recognition deeply shape the kinds of cases lawyers take on, their engagements with clients, and the ways in which they do (or do not) strive to make particular cases successful.

These everyday politics of recognition are fruitful sites to explore the performative logics embedded in refugee recognition, which are often elided in its formal juridical formulation. While "recognition" implies the authentication of an experience or personhood that, in many ways, was already there, in the juridical logic of recognition what is often *mis*recognized is the fact that this process itself serves to make persons recognizable as refugees. Recognition is performative in the sense conveyed by J. L. Austin (2001 [1962]), in that it both produces and enacts that which it signifies: the process of recognition itself makes the refugee real. Everyday processes of recognition can have many modalities. Sometimes, recognition can appear to be almost instantaneous, taking place during just one meeting, client interview, or even in one particular moment, as in the speech I described above. At other times, recognition unfolds through successive meetings and interviews, through the drafting of multiple documents, and layers of suspicion and mistrust; over a sometimes protracted series of encounters, one can see a refugee slowly carved and whittled out of a mess of information and uncertainty. Across these different modalities of recognition, however, the *refugee* always emerges in hindsight as a figure who appears to have been there all along.

For some lawyers and advocates, encounters with "real refugees" can serve to make both law and labor meaningful, as the moment of recognition is also, in many ways, a moment of redemption. For the speaker above, his remembrance of his encounter with the Somali woman carries him through the frustrations of his work. The moving response to his speech perhaps attests to a similar sentiment among others in the audience who, we can imagine, navigate tragic dilemmas and uncertainties much like those that ARS workers face, which persistently thwart their capacities to provide assistance. For Athenian refugee advocates, the cases of those whom they themselves recognize as refugees often provide moments of legitimization in often frustrating and deadening work. The possible (if rare) presence of the "real refugee" thus also makes legal aid and asylum advocacy legitimate, useful, and "real."

The Real and the Non-Real

The oft-discussed performative quality of law, which serves to produce the very thing that it names, is often taken to imply a binary between social constructedness and the "real," suggesting that law and legal categories have no grounding outside the semiotic systems in which they are embedded. During my field practice, I was perpetually reminded to temper my interest in how categories are "produced" and to consider them in their profound salience for the advocacy lawyers with whom I was spending my time: and to quote the ARS lawyer Phoevi, for many legal practitioners law describes and responds to the "real world."

Coutin and Yngvesson (2006) helpfully nuance discussions of performativity by considering how law does not simply produce but shapes and (re) configures social realities. They write that both "legal and ethnographic accounts retroactively instantiate realities that potentially existed all along" (63). From this perspective, the performative effect of refugee recognition is not that it creates refugees ex nihilo, but rather, that it consolidates a person's life history, country of origin, and the various elements of the asylum case and makes them legible according to this category. Nevertheless, that person *could* have been "recognized" differently—as an economic migrant, a trafficking victim, or a humanitarian case—through his or her encounter with the law.

Those found recognizable as refugees are particularly rare at the ARS, and even more so in Greece, given its historically extremely low refugee recognition rate (even as this may be changing in the wake of reform processes). This elusiveness does not emerge just from the prevalence of cases that may not meet the tightly defined criteria for refugee status (such as "economic" or "humanitarian" cases) but also from the persistent presence of *non-real* refugees, cases lawyers deem variously to be false, fake, or fantastical. Take, for example, my exchange with Dimitris on an afternoon in November 2006. As he prepared to conduct an eligibility interview with a man from Nigeria, he explained to me, "He is from Nigeria. He does not have a problem." He added that most people from Nigeria were economic migrants [not refugees]. But, he smiled, "they tell very good stories."

Heath: If you are so sure that he does not have a problem, then why do you do the interview?

Dimitris: Because there is a one in a thousand chance that someone might actually have a problem, and we don't want to miss them. There are real refugees out there—we have to find them. That is why we do interviews with everyone.

Later, when I asked him about the interview, Dimitris told me that it was more complicated than he had expected, not what he described as the "usual story" about Muslims and Christians. He explained that the interviewee had told him his father was a Satanist, who expected him to follow in his footsteps—but he did not want to. He had claimed his life was in danger from Satanists who wanted him to join them, and he had to leave the country, because there were people loyal to Satanists all over Nigeria. Evidently taking for granted that the story was untrue, Dimitris laughed and shook his head in what seemed like admiring incredulity. Then turning serious, he commented, nodding sagely: "No one tells the whole truth about his life. You have to look behind the curtains."

Here, Dimitris points to a crucial contingent of the *non*-real at the ARS: those who do "not have a problem" but nonetheless tell "very good stories." He expresses a certain admiration for these good storytellers, for both their creativity and their entertainment value. However, many of these stories could, on the face of it, make their tellers recognizable as refugees, closely resembling other stories that have been told by successful asylum applicants in the past, both in Greece and elsewhere in Europe. Dimitris refers specifically to the "usual story" about Muslims and Christians. During this period (late 2006), many Nigerians came to the ARS saying that they had fled conflict between Muslims and Christians in the north, in Kano province. A few months earlier, following a widely publicized exodus of Christians from this region, one Nigerian asylum seeker had been recognized as a refugee by the Greek state; he had even acquired refugee status from a first-instance hearing at the police, which was even more extraordinary. Yet as some of the key aspects of his story were repeated and reproduced in various forms by many Nigerian visitors to the ARS, this formerly legitimate narrative became the object of suspicion and mistrust as a likely fake.

These many similar stories about Muslims and Christians, which recall a story that was deemed to be authentic by the state, appeared to many ARS lawyers to be reproductions of that "authentic" story, without the aura of the actual or imagined original. Benjamin (1986 [1936]) famously explored how reproduction challenges the concept of authenticity, writing that "the authenticity of a thing is the essence of all that is transmissible from its beginning, ranging from its substantive duration to its testimony to the history which it has experienced." The reproducibility of these stories is what makes them appear fake, suggesting that the *real*, in part, may be located in the appearance of uniqueness and originality, with its history, duration, and testimony. In this specific instance, however, the extraordinary, even fantastical, individuality of this particular Nigerian asylum seeker's narrative about Satanists renders it non-real for Dimitris: its lack of precedent, and its dissimilarity to any other story through which it could appear grounded, substantive, or possible. The non-real lies in part in the appearance of reproducible, hollow, fake similitude, on the one hand, and extraordinary, but fantastical, individuality, on the other.

The suspected presence of fake and fantastical stories constitutes the terrain on which the recognition of "real refugees" always unfolds (see Mountz 2010). Bubant (2009: 556), borrowing Umberto Eco's phrase (1998), describes the "force of falsity" as the "efficacy and affectivity" of the false. Here, falsity defines the narrative terrain on which stories can be deemed authentic or inauthentic and even grants to particular nationalities and accompanying phenotypic characteristics and racial categories the aura of the fake and the fantastical (for instance, rendering Nigerians "economic migrants" who are "good storytellers"). Dimitris suggests that the task of finding "real refugees" centers, in large part, on weeding out that which appears false, getting at the truth behind the curtains people hide behind and the good stories they tell.

If, however, the *non-real* can span such a broad spectrum, this begs the question how a true or authentic story could possibly stand a chance of being recognized. If, indeed, reproducibility challenges the appearance of authenticity, we can see the difficulty entailed in ever making a story about "Muslims and Christians" appear authentic. Meanwhile, the other narrative's fantastical qualities recall the stories some recognized refugees tell, which often speak of all-permeating terror and persecution that extends everywhere; to some, such stories could appear paranoiac, exaggerated, conveying not just "actual" events, but also nightmares. The experiences of those who have fled violence may, in many cases, be beyond belief or comprehension for the listener (see Malkki 1998), and the real may have the apparent fantasy of fiction. Moreover, as I suggested in Chapter 4, for asylum advocates, not just the story and the content of the narrative distinguish "real" from "non-real" refugees but also the social aesthetics through cases takes shape. Thus, elements such as performance, language, textuality, emotion, and other much more nebulous qualities are crucial to making the "real" recognizable. Yet while in Chapter 4 I showed how such aesthetic qualities can often incite forms of mistrust and suspicion between lawyers and clients, here I consider how some cases do in fact become successful.

I now turn to two ethnographic accounts of the process of recognition that together gesture to the diversity of ways recognition can take place. The first account, which explores the case of Mahmud, focuses on the perspective of the refugee himself. This case highlights the extensive work many asylum seekers put into effecting recognition, in terms of both documenting and performing the "real." This case, however, also highlights how the process of recognition serves to instantiate and make "real" normative institutional, legal, and bureaucratic typologies. The second account, however, which centers on the case of Balram (introduced in Chapter 2), performs a reversal in these typologies. Focused on the perspective of the lawyer, Dimitris, this account demonstrates the protracted ways in which recognition often takes place. As he renders Balram's story into a legally salient text, Dimitris gradually begins to characterize the case differently. Most important, however, this case points to the flexibility of the category of the refugee, showing how bureaucratic and legal procedures themselves may effect the recognizability of surprisingly unlikely cases.

"A Good Actor"

I first met Mahmud at the ARS office, where he often came to chat and to pass the time. Numerous NGO workers had told me he was someone I "should" talk to, because he was a legally recognized refugee, and had a particularly interesting case. It was an unusually cold fall day; he was wearing a wool jacket, a sweater, and a scarf, an ensemble that, in combination with his neat mustache and thinning hair, made his appearance markedly professorial. I sat in a chair in front of him and introduced myself, and he answered with a wide smile.

We chatted, and he asked with puzzlement what I was doing at the ARS. I told him that I was doing a project on the role of NGOs in the Greek asylum process. He responded quickly, almost cutting me off: "I would be able to answer you in one word: '*Tipota*.' Nothing." He then explained that he had received asylum in Greece six years ago, but on his own, with no help from any NGO. When I asked him how, he responded with a sly smile: "Perhaps I had a very strong case. Or I had been a very good actor."

At the very beginning of our discussion, Mahmud thus introduced ambiguity into the question of what made his case successful, situating his own refugeeness tenuously between the inherent strength of his case and his being a "good actor." As Mahmud then told me in detail how he came to Greece and applied for asylum, it became clear that he framed his success in terms of both of these qualities. Specificities of his life history, both in Sudan and in Greece, emerged later, over multiple conversations, and in a three-hour recorded interview that we conducted at my flat, over dinner. Here, however, I want to focus on this initial meeting, in which he denoted a few elements that he himself found most important to his successful recognition as a refugee.

He explained that in Sudan he had worked in a white-collar job, and while he had not been very politically active, he had been caught up in a plot against the government, placing him in danger from the authorities. Rather than leaving at once, he took some time to prepare, collecting "papers and other things" to use later in his asylum claim. He explained that he came to Greece because of what he knew of the climate (warm, like Sudan), and because he had known Greek people in Sudan and liked them, finding them also warm. He explained that there was a large Greek diaspora population in Sudan, indicating that one of the workers in the ARS social department had, in fact, been born there to a Greek family.

Mahmud emphasized that he arranged to go to Greece legally, obtaining a Sudanese passport and a Greek visa, traveling not through smuggling routes but on a plane. Shortly after he arrived in Greece, he applied for asylum. Meanwhile, new acquaintances advised him to obtain a lawyer, so he went to the ARS, speaking with a highly experienced lawyer who agreed at once to take his case. But ultimately her services were unnecessary. Just thirteen days later, Mahmud explained, "Some policemen came to my door and asked me to come down to the main police station. I got my *adhia paramonis* [άδεια παραμονής] (residence permit). I took this to my lawyer and she could not believe it." He reached into his pocket and pulled out the passport-like document given to legally recognized refugees. The rapid process Mahmud describes here—thirteen days from initial application for asylum to recognition as a refugee—is almost unprecedented. Like the Nigerian case described earlier, his was one of those extraordinarily rare applications that received a positive decision at "first instance." Judging from the quick decision of not just the lawyer, but also the state, to recognize him as a refugee, Mahmud would appear impressively "real" even among "real refugees."

I asked him again why he thought he was so successful in his asylum claim, and he noted a few elements. First, he told me again that he made a strong effort to travel to and enter Greece legally, and he was convinced that this helped set his case apart. In his repeated emphasis on the legality of his movements, through both documentary legitimization and the routes and methods of his travel, he positioned himself apart from others who enter Greece through smuggling routes without passports or visas. His appreciation for and commitment to legality emerged also in other interactions, particularly in his open disapproval of the prevalence of drugs and drug dealing among young Sudanese asylum seekers and migrants in Athens. In a later conversation, however, he told me that when he applied for asylum, he had falsified his identifying information to ensure his safety. This additional information destabilizes the image of his fully documented, legal entry into Greece, which he emphasized so strongly in our first meeting. While he highlighted legality as key to making his case successful, it was ultimately unclear if this legality emerged more through substantive documentary legitimization or more through his being a "good actor" by carefully managing the appearance of documentary forms.

Mahmud then went on, citing the fact that he did not have an interpreter as crucial to his successful case. "I did not want them to hear my case second hand. When I went for my hearing, they said 'OK, we all speak English here, no problem.'" This may have enabled more precise communication, or it may have come at a price; while Mahmud's mastery of English is highly sophisticated, we do not know how well his interviewers understood every word. However, precision of word-for-word exchange is not what he emphasizes. Rather, he stresses the importance of directness, and thus also control.

Then he stated again: "I was a good actor."

Heath: "How did you act?"

Mahmud chuckled: "At the end [of the interview], I said [hanging head dramatically, looking weary], 'I am an old man, and I don't have the rest of my life to look forward to. All I want is to be able to drink my coffee in my house quietly with my family.'" Here, acting appears not as a strategy of dissemblance, but as a way to elicit sympathy from his audience. Mahmud's "good acting" conveys a notion of the "real" based not just on notions of authenticity, but on intimacy, affect, and emotional proximity.

Finally, he explained that his carefully collected supporting documents also strengthened his case. But then he added: "I must confess—some of the documents I had were real. And others—I confess—I cooked. . . . These ones would have come anyway, but I did not have the time to wait." Then he remarked with a sly grin: "They [forgers] can make some of them very well—they look very good." He thus cited, in rapid succession, the well-documented quality of his case and the clever production of fake documents that look real, but finally asserted that these were forgeries of real documents.

Mahmud is a recognized refugee who himself recognizes the importance of documents, asserting that he took the time to collect them before leaving Sudan. However, a "real refugee," whose life may be in even greater danger than Mahmud's, may not have such preparation time. Thus, at least in theory, an asylum case should be able stand on its own, without documents. Furthermore, as we see here, documents are easy to forge, and were always a point of suspicion in ARS and state assessment practices. When inspecting a set of questionable documents brought by an asylum seeker who had, nonetheless, a plausible and compelling story, Angeliki explained that people "can make anything," so she tried to focus on the interview, not the papers. Dimitris emphasized a similar ethic of focusing on the interview and the story, adding that if someone falsifies documents, it does not necessarily mean he or she is not a refugee. Likewise, for Mahmud, falsified documents did not undermine his case, because these documents were, in a way, real—they simply had not arrived yet. Moreover, these "cooked" papers perhaps looked *real enough* to his audience, and may have contributed to supporting his case. It is also possible, however, that like Dimitris and Angeliki, Mahmud's audience may have chosen to overlook these false documents, focusing instead on his interview.

As Mahmud emphasizes here, despite their physical fragility, replicability, and susceptibility to fakery, documents that look real enough can lend weight to the substance of a case. This weight is not just figurative, but rather, often emerges literally in the physical size and heaviness of a file or stack of papers. In September 2006, I did an interview with a former journalist from Iraq who was, like Mahmud, ultimately recognized as a refugee, though over a much more protracted period. During our interview, conducted in his one-room flat at a housing facility administered by another NGO, he used his hands to indicate the enormous pile of papers he had accumulated to support his asylum case, including documents brought and sent from Iraq, as well as newspaper clippings and other research he had done in Greece. Nasdar, the interpreter assisting us, explained that this man had had a "huge, huge stack of different kinds of proofs," and that when he went to his asylum hearing, his bag was so big the clerk initially told him to leave it by the door (thinking it was just a bag of belongings). Nasdar then added that journalists are "like old people, they save everything." Collecting, saving, preparing, even forging documents *can* make a case appear more *real*. Yet despite the, often literal, weight documents can lend to a case, the distinction between the "real" and the "cooked" is always slippery.

Mahmud's account provides a number of insights into the work that goes into becoming recognizable on the part of asylum seekers themselves. We can point to a number of elements that may be salient in effecting his recognition: his advance preparation of his case, his age, his education, his emphasis on legality, his carefully crafted sympathetic performance, and his class background all perhaps contribute to making him more likely to be recognized as a refugee. But we also see the complex shifts between conceptions of real and the non-real that, in his account, are also crucial to making his case successful. In our conversation, the elements behind his recognition as a refugee move fluidly between legality and illegality, substance and sympathy, and the real and the "cooked." Nevertheless, in recounting this first meeting with Mahmud, I am struck by the fact that despite his own description of the ambiguities of recognition, I never once doubted that he was a "refugee." Certainly, I was less concerned about his refugeeness than his ways of talking about his life in Sudan and in Greece, his excellent jokes, and his insights into numerous topics, including NGO work and the asylum procedure in Greece. Given his reputation as a "real," recognized refugee, the topic of his refugee status often emerged in our interactions. I always approached everything he told me about his asylum narrative with the confidence that it was "true," and thus, *real*, perhaps more so than I did with other interlocutors.

I have drawn on my own encounters with Mahmud because they highlight elements of the process of recognition that I cannot describe otherwise: recognition entails entering dialogically into a way of seeing. This is, in some ways, a kind of conversion. Susan Harding (2000), drawing on Althusser (1971), gives a memorable account of how she, as an ethnographer, experienced a moment of "conversion" when listening to a Pentecostal minister. As he delivers a powerful discourse on salvation, she feels herself gradually pulled into a narrative, imaginative, and emotional world that was, hitherto, alien. This process is realized only later, however, when she narrowly avoids a car accident after leaving the church, and she asks herself—without even thinking—"what is God trying to tell me?" Žižek (1989: 36) discusses the process through which subjects come under ideological authority also in terms of a conversion through which belief is rendered material. He writes: "the subject believes without knowing it, so that the final conversion is merely a formal act by means of which we recognize what we have already believed" (36). Through the moment of refugee recognition, a particular ideological world consisting of law, bureaucracy, and institutional practice is "materialized in our effective social activity," in how we experience our everyday lives and perceive other persons.

Likewise, my own increasing entanglement in the imaginative, emotional, and discursive climate of NGO legal aid work encouraged me also to participate in that shared repertoire of practices, categories, and sentiments. My engagement with ARS bureaucratic culture, and with asylum law more broadly, enabled me not just to see Mahmud as a "real refugee," but also, in a powerful way, to apprehend his refugeeness as something real, material, and essential—not as an imposed framework of legal and bureaucratic authority, but as a quality woven into his life, his body, and his person. The "real refugee" does not emerge just from the apparent facts and merit of the case, though these have an important role in anchoring, substantiating, and sometimes literally, adding weight to the real. Nor is the "real refugee" produced just through the work of good acting. Rather, only the act of recognition itself makes the real refugee "really real."

Reversals and Transformations

On a warm afternoon in July 2007 at the ARS, Rahman, the Bangla interpreter, stopped me in the hallway and introduced me to the young Bangladeshi man named Balram, whom we first met in Chapter 2. He had done an eligibility interview at the ARS a few months earlier, but he had not yet received a decision as to whether he was "eligible" for ARS legal aid services. Meanwhile, his asylum claim had been rejected, the police had taken his pink card, and he had received a deportation order demanding that he leave

Greece within a month. He needed to know if the ARS would support his case.

Searching for Balram's result, I sifted through the files of hundreds of Bangladeshis who had recently done interviews at the ARS. All—including Balram—had been rejected, with the formulaic phrase that interviewers had inscribed at the bottom of each interview form: "economic problems, ineligible." In a clear but nonetheless not wholly uncommon violation of ARS protocol, the interviewer had neglected to identify him/herself on the file, and had given no details about either the interview or the case. Furthermore, Balram had never even been notified of his rejection. Thus, unsupported by the ARS, unable to afford a private lawyer, and perhaps also unaware of the need for one, Balram had gone to his asylum hearing alone, and his performance had resulted in a rejection of his asylum claim. His situation had become urgent: as a rejected asylum seeker, he would soon be vulnerable to arrest or even expulsion. The only way for him to remain legally in Greece was to find a lawyer to apply for an annulment of the negative decision on his asylum application to the Council of State, a very expensive and labor-intensive procedure. Balram was again very much in need of ARS legal services.

But let us fast-forward a few months, to December 2007. By then, ARS workers had reexamined Balram's application for legal aid and not only found him eligible but determined that, according to the NGO institutional criteria, he deserved to be recognized as a refugee according to article 1A2 of the 1951 Geneva Convention. One of the ARS's most successful lawyers had taken on his case, and the Greek Council of State had granted him permission to remain in Greece legally while his case was under review. He could thus continue to live and work in Greece while his claim was under examination, and in the meantime, he might be able to acquire the necessary contacts and papers to employ other methods of regularization, in the event that his asylum claim was ultimately rejected. How did Balram undergo this transmutation from an "economic migrant" to someone who had become recognizable as a "real refugee" to NGO workers?

During much of my fieldwork, applicants from Pakistan and Bangladesh comprised approximately half the asylum cases in Greece,[1] and were the largest demographic of visitors seeking support at the ARS. However, these asylum seekers from South Asia were also generally assumed—by both state bureaucrats and NGO workers—to be "clandestine" economic migrants, owing largely to a fast-growing South Asian community engaging very visibly in labor activities, such as street vending, construction, and small-business entrepreneurship. Country of origin reports attest to political violence in Pakistan and Bangladesh, but they imply that, most often, persecuted individuals can relocate *within* territorial borders. Greek asylum policies routinely placed Pakistani and Bangladeshi applicants in an accelerated procedure reserved for cases deemed to be "manifestly unfounded," or when the applicant is from a safe third country or a designated "safe" country of origin. However, this also created a cycle, in which these applicants had much less time to prepare and appeal their cases. South Asians thus came to constitute ineligible cases par excellence at the ARS. Workers began streamlining the process of assessing the eligibility of Pakistani and Bangladeshi claimants, in a sense creating their own "accelerated procedure." Interviews were distilled to just two questions: Why did you leave your country? What would happen if you were to go back? These questions clearly grant asymmetrical emphasis to that person's narrative capacities and legal knowledge, as opposed to life circumstances that may also figure into an asylum claim.

My hallway meeting with Balram and Rahman the interpreter occurred after a few months in which Rahman had worked closely with Dimitris, interviewing large numbers of Bangladeshi visitors (15–25 a day). Dimitris invited me to observe and assist with their work, and thus we formed what some other workers jokingly called an *omadha* (team) on Bangladesh. While other lawyers characterized Bangladeshi cases primarily as a burden, Dimitris had volunteered to handle these cases, which initially surprised me, given his reputation as an experienced and successful lawyer both in asylum hearings and in trafficking courts. However, he insisted that he enjoyed working with Bangladeshi visitors, that he found Bangladeshis to be extremely pleasant and good-natured people. And so together, he and Rahman created a warm, even jovial atmosphere that contrasted almost absurdly with the seriousness of the proceedings, as they joked persistently about NGO work and the law. He also gave out information and advice to most of those he interviewed, educating them about the asylum process and their legal options; though he found most to be ineligible, he often put them in contact with private lawyers he knew to be reputable and honest.

Despite his jovial interactions with Dimitris, Rahman almost never intervened regarding the cases of aid applicants, usually treating them with neutrality as well as an apparent disinterest that veered on boredom. However, when I delivered the bad news that Balram was ineligible, he shook his head and responded: "I really think he has a problem. He is Hindu. Hindus have real problems in Bangladesh." Struck by Rahman's concern, I suggested that we should both talk to Dimitris, and as expected, Dimitris agreed to reexamine the case.

A couple of days later, Balram came to an interview to initiate the reassessment of his case. In a mix of English, Greek, and Bangla, and often with the help of Rahman, Balram explained that Muslim neighbors and local police had targeted his family because they were Hindu. He had moved to India for protection, but he had also had difficulties in India, because he was illegal there. So, returning to Bangladesh, he hid his wife with family and friends and left, spending some time en route in the Middle East, then ultimately traveling to Greece. Balram also explained that he had worked for a few years at an NGO in Bangladesh, though he did not give many details.

The story that emerged from this first meeting resonated with the religious persecution clause of the Geneva definition of refugee. After this first meeting, Dimitris said that he was convinced that some Hindus do have "real problems" in Bangladesh, but that he was not sure whether Balram was "really Hindu." He asked Rahman to call Balram and request some confirmation of his Hindu background. A couple of days later, Balram returned to the ARS with photos of himself and his wife as tourists in India and a letter from a Hindu temple in Greece certifying that he was a participant there. He explained in English about some Hindu beliefs and practices, pointing to his wife's clothing in a picture and a mark on her forehead.

However, the case quickly became more complex. A week later, he brought a thick stack of paper, in an envelope bearing the stamp of Bangladesh. These papers, including informational material and letters of reference, described his work at an internationally known Christian aid NGO. He also brought photocopies of multiple police documents attesting to "false accusations" through which police in Bangladesh had tried to arrest him on a charge of attempted murder. Finally, a few days after that—unsolicited—Balram brought Dimitris two DVDs. One of these contained home videos of him and his family engaging in Hindu celebrations; the other was a video of Balram taking part in a rally with the Awami League, the more progressive political party active in Bangladesh. At that time, its members reportedly had often faced discrimination and some harassment by the party then in power, the BNP (Bangladesh National Party).

This new information regarding Balram's work history, the "charge sheets," and his political activity added important new dimensions to his case, suggesting that he had experienced political problems, not just religious problems. But it also created points of contradiction, producing an informational and narrative gap between the existent account of this case—the text—and this new material. This also created a site of potential doubt, uncertainty, and even mistrust: why did he not speak about this before? Moreover, charge sheets like those that Balram brought are known among lawyers to be forged in Athens for a fee and are generally treated by ARS staff as part of a standard repertoire of false cases, owing to their wide circulation and apparent easy reproducibility. But the information regarding Balram's work history was material that no NGO workers had seen before, and the videos introduced an immediate vividness into his accounts of both religious and politically relevant activities.

In the meantime, over two weeks had gone by, and the deadline for Balram's application to the Council of State—if he were to make one—was drawing close. With this added pressure of time, Dimitris decided to accept Balram as eligible, explaining that he had decided to give Balram the "benefit of the doubt." He began to draft the application to the Council of State, or STE, which at that time was the court in charge of ruling on (and potentially nullifying) possible breaches of procedural matters in second instance asylum hearings. As the highest court of administrative law in Greece, STE had a very particular role in the asylum procedure. It did not officially rule on the merits of the asylum case, but instead on the procedural integrity of the adjudication procedure through which the case was assessed. If the court found a deviation from procedure, it would likely nullify the former asylum decision with the implication that the case be reexamined. Yet a positive decision from STE did not necessarily mean a positive asylum decision would result on reexamination.

Officially, grounds for applications to STE were always procedural, and in Balram's case, Dimitris claimed the asylum committee had misrepresented the interview Balram had given. And indeed, the asylum committee had been sloppy; the transcript of Balram's interview confirmed that he had given an account much like the one he had given in his ARS interview, whereas the wording of his negative asylum decision explained that *he* had said that he came to Greece for "economic reasons." Dimitris thus had concrete grounds for the application. Despite the official procedural focus of the high court, however, a number of lawyers told me that a positive decision at STE could unofficially lend weight to the merits of the applicant's asylum case and, thus, might have a positive effect on its reexamination. Moreover, shortly after each application was submitted, the lawyer had to file an additional application for suspension of deportation, which would grant the asylum seeker interim protection in Greece while his/her case was examined. In ruling on the suspension of deportation, the Court assessed the apparent danger or *vlavi* [βλάβη] (damage) that the applicant would face if deported to his or her home country. Not many applicants were granted interim protection—particularly applicants from Bangladesh and apparently "safe countries." Thus, in a backhanded way, the high court did render a judgment on the substance of the asylum seeker's claim.[2] This judgment had an immediate effect on that person's future in Greece and could impact further assessments of the case.

Interestingly, the structure of the applications to STE themselves reflected the important unofficial role of STE in the asylum procedure. The numerous applications of ARS clients I read place the narrative of persecution front and center, repeatedly returning to this narrative; the procedural material appears only toward the end. In crafting Balram's application, Dimitris drew on the diverse components of the file, the interview form, and his various meetings with Balram to create a text, a first-person life history narrative told in the voice of Balram, which is the standard format. And Dimitris himself delivered it to the Council of State on his motorcycle, his *mikhani*, on the very last possible due date. Balram's life history, as presented in his application to STE, is a narrative of a man targeted by police for his political and professional activities and who was *also* harassed because he was Hindu. If we take a closer look at the text itself, we see that the gaps are smoothed over, and the contradictions are made to work together to create a fuller and more substantive narrative of persecution. In the very first paragraph, both his activities at the NGO and his Indian origin are given as the reasons for his flight (reproduced in my own direct translation of the Greek text):

> In my country of origin I inhabited the area ____, and worked in ____, a worldwide Christian NGO which has as its key primary objective the help of those who have need, and I was an active member of this organization, as evidenced by correspondence which I attach. This activity of mine as well as my Indian origin forced me to leave my country and go abroad owing to fear of persecution and danger to my life in 2004.

The text goes on to describe a generalized condition of violence in Bangladesh, in order to substantiate his claim to protection.

> The unstable political situation in my country of origin, and the anomalous functioning of democratic process, had created during that period a particular tendency toward political violence. The state mechanisms of public order (police, army) were functioning in these contexts outside the framework of the law, serving various political goals.

The narrative then gives account of the events leading up to his flight to India (his first flight):

> During the elections of 2001 the BNP (Bangladesh National Party) came to power. The day after the elections when I was returning to my house I found the door marked [stamped], with a statement above that said "this house is now the property of Mr. ____" [a local BNP leader]. Both I and my brothers were arrested by the authorities and we suffered serious beatings during the period of our imprisonment. I was set free twenty-four hours after my arrest without any charge. Upon my return to my house I received threats on my life from my neighbors. Both I and my brothers went to India while I made arrangements so that my wife would be brought across the border.

Through a description of his return to Bangladesh and his second experience of persecution, the narrative then accounts for the "charge sheets," thus incorporating and rendering them legitimate through the internal integrity of the text.

> Because I was illegal in India I was forced to return to Bangladesh. Upon my return I tried to appeal the seizure of my home and property with the police authorities. Unfortunately, not only was the appeal not accepted but I was falsely accused of attempted murder [note pointing to the documentary evidence].

The next portion of the narrative focuses on the situation faced by Hindus in Bangladesh, thus substantiating his claim to a well-founded fear *throughout* the territory of Bangladesh on account of his ethnicity and religion:

> The situation for Hindus in the country of Bangladesh is extremely dangerous. . . . Although I tried to hide my Indian ancestry that was

> impossible, as physical characteristics, my surname, and my religious occupations suggest otherwise. The Muslim extremist group Jamaat Al Islam collaborates with the party BNP, and it is known that it is associated with terrorist attacks. The same applies to individuals who seized my home and my property, generally of a party belonging to the BNP. It is clear that both I and many others like me are in grave danger, while the situation in the country of my origin becomes more and more dangerous. I fear for my life throughout the territory of Bangladesh.

Finally, the narrative describes his flight to Greece:

> Upon hearing of these accusations, I ran away . . . because if I had stayed it was likely that I would be imprisoned without ever having the possibility of countering these unjust accusations.

The text closes by asserting that *all* these reasons combined constitute his fear of persecution.

> So, my fear of persecution is not based solely on the fact of my participation in this nongovernmental organization, but the particular circumstances of my case, circumstances related to my ethnic origin and the political situation in my home country.

Balram's life history thus shifted from that of an "economic migrant," with economic problems, to that of a "refugee," with "real problems," both political and religious.

Entextualization

Balram's application to STE—like his interview—is both a performance-based and a textual artifact. It emerged through a series of encounters involving multiple performers and audiences and diverse modes of representation. Bauman and Briggs (1990), however, have shown that texts serve to bracket off and remove discourse from its emergent, messy social contexts. They define "entextualization" as the "process of rendering discourse extractable, of making a stretch of linguistic production into a unit—*a text*—that can be lifted out of its interactional setting" (73). Entextualization can be initiated through written, oral, and visual and gestural signals—whatever serves to mark off a stretch of discourse such that the audience beholds it as a self-referential unit. The "texts" that interviewers produce on interview forms, and the text that Dimitris produced on the application, bracket off the asylum seeker's account, allowing the narrative itself to become the object of focus.

This process of entextualization plays a crucial role in rendering Balram recognizable as a refugee, though this does not necessarily mean that he will acquire refugee status. Entextualization, nonetheless, engenders a new range of potentialities for his case, a set of conditions in and through which recognition could occur. The text serves in a way to remake not just Balram's case but his legal personhood through this apparently seamless, coherent narrative of persecution. Yet the gaps, imperfections, and points of uncertainty underlying this text, which became visible as we reconsidered it in the context of its interactional setting, are also integral to effecting recognizability. Why, of so many cases, did Rahman intervene in this one? Perhaps he really thought Balram had problems, but perhaps he was paid (NGO interpreters are often offered bribes). Was Balram really Hindu? Were those charge sheets real? What exactly was the relationship between his religious orientation and his NGO work? Was he even from Bangladesh? Maybe he was a Bengali speaker from India. These gaps, on the one hand, may undermine his asylum claim, but on the other hand, they provide opportunities for crucial forms of creative work by each of the individuals involved. Dimitris's legal expertise, Balram's pictures and papers, and Rahman's intervention are all necessary to the production of the narrative. In the text, however, this creative work is elided and the narrative appears to be self-evident, smooth, seamless, a "matter of fact."

Shortly after our collaboration on Balram's case, I spent an evening with Dimitris, his wife Fani, and Stavros, at a bar in a suburb of Athens. A large part of our conversation centered on the topic of Bangladeshi cases. Dimitris had begun to do extensive research on Bangladesh, and he expressed surprise at the discrepancies between his findings and the assumptions among many lawyers regarding Bangladeshis and "economic problems." Citing both a UK Home Office Report and a report issued by the U.S. Department of State, he commented: "Bangladesh is a country that is in a state of emergency. And when a country is in a state of emergency, there are no trials, no nothing. There are many people," he explained, citing exact numbers, "who are in prison and who have not been to the court." He continued by highlighting that Bangladeshis are excluded from having legitimate asylum cases: "The UNHCR does not give any directives on Bangladesh. And England does not recognize anyone from Bangladesh [even though the UK home office recognizes that there are many problems there]". Finally, he concluded: "The Bangladeshi people we see are just poor, so poor they don't even know they have rights. Rights for humans—human rights. And some cultures do not allow for this idea, this understanding."

After working on Balram's case, Dimitris had begun to question the frameworks and assumptions through which refugees are most often made recognizable. He suggested that Bangladeshis might, indeed, have "real problems." Moreover, he considered that the concept of "economic problems," rather than signifying problems that are not "real," might indicate even particularly powerful forms of exclusion. He argued that many Bangladeshi asylum seekers in Greece lacked access not just to rights, but also to the knowledge and language of rights, owing to overwhelming poverty and in many cases also lack of education.[3] Dimitris thus began to shift somewhat the way in which he approached the everyday politics of recognition at the ARS. Months later, the ARS received news that the Council of State had ordered that Balram be given his temporary ID card back, allowing him to remain legally in Greece while awaiting the ruling. On telling me this news, Dimitris never mentioned his initial doubts about Balram, emphasizing instead the strength of the application (attesting not just to the strength of Balram's story, of course, but to his own expertise). Furthermore, by this time, Dimitris had also made Bangladeshi cases a project of sorts, taking on a number of other Bangladeshi individuals as eligible and bringing their cases to the high court. In ARS meetings, he expressed increasing frustration with the organization's practice of rejecting such cases routinely, and he had begun to advocate openly for a reconsideration of so-called "economic cases." As he explained to me, "I want to show that there are real refugees from Bangladesh too."

I do not want to assume a direct, causal relationship between Balram's case and Dimitris's changing approaches to his work. Yet it does appear that Dimitris had been pulled into a larger process of recognition through his frequent contact with Bangladeshi individuals, including Balram, through which he had begun to question ARS eligibility practices. Dimitris's recognition of Balram and other Bangladeshi applicants as possible refugees was incremental, cumulative, emerging also across multiple points of inconsistency. But just as the final text of Balram's application smoothes over narrative and informational gaps, when Dimitris discussed the case after the fact, he referenced Balram as a refugee who had, in a way, been there all along—Dimitris just "needed to find him." This process of recognition, effected through an ongoing dialectic between performance and entextualization, retroactively instantiates Balram's refugeeness. Meanwhile, just as Balram's case had a role in shifting Dimitris's own approach toward state and NGO policies, Balram's case could also change from the bottom up some of the assumptions of state actors regarding refugee status determination: perhaps people from Bangladesh could be real refugees too.

Conclusions

A successful asylum case involves much more than simply fitting into a precarved legal category; rather, performance, narrative, and entextualization are all crucial to effecting recognition. Through these many-layered, multivocal components of the politics of recognition, the category of "refugee" is made real: vivified, pulled, redelineated, and sometimes also reshaped. Yet while the "real refugee" always takes shape dialogically, the question of power is also always central. As Judith Butler (1997: 49) asks in her influential rethinking of Austin, "If performativity requires a power to effect or enact what one names, then who will be the 'one' with such a power, and how will such a power be thought?" Butler argues that this "one" is often, in fact, multiple, lying in the sovereignties of citizen-subjects. Yet in the politics of refugee recognition, this power is asymmetrically concentrated in the agents of the state and the law, highlighting the role of juridical and state sovereignty in uttering the "word" that, ultimately, makes subjects recognizable as refugees. Likewise, it is the lawyer's decision, not the asylum applicant's assertion, that ultimately makes that person's refugeeness recognizable to colleagues and, potentially, also to agents of the state.

The figure of the refugee finds its power precisely in this uneasy combination between an asymmetrical authority, which effects and legitimates recognition, and the fluid and dialogical encounters that lie behind it. In disarticulating the processes that underlie that decision or utterance, however, we see that the politics of recognition can throw into the domain of the "real" surprisingly fluid figurations of the category of refugee. To return to the initial vignette, the switch the speaker performs accomplishes the recognition of both himself and the Somali woman as refugees by his audience, enabling this category to move powerfully across diverse contexts, acquiring a broad, even "universal" resonance. Mahmud's case points to the complex tacking between "acting" and "substance" that underlies the process of recognition. Yet the engagements between Balram, Rahman, and Dimitris made a so-called "economic migrant" recognizable as a refugee, shifting also the parameters of what constituted the "real." While one who is structurally in a position of greater power may have a greater role in effecting recognition to agents of the state and the law, the question of whom and what that person recognizes, and why, is highly variable. This capacity of the category "refugee" to move both robustly and smoothly, to be both particular and general, to describe both specific and universal notions of human suffering, is how it acquires its peculiar power.

ACT III

Citizenship

May the dust never drink the black blood
Of fellow citizens, in their lust for revenge,
Hunting for murder to answer murder
To the ruin of the city.
Rather let them give joy for joy. . . .

—*The Eumenides*, 980–984

Chapter 6

Rearticulating the Ethnos

In March 2010, after months of intense debate, the Pa.So.K-dominated government of Georgios Papandreou passed an overhaul in the Greek citizenship legislation. This controversial bill introduced a new legal precedent for *jus solis* citizenship in Greece by easing the formal requirements through which alien residents and their children could acquire status as Greek citizens.[1] The practical and symbolic significances of this legislation remain topics of charged disagreement among lawmakers, advocates, migrants themselves, diverse groups of Greek residents, and the courts. In February 2013, the Council of State issued a decision framing the new citizenship law as unconstitutional—against the very nature of Greek citizenship (Council of State 460/2013). The court asserts that the legal category of citizenship must be grounded on a "real bond" between the "alien" and the Greek state and society. Greek society, insists the court, is not an "ephemeral creation," but "represents a timeless unity" with a distinct language, long cultural traditions, and relatively stable mores, which are transmitted across generations through family ties and in school.[2] The ruling thus insists that long-term residence and even birth in the territory of Greece do not necessarily constitute a "real bond" with the society at large.

It remains to be seen what the effects of the ruling will be, particularly for those who have applied for citizenship in the three years since the introduction of the bill. Current prime minister (as of October 2013), Antonis Samaras, of the conservative party New Democracy, is seeking to retool the citizenship bill in a way that will uphold the ruling. Yet these shifts in the realm of law between openness and closure, inclusion and exclusion, highlight how conceptions of citizenship in Greece are anything but stable—despite the court's insistence on the timelessness of Greek culture and society.[3]

The citizenship bill and the debates that surround it have thrown into question the entrenched *jus sanguinis* structure of Greek citizenship and the presumed inextricability of blood and soil.

Alongside recent debates in the spheres of law and policy-making, an increasingly charged discourse has emerged in Greece around race, racial difference, and *ratsismos* [ρατσισμός] (racism). Khrisi Avyi [Χρυσή Αυγή] or Golden Dawn, the neo-Nazi party that succeeded in placing eighteen representatives in Parliament in the 2012 elections, regularly holds anti-immigration demonstrations and other, much more violent activities.[4] In Athens, where the city center is increasingly militarized to discourage "illegal immigration" (see Cheliotis 2013), and residents of Greek origin often complain that they are marginalized by migrants, groups asserting claims to autochthony have carried out brutal attacks on foreigners. In May 2011, a Greek man was stabbed to death when two men from Afghanistan and one from Pakistan stole his camera as he headed to the hospital to film his wife and new baby. The aftermath of this event sparked attacks on migrants and persons of color that even the mainstream Greek press labeled "pogroms"; dozens were hospitalized and a young Bangladeshi man was murdered, his body rent with multiple stab wounds. Golden Dawn supporters have continued to target foreigners as well as Greeks on the political left. In late September 2013, anti-Fascist Greek musician and rapper Pavlos Fyssas ("Killah P") was fatally stabbed by a member of Golden Dawn. Greek authorities have since arrested four Parliament members, including the party's leader, Nikos Michaloliakos, on charges of founding a criminal organization. The government has also launched an investigation into the prevalence of Golden Dawn supporters among the police and armed forces. Yet long before the Greek authorities initiated this recent (and, one might argue, much too late) "crackdown" on right wing extremism, anarchist and radical left groups and migrant community organizations have been active and organized in responding to xenophobic violence, which they define explicitly in terms of *ratsismos*. This terminology does not draw on the Greek notion of *fyli* [φυλή], which is often translated as "race" to refer to groupings based on ties of blood (Herzfeld 1997), but invokes a more global discourse that highlights exclusion and discrimination based on phenotype and color.

The increasing racialization of the city of Athens is woefully predictable: in a time of economic instability, aggression toward foreigners escalates, as certain citizens seek to purge the body politic of "alien" substances. Yet alongside such forms of violence there is also a different story: of an Athens that is opening and being rearticulated in new ways, both exhilarating and violent. If one of the challenges of writing ethnography is to tell a history of the present as it currently unfolds, another is to ensure that other relevant histories are not erased by the events of the moment. This chapter seeks to track one of these alternative histories. I examine the rearticulation of the Athenian body politic by turning to a long-standing domain of belonging: language.

A language-based examination of belonging in Athens pushes against theorizations of nationhood in terms of entrenched, essentialized, even biologized notions of unbridgeable difference (Balibar 1998; Gilroy 1987; Stolcke 1995). Language was one of the early domains in which discussions of exclusion, inclusion, and incommensurability surfaced in the human and social sciences, particularly in terms of cultural and national identity. From Herder and German Romanticism's take on the entanglement of language, thought, and nation, to the so-called Sapir/Whorf hypothesis, language has long been cited as a crucial element through which differences in social worlds and cultures have emerged. Yet while it draws boundaries, language also has a curious openness. Renan outlined the limitations of language as a ground of nationhood, observing that "language may invite us to unite, but it does not compel us to do so." Likewise, Étienne Balibar (1998: 98) writes that language is "by definition, open"; while one does not choose one's mother tongue, one can learn new languages and thus enter new social worlds. Thus he claims nations are based on notions of blood, of *race*—"a principle of closure, of exclusion." For Balibar, the openness and plasticity of language and language acquisition disqualifies it as the stuff through which the nation can be bound. Yet this openness also gives language a peculiar power to transform consciousness, as nations are opened and articulated anew. I examine how practices of speech itself, and in particular, multilingual communicative events accompanying increasing immigration, are reconfiguring everyday conceptions and practices of belonging. I begin my discussion by tracing the relationship between national memory, language, and inclusion/exclusion in the modern Athenian polis. Then, through some of my urban travels with Hussein, a Sudanese refugee, I ask what new exclusions and connections multilingual communicative practices enable among both Greek and non-Greek Athenians, and how these reshape and rearticulate dominant notions of nationhood.

"A Serious City"

One evening in early spring, I sat with my friend Mihalis on his dusty balcony drinking throat-burning *raki*, swatting at the first *kounoupia* [κουνούπια] (mosquitos). His balcony opened on an empty lot and a small street, and except for the buzzing of insects, it was quiet—a rarity in central Athens. He gestured to the view in front of us: a streetlamp illuminated the stucco façade of the house opposite like a stage set, catching the branches of a single tree in its light as if it were a Japanese gold painting. He asked me what this view made me think of. I replied that it looked very peaceful but lonely, as though there should be a dog barking. He laughed and responded: "It reminds me of what Athens must have been like 50 years ago." I asked him what he meant. He went on: "Before urbanization. Before Athens became a serious city. Before there were neighborhoods. Now there is traffic everywhere. My mother told me how in her house in Nea Smyrni, where she grew up, there were butterflies in the spring. Now, there is nothing like that."

"But there are mosquitoes," I offered. He laughed. He explained that it was not necessarily bad, that now people are more educated, more aware, and there are more different kinds of people—immigrants and refugees (he gestured to me). But he qualified that now there is a lot of noise and less green.

This conversation unfolded in a fluid combination of Greek and English. Mihalis and I had met each other shortly after I began my fieldwork, at a presentation I gave for students interested in doing "postgraduate" (graduate) work in the United States. Like many young people I know in Athens, Mihalis, a recent graduate of the Fine Arts School in Athens, spoke frequently of getting a second degree elsewhere, and he had spent a memorable year in the Erasmus program in Portugal. He speaks English, Portuguese, and German (indeed, he is now an artist living in Berlin), and he later joked that he had pursued a friendship with me partly as a way of improving his spoken English. While he was eager for practice in English, however, I wanted to speak in Greek, so we often spoke in a mixture of the two languages, playing with the array of words available according to the social situation and often quite simply our moods.

When I wrote down this conversation later, I found myself, as I often did, having difficulty remembering what language we had been speaking. I remembered Mihalis speaking about *petaloudes* [πεταλούδες] (butterflies), but I also remembered the striking phrase he had uttered in English—"a serious city." Given our background of multilingual communication, "serious" here references not just English meanings, but also the Greek word *sovari* [σοβαρή], which, much like the English, connotes not just *serious* in the sense of somber, but also important, major, real. Athens is a city not to be trifled with: bigger, more diffuse, with more neighborhoods and less green, but also more impressive, more diverse, with more people and more going on—a global city, with accompanying problems and benefits.

Like Mihalis, many people explained this new Athens to me not only in terms of more traffic and loss of green, but through the presence of new people and languages—not just tourists, but more often migrants and refugees. And despite the often hidden but nonetheless profound heterogeneity of Greece's cultural past, there is a strong sense that with these new migrations, languages, and cultures, Athens has changed irrevocably. Mihalis, with his own desires to travel and live elsewhere, welcomes the new urban experiences that the presence of new people brings. But for many, the coming of new "foreigners" and the emergence of Athens as a kind of global city are very frightening. Haris, the kind-eyed older gentleman whose family ran the vegetable store around the corner from my flat, also told me of this changing Athens. He explained to me that "before": "Greeks had good families. Greeks were not afraid. In their gardens and courtyards, they left things—even money. They left their doors open. But then the war came—Germans and Italians—they stole from us! And now there are many foreigners—immigrants. Many make trouble."

Haris has experienced much that would make one afraid. He has lived through the devastating famine of World War II, the civil war, the Junta and its fall, the student rebellion at the Polytechneio. But here, he narrates the changes and the suffering that he has witnessed primarily in terms of different waves of *kseni* coming into Athens—first Germans and Italians, now immigrants—making the city a place he does not recognize. Likewise, much as Haris expresses a longing for a time with open doors and courtyards, as Mihalis recalls his mother's narrative of her childhood, there is a certain wistfulness in the way he imagines the butterflies. Athens has perhaps become heavier, a more difficult place to be—a serious city.

Nadia Seremetakis (1996: 4) writes, "*nostalghia* speaks to the sensory reception of history." Nostalgia also reflects how that history, and its imprinting on sensorial memories, is remade in juxtaposition to the particular sociopolitical climate of the present. Wistfulness and nostalgia for a lost city with more solid boundaries and borders, coupled with excitement and anxiety for the emergence of a new global city through immigration, is replicated in many different sites in Athens, and with many mixed messages. Newspapers report the plights of migrants and refugees while simultaneously highlighting their involvement in crime. Documentaries and news reports seek to put a "human face" on immigration while also bemoaning the city's transformation. A particularly curious series of broadcasts from October 2008 produced by *Erevna*, a news show on the major channel MegaTV, entitled "5 minutes from Omonia," documents the city center "ghetto" emerging near Omonia Square. The first of these reports features interviews with migrants who tell of sleeping in the street, as well as the commentary of Greek shopkeepers who say that they are afraid, complaining that they can no longer walk down the street or enter their shops—the neighborhood is so crowded with migrants. This broadcast also features an old woman who has lived in the neighborhood since before World War II and is apparently the only Greek woman still living on the block. Although the voiceover explains that the neighborhood became, suddenly, a "ghetto" and she is all alone there, she tells the interviewer emphatically: "They are good people," explaining that "they" always greet her on the street: "Grandmother, how are you doing, how are you?" She also cooks for them sometimes. Thus, the words of the elderly Greek woman alleviate the hyperbolic commentaries of the shopowners (and the interviewer). The interviewer then recounts how a "new life" has emerged in this neighborhood, cutting to scenes of these now culturally diverse streets, with new foods and items for sale. Such contradictory messages underscore the ambivalence beneath the story of changing Athens, tinged with both nostalgia and fear but also excitement around a kind of *polipolitismikotita* [πολυπολιτισμικότητα] or multiculturalism (Tsibiridou 2006b Yiakoumaki 2006b), consisting of new foods (Yiakoumaki 2006a), new languages, new economic practices (Rosen 2013), and new encounters and experiences becoming possible.

Purification

Recent migrations into Greece are often expressed in terms of a dramatic injection of "difference" into a largely homogeneous cultural space. This assumption of homogeneity is remarkably widespread, as many continue to describe the modern Greek nation in terms of remarkable uniformity of religion, phenotype, and language. Scholars also have marveled at the "triumph" of the Greek *ethnos* (Herzfeld 1997, Just 1989) and the markedly monochromatic picture of Greek culture and nation that has emerged out of the complexity of its multilayered histories. Michael Herzfeld (1997: 85) has pointed to Greek nationalism's peculiar power to incorporate rather than contradict local and regional identities, though this must not be mistaken for inclusiveness. Indeed, until the recent "crisis" of immigration, the presence of minorities in Greece had entered the realm of public concern and debate primarily in the context of border struggles: the Turkish and the Macedonian minorities (see Danforth 1995), amid persistent Greek fears of encroachment in the Aegean and the North. Even many so-called minorities nonetheless identify as Greek, particularly when their Greekness is under question (Cowan 2001; Herzfeld 1997). Whether it is illusory or triumphant, the narrative of Greek cultural uniformity is remarkably widespread, and its power and persistence are crucial to consider when examining the significance of new migrations into Greece.

This monochromatic image of Greekness has, however, been wrought through difficult work and often violence, and with just a bit of probing we can begin to see its fissures. With the construction of the Greek nation also came projects of national *katharismos* [καθαρισμός], cleansing or "purification," aimed at constructing the Hellenic ideal through the erasure of the Ottoman past. Archaeologist Effie Athanassopoulou (2002) explains how the emerging field of classical archaeology was colored by the binary of Hellenism versus Orientalism, as the Acropolis, in its white, solitary splendor, was (re)constructed as Ottoman buildings were razed. Such projects of cleansing reached perhaps their most violent zenith shortly after World War I, in 1923, when thousands of ethnic Turks were displaced in the infamous "population exchange" with Turkey. Continued disputes over Cyprus make clear the persistence of this complex, but also intimate, antipathy between Greece and Turkey, and perhaps also the continuation of a divide between the Hellenic and the Oriental. Fissures in the Greek national narrative cannot always be traced along the Hellenic/Oriental faultlines, however, as the dominant history of Hellas powerfully excludes also Slavic histories (Karakasidou 1997).

Ethnographic scholarship has, nonetheless, increasingly called attention to the diversity that simultaneously underlies the monolithic image of Greekness (Faubion 1995), and the experiences of alterity, fracture, and also tolerance, which often go unacknowledged (Dalakoglou 2010; Karakasidou and Tsibiridou 2006; Papataxiarchis 2006; Papataxiarchis et al. 2009; Rozakou 2009). Papataxiarchis (2006) examines the various waves of migration into Greece that have occurred since the fall of the "iron curtain": first Albanians, but now people from throughout the Balkans, Middle East, and Africa, manifesting now in a distinct sense of the presence of new cultural others. Importantly, however, he reminds the reader that notions of difference are not simply new in Greece; rather, the appearance of new "others" maps onto and reconfigures long-term histories of alterity in the Greek, Ottoman, and Balkan pasts. This complex mix of presumed cultural homogeneity and, often silent (and silenced), alterity and tolerance, forms the backdrop against which new encounters with "difference" in the context of immigration now unfold.

Yet even if the Greek nation (like all nations) did not realize its dream of homogeneity, much of the nation, nonetheless, seems to insist that it did. And in this dream, Athens has a crucial place. While Athens is well known for its centrality in Attic Greece, Constantinople was the undisputed heart of the Byzantine Greek world and still holds a spiritual significance as the "lost homeland" of a diasporic Greek people. During Ottoman rule, Athens became a backwater of Attica, particularly in comparison to the lost center of Constantinople and the trade crossroads of Thessaloniki, a nexus for Greek, Ottoman, European, and Slavic worlds. With Greek independence, however, following the provisional capitals of Aegina and Nafplio, Athens was transformed into the new center of Modern Greek nationhood through a protracted alchemy involving the ancient past (particularly the archaeological landscape) (Hamilakis 2007), Europeanized ideals of Greek history, neo-Hellenic nationalist intellectualism, and the Orthodox church (Bastea 2000; Gourgouris 1996). As the Athens subway has expanded, construction has sparked the creation of small subway museums displaying Classical and Byzantine layers, beneath the messy sprawl of a city that somehow continues to circle around the pristine columns of the Acropolis and the domes of Byzantium, with very few visible traces of its Ottoman (and Muslim) histories. Following World War II and the Civil War, Greeks from the islands and the provinces (*eparheia*) relocated to Athens in search of economic viability, sparking a population explosion and rapid urban development in the 1960s, 1970s and 1980s. The city is now known throughout Greece as a place where very few people are "from" but almost everyone has a connection.

Athens is also, as we know, a central site in the movements of—largely Muslim—migrants, asylum seekers, and refugees, who travel to Athens directly from border detention centers, in seasonal movements from agricultural jobs, and in daily commutes from factories at the edges of the city. In northern Greece, near the Bulgarian and Turkish borders, but also in

Thessaloniki, minarets and mosques are much more common to the passing eye than archaeological sites. But in Athens, no formal mosque has been built since Ottoman rule (though there are many informal worshipping sites) (see Antoniou 2005, 2010), and Muslim migrants now find themselves caught in these pasts that drive their worship underground, to community centers, flats, and basements near Omonia (Triandafyllydou and Gropas 2009; Tsitselikis 2004).[5] Amid the ambivalence of longings, fears, and excitements around a more "global" future, Athens has become a site of encounters that might not have been possible even just a few years ago.

Language, Opening, and Rearticulation

In projects of purification accompanying the building of a Greek national narrative, language has been a central marker through which Greeks were made and made recognizable, but it has also been a battleground where the contours of the Greek nation have been repeatedly drawn and contested. After independence, nationalist intellectual Adamantios Korais drew on notions of European romanticism to advocate an active "cleansing" of the Greek language, insisting, following Herder, that language is a "sacred property," by virtue of which a nation's character can be known (Gourgouris 1996). The puristic language that resulted from these nationalist projects was known as *katharevousa* [καθαρεύουσα], and it was framed as a Greek purged of "barbarous" forms: words with origins in Turkish, Slavic, Albanian, Arabic, and other languages not associated with the European imperial core. While presented as a simplified version of Ancient Greek, it in fact drew heavily on Western European visions of the Ancient Greek language as well as certain Western linguistic forms (in particular, from French) (see Mackridge 1985). *Katharevousa* thus was founded on a vision of commensurability with the linguistic knowledges of Western Europe (Herzfeld 1987a). This created, as Herzfeld shows (1987a: 51–52), not just a symbolic entry point into a Greek nation imagined as a progenitor of Europe, but also a "supracultural" code that would facilitate Greece's movement onto the plane of international communication with the West.

Katharevousa is the original language of the Greek constitution, persisting as the official language of Greece until 1976. Yet its antiquated, artificial quality was underscored by the persistence of *dhimotiki* [δημοτική], the demotic, which many poets and writers, such as Kavafy, enlisted in literature, and which ultimately replaced *katharevousa* as the official language. In today's spoken and written Greek, however, both versions are entangled, as is evident in the persistence of words and grammatical forms (documented in detail by Mackridge [1985] in his masterful description of the Athenian language), and in the persistence of what some of my Greek interlocutors have described to me as a semi-*katharevousa* in academic texts and in the newspaper, a characterization that highlights not just the formality of the genre but its dissonance with spoken Greek. Despite all attempts at "cleansing" and closure, the Greek language is the subject of ongoing discussion, debate, and contention—the dream of a "purified" Greek nation intermingling with the vernacular traces of its "Oriental" past.

The contested history of the contemporary Greek language points to the centrality of language ideology in contests over Greek nationhood. Now, however, the terrain of language in Greece is being further reconfigured through new formations of power, which simultaneously heighten and contest the apparent closure of the Greek language. EU governance has given rise to new overlapping regimes of policy and language. While EU bureaucratic practices are always inflected through the careful and intensive role of interpreters and translators, policy papers tend to couch European goals first in English and French, even in policies that implicate Greece. Furthermore, with EU policies that encourage freedom of movement and labor, and particularly given the extraordinary challenges Greeks currently face with the financial crisis, many Greeks increasingly seek education and work abroad. Well-traveled young Greeks often emerge as polyglots, switching between English, French, Italian, German, and of course Greek with remarkable comfort and ease. The prevalence of English terms and the Latin alphabet in spoken and written colloquial Greek has emerged in the humorous denotation "Greeklish" or "Greeglish," a hybrid language that jumps playfully between the registers of English and Greek.

The effects of Europeanization on language, however, must also be understood alongside emerging global reconfigurations of capital and labor, particularly in the context of immigration. New languages and the multilingualism of migrants themselves are making Greece—and in particular Athens—an increasingly multilingual space. As foreigners themselves learn Greek, sometimes almost perfectly and at other times not so well, new pronunciations, accents, inflections, idiosyncrasies, and "mistakes" begin to emerge in the everyday practice of the Greek language. The terrain of language thus reflects shifting constellations of power and exchange, which are constitutive of the everyday encounters through which language unfolds and takes shape (Sapir 1921).

Despite this emerging multilingualism, the Greek language, nonetheless, at times seems to function as an instrument of identification, taking on an almost racialized capacity to mark persons as recognizably Greek, particularly in encounters with foreignness. During my fieldwork, I was perpetually baffled by the apparently self-evident qualities through which native Athenians would claim to recognize Greekness against similarly self-evident notions of the foreign and the foreigner—a distinction often expressed through a melding of phenotypic cues and language. Many Athenians would address me in English before I even opened my mouth. When I asked why, I received variations of the response that a Greek teenager gave, as she gestured toward me and shrugged her shoulders, then answered in Greek: *you are not Greek* [δεν είσαι Ελληνίδα]. My foreignness was so self-evident (presumably not just in my clothes, but in my fair complexion) that no further explanation was necessary. When I explained this to a Greek acquaintance with red hair and blue eyes, he laughed that at least once a week someone approaches him in English; similarly, a dark-complexioned Italian friend visiting Athens was frequently addressed in Greek.

The self-evidence of my *non*-Greekness was also frequently reflected in the presumed impossibility that I was learning the Greek language: "Why are you learning Greek?" was a common response from Greek speakers who often emphasized that "only Greeks speak Greek," or as most of my younger friends and acquaintances would carefully underscore, "*We* speak English" Others would emphasize the difficulty of Greek—"a difficult language, a rich language." On multiple occasions, I was told that Greek has two times (or three times, or five times) the number of words as English, and that Greeks themselves use only a fraction of them (an account I have also heard to describe Italian and even English). Greek was framed simultaneously as inaccessible and also, in many ways, as useless: a precious linguistic world confined to ethnonational lines, in stark contrast to the accessibility—but also poverty—of the English language. As I myself have spent more and more time interacting in Greek and moving through the streets of Athens, I too have begun to embody certain markers in how I speak and carry myself. While I am never mistaken for a native speaker, I am often asked whether I am of Greek origin. Unlike my earlier discussions with Athenians about my interest in the Greek language, this question implies inclusion rather than exclusion, yet it still presupposes that the Greek language maps onto lines of descent and blood. It is, however, important not to dismiss this closed, even exclusionary nature of contemporary Greek language ideology as "mere" nationalism or xenophobia. Given the history of Greek nationalism's entwinement in the imperial projects of western and northern Europe, suspicion toward encroachment by Anglophones like myself on the intimate terrain of contemporary Greek could also be interpreted as a lasting, embedded practice of resistance.

The assumed phenotypic and linguistic distinctions between Greeks and northern European foreigners (most often tourists) are, however, very different from the new constellation of foreignness that is emerging in the context of immigration. While tourists are, in many ways, problematic figures (Herzfeld 1987b), owing to the power dynamics that they introduce, they are most often assumed to be white foreigners from the global North, who move with passports, legally and legibly to the law, bringing money and business. However, migrants, asylum seekers, and refugees represent a new kind of *ksenos* whose presence is highly racialized and strongly ambivalent, introducing powerful dilemmas into the local/foreigner dynamic. In this emerging configuration of difference, language emerges as a terrain on which Greekness is defined but sometimes also muddied. Alongside the increasingly multilingual climate of Athens, there is also the fact that many foreigners do learn to speak Greek, which is a similar source of ambivalence. My neighbor, in warning me to be careful of foreigners, told me to be especially careful of foreigners who speak Greek, asserting solemnly that not everyone who speaks Greek is, in fact, Greek. I have frequently heard Albanians described as particularly dangerous foreigners precisely because many speak Greek and also, in many cases, are presumed to "look Greek" (or as I was told a number of times, they "look the way Greeks did fifty years ago"), thus complicating those supposedly easily apprehensible elements of Greek identity: language and phenotype.

Language, while traversing the body of the Greek *ethnos*, is also a site where it might be falling apart, as new languages and new foreigners transform how the boundaries of Greekness are configured. The presence of new languages and of foreign speakers of Greek contests the representation of the Greek language as a closed system that can easily define the boundaries of inclusion and exclusion. Furthermore, while the Greek language often continues to serve as an instrument of identification and differentiation, it also increasingly enables intercultural encounters that undermine these very forms of closure and exclusion. Alongside entrenched assumptions of homogeneity and increasing forms of racialized exclusion and violence, the Greek *ethnos* is also being opened and rearticulated.

Hussein ("not Saddam")

I first met Hussein at a Sudanese community organization that had their "office" above a shuttered storefront near the central Athens market. David, an NGO client from Sudan and a part-time interpreter, had offered to take me there, suggesting that perhaps I could help them write a grant application, or that I, as an anthropologist, could help them learn more about their "black African history" (an assumption I emphatically contested). We walked through a street littered with vegetable refuse where earlier a bustling market had taken place, then up a dank stairwell to the fifth floor. A handwritten sign indicated which door to enter. I was somewhat apprehensive at what kind of office I would find, but I was surprised and delighted to see not so much an office as a café or bar: a large, sunny apartment, with a fridge stocked with beers and juices, and a makeshift kitchen staffed by an attractive woman who was busily cooking and serving (the only woman there besides me). There were overstuffed leopard print sofas and tables with candles and bright colored plastic tablecloths. The front room was populated by a group of young men wearing oversized t-shirts, some with dreadlocks, smoking *nargileh*; the air was sweet with tobacco smoke and incense that I had never smelled before. A larger adjacent room was set up less like a lounge and more like a café, with many more tables and a television playing news in Arabic. In this room, the men looked older, and most were watching TV, though there were also men playing chess amid a small group of onlookers.

David and I drank sweet red tea as he told me about the work of this community organization, which was focused specifically on addressing the challenges faced by Sudanese refugees; he was an active member and had a number of plans he needed help with: he wanted to start a website and letter-writing campaigns to inform the world of the problems of Sudanese refugees in Greece. As we were talking, a broad-shouldered man who appeared to be in his early forties approached us. With long thick dreadlocks, he wore an oversized yellow coat and walked with a slight limp, but he nonetheless managed to move with a cool, relaxed fluidity. He had notably lighter skin than most of the other men in the room, and his face was striking for the pronounced dark shadows beneath his eyes. "This is Hussein," David said. "He is the president of the organization." Hussein put out this hand and answered in English, with a deep voice and serious expression that increased the ironic humor of his introduction: "Hussein, not Saddam." I told him briefly that I was doing research on the asylum procedure in Greece, and while he did not remain at the table, we exchanged contact information. Then he joined a group of older men playing chess, rather than the younger, dreadlocked group smoking from the water pipe.

After that first meeting, Hussein and I began meeting frequently for coffee or food in the afternoons. I learned that he had been granted asylum in Greece a number of years earlier, after experiencing persecution in Sudan for his political and religious beliefs. I also learned that he and David did not like each other, which was why he had not remained at our table that first day. He told me to be careful of David, complaining that he was all talk and no action: "blah blah blah," he mouthed, then laughed; I later found out that David was a contender for replacing Hussein as leader of the community organization, and he ultimately succeeded.

Hussein and I initially spoke English together, but I quickly learned he was more comfortable in Greek; he told me that while he had spoken English before, after his years in Greece he had begun to forget it. He spoke fluent Greek, peppered with colloquialisms despite frequent grammar mistakes, and he often spoke extraordinarily fast, with a strong throaty "R" I recognized from Sudanese Arabic. At this time, early in my fieldwork, I frequently returned home at night exhausted from the effort of thinking, speaking, and listening in Greek. Our conversation would break down sometimes, but most often these points of misunderstanding became sources of laughter. No doubt we formed a funny spectacle for outsiders, spinning our own world of mutually intelligible Greek rife with different accents and occasional grammar mistakes. As one server at a coffee shop we frequented asked laughingly, in Greek: "What language are you speaking? Greek?" Or as another Greek friend observed, "You don't talk, you communicate."

Hussein moved with ease and visible comfort in Greek and among Athenians. He told me he had a Greek girlfriend, though he asserted that it was an occasional relationship, not a "serious" one. He served also as a frequent liaison to the hospital and the police station for people newly arrived from Sudan, accompanying some as an interpreter, or going alone, to assist on different cases. One afternoon, he and I spent an hour waiting for a notary to sign documents for three Sudanese men recently arrived in Greece. He and the notary joked together and parted with a warm handshake—Hussein was a frequent customer. At the police station, he was frequently encouraged to cut his dreadlocks and work for them as an official interpreter, but he did not want to work with the police—he did not want to cut his hair, he said. But he cultivated good relationships with certain police officers: on a couple of occasions, I saw him shake hands and chat with police officers we passed on the street. I suspected that the people he helped (fellow Sudanese) paid him for this work, and that in a way he gate-kept access to bureaucratic apparatuses, though I never was certain. I do know that he did not have a regular job, and he spent most of his time traveling around Athens and even outside, helping new Sudanese arrivals navigate Greek bureaucracy, a kind of unofficial advocacy that both his language capability and his connections made possible.

Together, we occupied a semi-comfortable space of shared foreigner's Greek, and he moved with ease among persons who, through their jobs, dealt with migrants on a daily basis. For some Athenians, however, Hussein—and Hussein and I together—were a strange, remarkable, even unpleasant sight. Hussein and I took two taxi rides together, which were the settings of two particularly memorable encounters. Both rides took a similar trajectory: from Plateia Amerikis (known among Athenians for its large migrant population, where many of Hussein's friends lived) to neighborhoods just a little south of the city center, where we had our respective flats. On both occasions, the drivers displayed strong reactions toward both Hussein and myself, but in very different ways.

The first ride occurred in the evening, after a meeting of an African women's community organization. We spoke quietly among ourselves in the back, in Greek, until the driver interjected with a smile: "Are you from Ethiopia?" Hussein replied that he was from Sudan. Citing Hussein's light skin, the taxi driver commented that he looked more like he was from Ethiopia. Hussein laughed, and explained that many people think he is Ethiopian, but that people in Sudan have many different skin colors. "You must miss it," said the man wistfully. "It is better in Africa." The taxi driver went on to explain that he was from Athens but his wife was, in fact, Ethiopian. They met in Athens, but were married in Ethiopia, and they had lived there together for a while. He came back to Athens to make money to support her while she remained in Ethiopia, but he was trying to go back soon. "Life is better there" he added.

The journey ended before we could hear more of this man's story. But I was amazed at the remarkable account of cross-cultural intimacy that Hussein's presence and "lighter skin" had evoked. The mustached taxi driver, whom I had mistakenly taken to be just another "regular Greek," in fact was turning the expected migration pattern on its head: working to support his wife back "home" in Ethiopia, much like many other single migrants I met in Athens. Yet this man was working in his *home* country, which was itself a new migration destination, and he was working in order to go back to Ethiopia, thus contesting also the desirability of Athens and of Europe as a central migration destination. While Athens provides certain opportunities for livelihood—facilitating also his movement away from Athens—he insists, as I heard many migrants and asylum seekers assert, that life is "better" in the home that is not Europe. This man was, of course, unusual, but his story attests to multilingual lives and families that are becoming increasingly possible in Athens.

Our second taxi ride together was very different. This time it was quite late at night, after dinner with some of Hussein's friends, and we were smiling after an evening of good food. We flagged down a taxi, and a strong-jawed, thick-mustached man stopped for us. Before we got in, I spoke through the open window, using the subjunctive to indicate politeness, asking the driver if he would make two stops, as we were both headed directly home, and our neighborhoods were easily reachable on the same route. The man nodded, so we got in, and we chatted quietly among ourselves in the back until the first stop, when Hussein waved goodbye. Sitting alone in the back, I noticed the driver glaring at me through his rear-view mirror, and I grew increasingly uncomfortable. As we drove up the hill above the old Olympic stadium, toward my flat, he addressed me coldly in Greek with a strong accent, pronouncing his Rs in a guttural fashion: "Foreigners have to learn how it is in Greece [οι ξένοι πρέπει να μάθουν πως είναι στην Ελλάδα (*I kseni prepei na mathoun pos ine stin Ellada*)]. A taxi is not a bus. You cannot [δεν μπορείτε (*dhen borite*)] ask for multiple stops."

This statement was made even colder by his use of the formal address—one of the few times I was ever addressed formally. Most strange men—particularly older men—readily approached me in the intimacies of the first person, with masculine paternalism, highlighting both my gender and my age, calling me also *koritsi mou* [κορίτσι μου], *kopelia* [κοπελιά], *ghlikia mou* [γλυκιά μου]—my girl, missie, my sweetie. Through the guise of politeness, not only was this man's formality a clear distancing move, but it also contained more than a hint of irony. Taken aback, I apologized, but flushed by his unexpected bitterness I pointed out that we had asked him beforehand, and he had taken us anyway. "You have to learn how it is in Greece" (*prepi na mathite pos ine stin Ellada* [πρέπει να μάθειτε πως είναι στην Ελλάδα]), he repeated. I sat quietly, waiting anxiously for the ride to be over, but he spoke again: "What are you doing with those blacks? How do you understand each other? Speaking Greek. A mess [χάλια (*khalia*)]." While he had initially directed his anger toward both Hussein and me collectively as "foreigners," he turned immediately toward a question of race, implying also that my being with "those blacks" was somehow inappropriate. But worst of all, it seemed, was the fact that we were speaking Greek, and that Greek had become a common language for foreigners: a "mess," signaling a mixing and even contamination that offended the cosmological ordering that reserved "Greek" for "Greeks" (Douglas 1966).

These two very different encounters highlight what I would characterize as rather exceptional reactions generated through meetings between Greeks and foreigners in Athens. Both of these encounters, involving persons from multiple linguistic and cultural backgrounds, transpired in Greek, and in both, questions of race figured centrally. For the first man, Hussein's dark but light skin, as well as his African origin, evoked a discussion of a new home and family that had emerged through the transcultural, multilingual encounters that have become possible in Athens. In the second meeting, however, both race and language are nodes of anger. For this man, the discomfort that he associates with Hussein's blackness (particularly when combined with my whiteness, my gender, and perhaps also the hint of a possible sexual relationship between myself and Hussein) is heightened through what he describes as the *mess* of us speaking Greek. The possibility not just of multiracial and multilingual intimacies, but also that Greek could be a common language for foreigners, is framed as extremely problematic. These exchanges point to the ambivalent possibilities of multilingual encounters emerging in Athens. Language provides a point of opening, through which new connections and lives become possible, but it also incites new racialized points of closure and exclusion.

"All One Family"

Hussein met me one afternoon with an envelope: an invitation to a wedding. Two of his friends, Temima and Samir, were getting married, and he told me I was invited not just to the wedding, but also to the party the night before, when the groom's hands and feet would be painted with henna. I had met both Temima and Samir on a number of occasions, but only in passing.

Temima was from Addis Ababa and Samir from the region of Darfur; I was particularly impressed by their relationship because they did not share a common language. According to Hussein, Temima did not speak much Arabic, though she was learning, and neither of them spoke much English or Greek. But they had been living together for a few months, and were now starting a family (she was, in fact, a few months pregnant).

I knew from my experiences at the ARS and other outings with Hussein that many Sudanese men and Ethiopian women had started families together in Athens, forming common communities. Most of the women I met through Hussein were from Ethiopia, and all were involved with the men in his inner circle of friends. Samir's biological brother was, in fact, married to one of Temima's close friends, and they had a small son together. At the ARS, I also met numerous Ethiopian women with children who told me that their children's fathers were from Sudan, though I rarely met whole families there; rather, women mentioned husbands and boyfriends who were busy, at work, or in another European country. Getting the sense that Hussein was really the one inviting me, I was not sure if I should attend such important gatherings, but he insisted that not everyone had received a proper invitation with a card. I looked again at the envelope and saw my name: *Mrs. Heath* written in careful script. And so I accepted.

A couple of days later, accompanied by my American friend Maria, who had also been invited as a friend of Hussein, I took the trolley to Plateia Amerikis, near the home of friends of Temima and Samir, where the henna party would take place. Hussein was waiting at the trolley stop with a group of other men; at the center was Samir, the only one among them wearing a Sudanese robe and skullcap, which his companions grabbed and tossed playfully. Surprised that we were the only women, I asked Hussein if it was appropriate for us to be there; he answered that the other women were preparing the dinner—and also preparing themselves, he added laughingly. We walked just a couple of blocks, moving slowly as Samir stumbled in his robe, stopping at a nondescript building on a quieter street off the large boulevard of Patission. A man greeted us in Arabic at the door of a basement apartment. As we walked in, I saw a number of women I recognized from other outings with Hussein, cutting onions and other vegetables in the kitchen and hovering over the stove. Through the open bathroom door, I also caught a glimpse of the woman Hussein explained was the "lady of the house," also from Ethiopia, with wet hair, bent over the sink; she laughingly shut the door.

Maria and I sat with the men and two other women in the living room, all rapt, watching an Egyptian musical about a marriage. On the mantel behind the television, above a defunct fireplace, I saw two photographs. One was a posed photograph against a blue background of the couple who lived in the apartment, the woman sitting in the man's lap, with an arm wrapped around his neck in a grip both sweeping and tight, appearing to convey both love and possession. The other was, in fact, two photographs that I realized had been placed together to appear almost as if they were one: a white-bearded man with a stern expression, dressed much like Samir in a long robe and skullcap, and an older woman wrapped in colorful robes and a headscarf, who looked unsmilingly at the camera. Noticing me, the man whose apartment we were in explained in English that these were his father and mother. I was struck and somewhat touched by the difference between these photographs: the affectionate physical closeness he and his wife performed in their poses juxtaposed against the formal expressions of the elderly man and woman, who did not even occupy the same photographic space.

Shortly, more and more people filed in until the small living room was packed, and the "lady of the house" appeared, her hair in curlers that were hidden by a scarf, but decked out in a short pink dress, a big beaded necklace, and jeweled heels. Her husband embraced her and placed his hand protectively around her belly—she too was pregnant. She made a gesture toward the stereo, and someone put on music—Arabic pop—and a few of the guests began to dance, she at the center. Samir sat on the sofa, flanked by his compatriots, who brought him beer and whiskey. The women who had been preparing the food brought in *injera* (Ethiopian flat bread) and spicy chicken, which we ate in groups of five and six off shared plates. Then Temima and three of her friends arrived. Unlike the other times I had met her, and in stark contrast to our hostess, she was dressed simply, in jeans and a sweater, wearing no makeup. But she and her friends lifted their sleeves to display the henna that had been applied to their arms and hands, and to Temima's feet: intricate, dark brown, curling designs that danced as they moved. They had just come from their own private henna gathering. As Temima pushed through the crowd to squeeze in next to Samir, Hussein leaned over to me and explained that when "Fatimah," the henna artist, arrived, Samir would have henna applied to his own feet.

The guests danced, sang, drank, and talked. Communication unfolded in partial mixes of a number of languages: Arabic, Greek, English, and Amharic. A couple of women from Sri Lanka also arrived, with Sudanese men, and these couples spoke in a mix of Arabic, Greek, and English. Hussein spoke to me and Maria in Greek, but most of the other guests addressed me in a mix of Greek and English. Overall, however, the party was centered less on conversation than on eating, music, and dancing. At some point, the music switched from Arabic to Ethiopian pop, and the hostess and her friends danced in an informal performance.

Finally Fatimah arrived, in colorful teal robes and a matching headscarf. The only woman from Sudan who was at the party, Fatimah, I was told, did the henna for many of the marriages in Athens involving Sudanese people. Smiling, but without speaking to any of the men or women, she mixed the henna, and setting herself up on the coffee table, plastered the bottom of Samir's feet with the dark red clay. Expecting the intricate designs I had seen on the women, I quickly realized that this was a very different style—broad, deep red on the dark feet of the men. One by one, she also plastered the hands of the male guests, and finally my hands and Maria's. Reluctantly at first, but under the urging and laughing of Hussein and some of the other men, she did our hands just as the men had been painted: the palms, and thin stripes on my fingers.

As we waited for the red plaster to dry, Hussein turned to me and said, gesturing to the group around him: "imaste oli mia ikoyenia" [είμαστε όλοι μια οικογένεια] (We are all one family). He put his arm around a quiet man next to him with downcast eyes, wearing a baseball cap: "o adherfos mou" [ο αδερφός μου] ("my brother"). He pointed to a number of other men and then to Temima and her friends, saying: "They were all in Lebanon together, and now we are here together. We are all one family." He explained that many of the women and men in the room (both Sri Lankan and Ethiopian women) had met in Lebanon as they were en route to Europe. Some had even entered Greece together.

In this multilingual space, multiple kinds of intimacies had emerged. Men and women, across lines of language, religion, and ethnonational identity were forming families that may not have been acceptable at home, but which had become possible in Lebanon and then in Athens. The broader "family" of which Hussein speaks was not just a friendship group; many of these men also worked together, and Hussein had "helped" many of them with their papers in Greece. Some of the men had helped one another access other countries in Europe through smuggling networks, only to be deported back to Greece, where they found each other again. These relationships also transected tribal divisions. During one of our afternoon meetings, Hussein was careful to underscore the significance of this, explaining that they speak

Arabic together because they are from very different tribal groups as well as different regions in Sudan; but sometimes, he added, they tell secrets and jokes in tribal languages. These were families formed across many lines of difference, emerging in the common experiences of transit and exile. In conversations that night and at other gatherings, I learned that these women and men had extraordinarily diverse reasons for being in Athens: some were asylum applicants, and others (including asylum seekers) described themselves as "there for work." But all had faced the common experiences of clandestine travel and of having to survive in extraordinarily difficult circumstances, and in these contexts, these intimacies—with their many evident joys—also emerged.

Certainly other much less sunny stories also undergird these intimacies. When Hussein told me that most of the men and women there had met in Lebanon, I knew well of Lebanon's reputation as a site where migrants—in particular, female Ethiopian domestic workers—frequently encounter exploitation, with highly organized smugglers or "traffickers" who facilitate these migrations; inquiries and reports by NGOs (Human Rights Watch, in particular), have lambasted the government of Lebanon for turning a blind eye to these abuses. In another conversation, on a different day, Hussein explained to me that these marriages were sometimes a kind of protection for women; at the ARS, such arrangements were frequently described in terms of a kind of "trafficking." Meanwhile, many of the men I met were closely involved in various informal economies in Athens. A year and a half later, there was a drug-related dispute involving this very "family," in which the man whom Hussein referred to as his brother was badly injured. There are many forms of suffering and violence that inform these multilingual intimacies, and the zones of illicit travel and illegality that these women and men navigate (the difficulty of moving across closed borders and surviving in a site where one is either illegal or in legal limbo). But with the ambivalence that characterizes the multilingual worlds of Athens, the very contexts that incite these violences also produce these families.

"My Golden Fish"

At the end of the evening, Samir, Temima, and most of the guests headed out. Hussein, Maria, and I remained with just the couple who lived there and two of our hosts' friends. Hussein turned to me and said that they were talking about going to a club, Axum, where the wedding would take place the next day. Though it has since closed, at the time Axum was one of Athens's only clubs playing African music, often serving as the location for events organized by various formal and informal African community organizations, becoming a pan-African gathering place. Hussein explained that Axum got its name from an ancient kingdom that was made up of both Ethiopia and Sudan.

Our hostess went to get changed to go to the club, and as we waited, two other women arrived, also from Ethiopia. One of them, middle-aged, nodded at me uninterestedly, but her companion immediately started interrogating me in fluent English. As we talked, our hostess reappeared, wearing a short glittery gray dress, black sparkly tights, and red boots. From behind the door, she dragged a huge hair dryer of the kind one finds in a hair salon, which she sat beneath, sipping a drink. We all sat quietly, waiting for our hostess's hair to dry, until one of her friends, who had left earlier with the bride-to-be, returned—a burst of energy and noise. She squealed when she saw her friend thus transformed for clubbing, chatting to her in Amharic, then kissing her. Still squeezing her friend's hand, she turned to me and said in English: "Isn't she beautiful? She is my sister."

The woman who spoke fluent English interjected, a hint of aggression in her voice, correcting her: "No, she's not your sister."

"She is my sister," was the smiling response, still holding her friend's hand.

"No she is not your sister. She is not your actual sister. She [gesturing to me] will not understand what you mean when you say that."

I interjected, protesting lightly that I did understand, but neither woman paid much attention. Then, still holding her friend's hand, the first woman turned to me again and insisted:

"*You understand.* She is like my sister. She's my golden fish. She helps me so much—I could not live here without her. She's my golden fish."

The other woman ceased her interventions, as our hostess and her friend removed her curlers and teased her hair.

In this exchange, the first woman initially enlists the polysemic kinship term *sister*, but the other interlocutor in the conversation emphasizes the literal meaning of the word in its English linguistic and cultural specificity. I encountered this language of sisterhood many times during my fieldwork, among African women from many different countries, even women who had just met each other. Among some of the Ethiopian women I knew, "sisterhood" did not seem to depend on ethnicity or race; some women addressed me as sister, highlighting our gendered connection. But kinship-based expressions of intimacy and solidarity among African individuals from many sites frequently furnished points of miscommunication with Greek audiences. For instance, one of my first days at the ARS, a volunteer spoke with a woman who referred to a man as her "brother," and a senior lawyer interjected, explaining that this probably was not *really* her brother. Similarly, the explanation that this is not an "actual" sister can be seen as a kind of translation work, through which the woman parses distinctions between what this term might mean for the speaker and the listener (me). But her translation strategy, through which she also asserts her own language competence and cultural fluency, entails a form of closure, squeezing out the complexities of her friend's use of language to establish a certain standard of clarity in English: "she is not your *actual* sister" (my emphasis).

The first woman then adjusts her response. She asserts, in English, that I do understand: her friend is *like* her sister. But then she uses a phrase that is untranslatable. The intriguing utterance "my golden fish" is perhaps imported into English from a different linguistic realm. Perhaps it comes from some Amharic or local expression, or is an English idiom translated into Amharic and back into English; it may be an error (does she mean "my gold fish?"), or maybe she said exactly what she meant to say. Regardless of its origin, however, this phrase creates a gap in our exchange, a space of extraordinary indeterminacy, but combined with other, non-linguistic signs—holding her friend's hand and kissing her—it nonetheless conveys intimacy, friendship, and affection. And so she is right, I do understand, through an emotional response to the elements of her speech that I do not fully understand. This moment of imperfect translation, through its very opacity, sparks emotional engagement: between the speaker, her friend, and the listeners.

This short exchange points to some of the productive possibilities of multilingual encounters: gaps in linguistic and cultural worlds leap out, causing people to meet the edges of their understanding. Sometimes this manifests in moments of closure, such as the translation strategy of the woman here. But sometimes, when languages bump up against each other in such transcultural, multilingual spaces, language also ruptures. At these points of rupture, communication may not have the smoothness or transparency that is often the presumed goal of speech, but it can provide openings into other forms of communicative practice that are not clearly language based, but which may be sparked by language.

The linguistic anthropologist and poet Paul Friedrich (1986) asserts that "poetry" arises from the disjuncture between the formal structure of a language (its closed, determined, clarity of meaning) and the "indeterminacy" that individual speakers and listeners introduce to that structure. Friedrich's focus is primarily on the imagination of the creative individual who plays with the structure of speech, but he also returns repeatedly to sites of translation, where languages meet, as nodes of unusual power: where the disjuncture between languages is heightened, it also encourages new forms of creativity from listeners and speakers. Such "poetic" moments simultaneously highlight the untranslatability of languages while increasing their accessibility through forms of communication that emerge from impact and affective engagement: what he describes as the "virtuosity" of the speaker, and the response of the listener (53). I repeatedly return to this phrase, "My golden fish," with its strange poetry, as a particularly potent example of the openings that can occur through multilingual speech acts. As the English language is jostled and creatively twisted by the speaker through the introduction of new elements, in some ways she gives voice to an emergent language, melded through the creative mixing of diverse repertoires, feelings, and associations. Meanwhile, for me, the listener, this phrase is left to hang as a blank spot, a lacuna. While I asked other Amharic speakers later about this phrase, I never found out what it meant. But rather than being a limit to our conversation, this gap is a site of opening, a small window into a world that I cannot see, but where words, fish, friends, and sisters are arranged differently.

Openings

As the relationship between blood and citizenship in Greece is increasingly thrown into public discussion and debate, multilingual encounters are creating openings, lacunae, in crucial sites where belonging is constituted: in languages, friendships, families, neighborhoods, and cities. With the transformative potential of language to create new worlds of experience and sociocultural connection, the nation, as such, is opened and rearticulated from the inside out, through the everyday intimacies of these encounters. Athens is a city shot through with openings: in emergent linguistic and cultural worlds, in notions of kinship, in narratives of the past and the present, in histories, memories, and longings. Violent closures at the frontiers of Fortress Europe, legal alterity, racialization, and xenophobia exist simultaneously with points of opening that enable new connections and forms of virtuosity across linguistic and cultural difference. Greece has long been caught up in diverse movements of peoples and cultures throughout the Mediterranean, but Greece is very often still framed as a nation with extraordinarily clear insides and outsides. The nation, however, does not necessarily emerge through closures. Instead, openings—imperfections, indeterminacies, lacunae—constitute the topography of a city and a nation always rearticulating itself.

Chapter 7

Citizens of Athens

> We started the protest against the government of Greece. . . . I really tried to explain to the media . . . CBS, CNN, BBC, by Internet, by interviewing on the streetside. We tried to explain these problems to them and they showed in their countries—not only their country but in three hundred countries they showed this situation, this crazy situation. . . . They showed the European Union and many humanitarian organizations the situation in Greece. . . . and after us, many of the other groups of refugees started to do the same—I had cooperation with the Afghans, for three months to guide them . . . and after that three hundred persons behind the *panepistimio* [university].
>
> —Bashir, former hunger striker and now recognized refugee, interview with the author, Athens, July 21, 2011

The past few years have marked a period of intensive civic engagement, unrest, and institutional instability unprecedented in Greece since the uprisings that drove the Junta out in 1974 (see Alivizatos 1996; Xenakis 2012). Since the late 2008 protests following the murder of Alexi Grigoropoulos, Athenians of diverse generations, origins, and political persuasions have sought new ways of claiming a presence and voice in the public sphere. During the economic collapse in May 2010, and the subsequent international push for top-down EU austerity measures, massive demonstrations and general strikes took place across the country, but nowhere more powerfully than in the Athens city center. These protests were aimed not just at the Greek state and politicians for mishandling and misappropriating funds, but also at the European North (particularly Germany), and the broader specters of intervention, inequality, and capitalist consumption associated with the International Monetary Fund (IMF), the World Bank, and other financial institutions.

The spring of 2011 witnessed the emergence of the *ayanaktismeni polites* [αγανακτισμένοι πολίτες] (indignant citizens), and a series of explicitly peaceful protests organized by the grassroots association Amesi Dhimokratia Tora! [Άμεση Δημοκρατία Τώρα!], Direct Democracy Now! Protestors occupied Syntagma Square, in front of the Greek Parliament, creating a forum for public debate about the adoption of austerity measures as a prerequisite for "bailout" money. The protest brought together Athenians on all sides of the political spectrum and across generations; there were even participants from migrant communities, though the level of their inclusion was questionable by some accounts. Greece has since, in many ways, emerged as the beating heart of largely leftist grassroots movements throughout the world (notably the now pan-European Indignados, and the Occupy movements).[1] Importantly, however, this intensification of political activity and activism must not be associated purely with the Left. The increasing presence of Golden Dawn has also included what could be described as outreach work, such as soup kitchens and blood drives (Tsimouris 2013), though these are available only to those of Greek heritage, and thus are notable for their racializing and exclusionary qualities.

Just as this vitalization of Athenian civic activity is taking place across political and generational divides, it is also emerging among those who, legally and socially, have been relegated to the edges of the body politic. In January 2011, 300 undocumented migrants, largely from North Africa, many of whom had lived and worked in Greece for as long as a decade, took the ferry to Athens from their jobs in Crete and occupied the Law School. Calling themselves the "300," in reference to the 300 Spartans who defended the Greeks against Xerxes in the battle of Thermopylae, they invoked the law of "academic asylum," through which universities provide safe haven against police intervention to protestors.[2] They initiated a hunger strike that lasted for forty days. Their demands were clear: *nomimopiisi* [νομιμοποιήση] (legalization). Eventually, the strikers were forcibly relocated from the law school to the nearby Hypatia Mansion, where in early March 2011 they received news that the Greek government would, in part, honor their demands: they would be offered six-month renewable residence permits, based on a clause in Greek immigration law allowing for anomalous, ad hoc legalizations in "extraordinary" circumstances. By this time, despite their close monitoring by medical volunteers, a number of the strikers had reached the point of organ failure, though there were no fatalities. The "300" thus acquired legal status in Greece by pushing life itself to its limits.

The "300" became a cause célèbre for anti-racism movements and those in solidarity with *sans-papiers* throughout Europe and the world. The protest recalled the tactics of hunger striking that undocumented persons have long carried out in France (see Ticktin 2011), Ireland, and other sites in Europe. Their blog, which was regularly updated throughout the strike, bears entries not just by the strikers but also by their supporters, including letters from Noam Chomsky, Immanuel Wallerstein, and Étienne Balibar. Given its scale and level of organization, the strike marked a moment when migrant political action in Greece achieved global visibility, "laying bare" the workings of power (Zavos 2011) on what became a global stage. This protest, however, must also be located within a series of hunger strikes that were initiated in Greece between 2008 and 2011, largely by asylum seekers and refugees, who demanded recognition of their requests for political asylum. The participants were different (primarily Afghan and Iranian), and in many cases the tactics they used were even more striking, including, in particular, sewing their mouths. The first strikes were carried out by detainees at the border sites of Samos, Lesbos, and Evros, but this changed in July 2010 when a small group of Iranians conducted a hunger strike in front of the UNHCR offices in Athens. In October 2010, a group of 49 Iranians went on hunger strike in front of the university, invoking the university as a site that grants "asylum" to radical protest. This was followed by a widespread strike of Afghans in Athens and Thessaloniki in November 2010, and finally, the largest and most widely publicized: the "300."

Bashir, an asylum seeker from Iran who eventually acquired refugee status in Greece, was among the participants in the October 2010 hunger strike. He granted me important insights into how hunger striking serves not just as a bid for legalization, but also as a way to expose the situation in Greece to wider publics. I first met him in 2006 while he waited at the threshold of the ARS for an appointment with a lawyer. When I later ran into him on the street by chance in July 2011, he announced happily that he had just received his "passport," or rather, he clarified, his refugee travel document. He explained that like many of his fellow strikers, he had ultimately received asylum as a result of the strike. He invited me to conduct an interview with him about his experiences in Greece, explaining that he had important things to tell me.

We met for coffee the next day at a café that also seemed to function a bit like his living room: the proprietress took good care of him, bringing him discounted coffees and chatting with him in a mix of English and Greek over the constant stream of classic rock that emanated from the speakers. He explained that he lived with forty or so other men about ten minutes from there. In the interview we conducted—which I recorded on his request—he gave me a nightmarish description of how, as he had waited for his asylum claim to be examined, Greece became a "prison" shaped by bureaucracy, in which he had no services, no rights, and no dignity. He explained that overwhelming helplessness and frustration in the struggle to survive drove his participation in the strike. Thanks to his education and fluent English he had served as a kind of media representative, giving interviews and statements to the press and producing content for the blog associated with the strike. The problem, he clarified, was that "normal" Greek people, and people outside of Greece, do not understand the "crazy situation" facing asylum seekers. Others—especially, he added, social workers and NGOs—"know about these things, but they hide it." For Bashir, hunger striking served as a way not just to claim entitlements, but also to expose the shadowy underbelly of the world in which he had struggled.

I focus this chapter around two long-standing acquaintances, Bashir and Azar. When I first met each of them early in my fieldwork, neither mentioned having been particularly politically active, either in Greece or in their countries of origin. Yet the new forms of civic engagement taking place in Athens have been accompanied by what Neni Panourgia (2012) describes as "the emergence of a polis": a center of political action for persons who may never before have deemed themselves "political." In very different ways, these two men—one from Iran, one from Afghanistan—have begun actively to claim rights for themselves and for broader groups of migrants, asylum seekers, and refugees. For Bashir, the tipping point was the bureaucratic "prison" of the asylum procedure, while for Azar it was the worsening forms of race-related violence that have accompanied the financial crisis and its aftermath. The accounts of these two men do not by any means "stand in" for the diverse experiences of foreigners in Greece; there are many voices missing from this chapter, specifically those of women. Moreover, these particular individuals could, in many ways, be said to be idiosyncratic or even extraordinary (Crapanzano 1980), though in different ways, taking on the roles of cultural brokers or even, literally, interpreters. Yet, since they are active and visible members of their communities, their stories also serve as openings or thresholds into the actions through which "aliens" have increasingly claimed a presence as *citizens* of Athens.

Politics of Exposure

> *Ekkyklema*: "in classical Greek theatre, stage mechanism consisting of a low platform that rolled on wheels or revolved on an axis and could be pushed onstage to reveal an interior or some offstage scene such as a tableau. . . . Because violence was prohibited from the Greek stage, it is thought by some that murdered bodies may have been displayed on the device." (*Encyclopedia Britannica* 2008)

In this chapter, I explore emerging political practices through which "alien" residents have sought to bring to light the "crazy situation" in Greece and claim forms of civil membership, rights, and entitlements. Across their many manifestations, these actions serve to *expose* the entwinement of life, law, and citizenship: the ways in which human capacities for survival have become inscribed into the "matrix" (Agamben 1998) of law and rights. In Greece, the capacity for mere survival—the ability to claim even minimal rights and services—is pushed to the very edges of the possible for those without access to legal status. Moreover, amid increasing forms of xenophobic violence, irrespective of their formal legal status foreign residents are now, perhaps more than ever, vulnerable to forms of brutality that make everyday survival an even more urgent matter of life or death. From the perspectives of many asylum seekers and refugees with whom I have spoken, both NGOs and the state often turn a blind eye to these problems. In this book, I have looked carefully at how service providers themselves deal with the structural and ethical dilemmas that perpetuate "this crazy situation." Here, however, I consider how foreign residents of Athens seek to expose, and thus interrupt, the modes of practice and knowledge that turn tragedy into "common sense" (Gramsci 1992; see also Rabinow 1977).

This chapter, in some ways, contrasts with my earlier analyses of asylum-related adjudication and service provision, which emphasized the ghostly indeterminacies of knowledge, rights, bureaucracy, and law. In this book, I have shown that encounters that take place in sites of "anti-politics" (Ferguson 1994; Fisher 1997; Ticktin 2011) (the worlds of aid encounters) *can*, in fact, have important destabilizing effects, undermining systems of exclusion from within, even as they may produce further forms of violence. Here, however, I consider concrete, intentional, and proactive ways in which "aliens" contest the frameworks through which they are figured as "victims" or "ghosts." These actions can be said to be political (Ticktin 2011), even revolutionary: intentionally aimed toward radical change that disrupts "an established order" (19). Despite their moments of excess, "lines of flight" (Deleuze and Guattari 1987), and even redemption, aid encounters take place within a broken system that persistently gestures to and yet veils its own brokenness; the political actions described here, in contrast, seek to *expose* the suffering, pain, and violence that take place "behind the scenes."

In many cases, migrants, asylum seekers, and refugees in Greece seek not to reject but to reclaim and remake regimes of law and rights. From mundane to more radical activities, from archival practices to hunger striking, "alien" subjects strive to carve out space for themselves as citizens through the exposure of fundamental forms of injustice. These citizenship practices include claims to official legal status, yet they also exceed the formalities of legal process and bureaucracy. Through a politics of exposure, migrants, asylum seekers, and refugees assert forms of civil membership as persons entitled to lives that surpass the task of mere survival. They also seek to take into their own hands bureaucracy and service provision, attempting to do this work in a manner more accountable, equitable, and transparent. Perhaps not surprisingly, many of the tactics comprising this politics of exposure share in the very regimes of practice and knowledge that have held these persons "prisoner." Bashir collects documents—thousands of documents, he says—as a way to substantiate his own mistreatment at the hands of state and NGO bureaucracies. Others cite rumors about NGO misuse of EU funds that recall the accounts many Greeks give of their own state. Some found community centers, encourage cross-cultural communication and debate, and institute community-based support, citing values of multiculturalism also dominant among Athenian NGOs. They draw on existing media outlets and create new ones (blogs, Indymedia[3] articles, Facebook pages) to circumvent the Greek media's lack of attention to the struggles of refugees and migrants. For those seeking revolutionary change, there may be certain costs to participating in such dominant repertoires of political action (Chatterjee 1993). Yet, in part, both native Greek citizens and "alien" subjects share in a similar political milieu: a newly emergent polis, a shifting landscape of citizenship. The "300," writes legal scholar Costas Douzinas (2012: 39), became "the only truly free people of Athens."

Fakeability and Transparency

Nobody knows where does it go . . .

It was back in 2007 that an ARS aid candidate first told me that NGOs in Greece were stealing money from asylum seekers and refugees. Numerous people repeated this rumor to me, including some interpreters at the ARS, themselves asylum seekers and refugees. The story goes something like this: NGOs receive money from the European Union to provide services to seekers of refuge—sometimes 1,200 euros per person, sometimes 2,000, depending on whom I talked to—but the intended beneficiaries never receive the money or the services. This story was strikingly similar each time I heard it, and it was replicated across multiple scales. It is structurally similar to that which Hadi told me, discussed in Chapter 3, about how the Greek state steals money from NGOs. It also recalls the exposés, which emerged a few years later in 2010, of how Greek politicians stole money from Greek citizens.[4] The common theme is that money is coming in from somewhere (usually the EU), but it does not find its way to its intended recipients, be they refugees or pensioners. As Bashir put it, in a distinctly ironic tone: "nobody knows, where does it go. This budget, where does it go? Nobody knows. Nobody knows."

Bashir identified a corrupt bureaucratic apparatus, consisting of governmental and nongovernmental offices, as lying at the core of his problems in Greece. He told me how a "useless" shadowy bureaucracy, perpetuated by equally useless documents and governed by smiling but "lying" service providers, kept asylum seekers and refugees in a kind of "prison." He also described how bureaucratic sleight of hand served to hide and deflect attention from "thefts" of money and services. Yet despite his insistence on the uselessness of bureaucracy, he himself had become a bit of an archivist. He had not only collected and saved carefully, almost lovingly, all of the documents that he had received in Greece, but he had also searched for documents that would, somehow, provide a way to expose the thefts and the lies. With a gleam in his eye, he told me that he had found such a document. "I made some copies. Tomorrow I will show it to woman [a social worker at the ARS]—to show it, just to prove it to their face, to say: 'You lied to me. You are a liar. Why do you lie?' "

Bashir's tactic of enlisting documents themselves to expose the corruptions, thefts, and lies of bureaucracy points to the important role of transparency in the politics of exposure. His archival practices are very much in the spirit of what Kregg Hetherington (2011) describes as "guerrilla auditing." Hetherington shows how rural Paraguayan *campesinos* built archives as ways of contesting a state that sought to dispossess them of their land. *Campesinos* embraced a politics of transparency dominant among urban elites, even as *campesinos* themselves were framed, among certain publics, as representing cronyism, arbitrariness, and corruption fundamentally counter to transparency politics. Similarly, asylum seekers, who are often characterized as practitioners of deceit who attempt to "game the system," frequently enlist documents, the tools of bureaucracy, to expose deceits within this very system. As an archivist of sorts, Bashir was not particularly atypical. I met many asylum seekers who offered to show me the documents they had collected and the file folders that they often lugged around with them. As might be expected, literacy in English or Greek facilitated such archival practices—but it was not crucial. Bashir himself did not have solid written knowledge of Greek, and I was often shown a flush of documents by people who were not literate even in their native languages. Those who were even semi-literate, however, often acquired in-depth, even expert, knowledge of bureaucratic processes through their personal encounters with bureaucracy, conversations with compatriots, and the occasional helpful bureaucrat or NGO worker.

In Chapter 5, I discussed how documents that substantiate accounts of persecution may provide weight and credibility to an asylum claim. Similarly, documenting one's bureaucratic encounters in Greece also serves to protect or arm oneself for future encounters with bureaucracy. Archiving documents is also, in part, a way of being a cooperative, prepared, and organized client or asylum applicant. Yet such mini-archives also speak to a deep mistrust of bureaucrats and service providers and the sense that one must take care of oneself, because no one else will. Take the case of Joshua, an asylum seeker from Sudan, who photocopied for me what he described as his "case file," which he himself had assembled. Over a number of years, he not only had collected documents, but had lodged his own appeals with the police and the high court, though with the assistance of ARS lawyers; he explained that the lawyers, while helpful, did not always meet deadlines, so he did it himself. Ultimately Joshua received asylum, a fact that itself attests to the power of these practices and the ways asylum seekers willing to know bureaucracy can often better it. Yet such canny and knowledgeable archivists were also threatening to both bureaucrats and service providers. An ARS lawyer flatly refused the request of a Somali asylum seeker who demanded a photocopy of his eligibility interview form by insisting that the interview itself was ARS property; he later explained to me that if the form circulated openly, it might increase the risk of people misrepresenting themselves in their eligibility interviews, since they could examine the form and rehearse their responses beforehand. Yet over the next few weeks, a number of Somali asylum seekers made similar requests, which did not eradicate but certainly brought into the open this ARS policy *against* transparency, placing workers in the uncomfortable position of having to articulate it explicitly.

In what follows, I consider Bashir's account of how he sought to contest bureaucracy through his own collection of documents. Bureaucratic transparency—itself a core value in cultures of law and rights—has a central place in the politics of exposure.

Greece, the Prison of Europe

> [Greece] received the budget from the European Union to prevent the invasion of the refugees from Asia and Africa, prevent them from invading the European countries. They used this country as a prison. They used this country as the prison.

When I first met Bashir in 2006, his easy sociability, intelligence, and clever humor charmed many of the ARS workers. According to his ARS interview, he had been an intellectual and an author in Iran, who had converted to Christianity and written a book about his conversion; his case had been compelling for staff across the board, and he was quickly found to be eligible for ARS assistance. He used to stop by the organization just to chat, and I often found him sitting in the afternoon at the entryway with Luc, passing the time. He spoke sophisticated, if somewhat quirky, English, and over time he learned some basic Greek. When we reconnected in 2011, the sociability and humor were still there, but I was struck by the palpable, hardened anger that undergirded his account of his experiences in Greece. Bashir, like many others I met, was initially arrested for entering Greece illegally, and he was detained for three months. On release, he was given a deportation order, with instructions to leave Greece voluntarily within a month, but when he learned of the Dublin II Regulation he decided to stay and wait out his asylum application in Greece. The physical immobility he faced as an asylum seeker in limbo made Greece itself into a kind of prison: "So, it means you're stuck here. You belong to this country. . . . If someone says 'fige apo 'do' or 'leave this country' . . . [We say] We want to leave! But we have no passport to leave. We can't go. We are trapped here, we are stuck here. . . . It's some kind of paradox. You want to leave you can't, they will arrest you. You want to stay you can't."

For Bashir, the *prison* of Greece did not consist only of physical immobility but was instantiated perhaps even more powerfully through the bureaucracies surrounding social services and support, both governmental and nongovernmental. Speaking not just of "the government" but of "NGOs under the authority of the government," he described a diffuse, flexible, yet unwieldy bureaucracy, through which foreigners "run in circles" for nothing. He himself had "run in circles" multiple times, from his attempt to get a work permit to his search for medical care. "For instance, if you want to renew your work permit, you go to the work permit organization—they will send you back to the state office for a tax statement. But then they will send you to IKA [insurance office], and they will continue to play with you, waste your time. . . . And after you do this a few months running you could not find any work."

With the stress of his life in Greece, he had developed stomach problems—chronic diarrhea and an ulcer—so he went to Evangelismos, the largest public hospital in Athens, where he underwent numerous tests. As the holder of a pink card, he was entitled to medical care, but it appeared that in practice this care would be minimal: the doctors told him they would treat him, but he had to cover any rehabilitation costs himself. He visited a number of NGOs, including the ARS, to ask for financial assistance to go forward with the treatment, but he was told they did not have enough resources for him.

This convoluted bureaucracy in Greece, for Bashir, consisted of both state and NGO offices, which often appeared to him to collaborate in keeping asylum seekers stuck, preventing them from acquiring both status and services. In describing his treatment at NGOs, in particular, he drew on a Persian expression he translated as "playing cats": "whenever someone plays with you for nothing, whenever, you know, you make a cat play for you for nothing. . . . They do something like this with you." He spoke of one ARS social worker, in particular, whose job was to help asylum seekers find employment. She sent him to get a work permit and collect all the paperwork involved, which took six months, then sent him to learn Greek, which took another few months:

> After that one year running . . . you will return to her and say OK I have ten documents which I have gotten step by step, I know Greek

> language (and I have a certificate to prove it), I know this profession, I know this kind of work, and she will say to you: "You have these documents, all OK. And you know Greek language. So go and buy a magazine and find a job in a magazine."

In trying to sum up the peculiar character of NGOs in Greece, for him almost indistinguishable from the state, Bashir coined his own, powerfully descriptive term, explaining that these organizations are "fakeable." He described NGOs in Greece as comprising a chain of *like* organizations, which may appear under the aegis of another, but where one can find no substantive help. "If you go to the Red Cross here they will send you to another organization which is under the authority of the Red Cross but it is *fakeable*. It doesn't work. You couldn't receive any kind of human social services or something like that but just the excuse that 'we have not any kind of budget.'" This 'fakeable' quality of service organizations in Greece, for Bashir, centered particularly around the "excuse" that they cannot provide services—that familiar sense of tragedy and limited resources, which I have discussed elsewhere from the perspectives of service providers themselves. For Bashir, however, what many service providers may describe as ethical conflict is read as "fakeability," a strategy of dissemblance through which NGOs *steal* services from claimants.

From our interview, which itself served as a vehicle through which to narrate and perform his anger, frustration, and disappointment, Bashir's life in Greece appeared to be circumscribed by paper: the promise of documents that signified the hoped-for capacity to acquire services and refugee status, and perhaps finally, to move and travel. But more powerfully perhaps, documents were relevant in the small, incremental elements of his everyday life, representing the opportunity to work, to access healthcare, and acquire some financial support. As he ran in circles, however, through governmental and nongovernmental bureaucracies, he accumulated paper after paper only to find that they did nothing for him: organizations are "fakeable," and social support consists of lies. Moreover, these documents, rather than facilitating the distribution of services, further ensure that seekers of refuge in Greece do not acquire recognition as politicolegal subjects entitled to rights; instead, they remain perpetually faced with the problem of mere survival. "Believe me, I have hundreds of documents—*dhilosi*, *vevaioci*. But this kind of bureaucracy is useless, useless. . . . Just you are running for nothing. And you are hungry, and you are sleeping on the street-side. What could you do . . . ?"

Cornelia Vismann (2008: 72) writes that documents differ from records in that they "are not designed for any administrative use; rather, they are made to impress . . . legibility is of little concern." Although these documents are designed as if they have an administrative use, in practice they have little relevance. Instead, what is impressive is their fakeability, their lack of substance. These documents do not encode administrative services or rights that can be claimed, but remain, like the organizations that issue them, self-referential to the bureaucratic world, in a recursive chain of documents that demand further documents (see Hull 2012). Significantly, in our interview Bashir's use of Greek was largely restricted to his denotation of bureaucratic terms and documents, perhaps highlighting not just their untranslatability but also their lack of intelligibility. Yet despite these documents' "fakeable" qualities, Bashir had saved them all. At his own request, we met the following day, expressly in order for him to show me his files.

He opened a large folder and pulled out documents that he had collected over the years, arranged neatly in chronological order. These were just some of his documents, he explained—the most important ones; the others were at his apartment. He had also made copies of many of them, which were also in his living quarters. He passed the file over to me, insisting that I handle the documents myself, and as I leafed through this archive of his bureaucratic encounters in Greece he narrated each of them. Most of the papers were various forms of *dhilosis* [δηλώσεις], which state or *declare* a set of circumstances (for instance—that he had applied for asylum, that he had not worked for months, or that he had registered for insurance); others consisted of *veveosis* [βεβαιώσεις], which *certified* that these circumstances were true; all were, of course, double certified with seal. Bashir laughed that in Greece "they never believe you—they need a document." Finally, he called my attention to a document that was filed away at the very end, which he explained he would use later that day to confront the social worker and expose her "lies." This document, he explained, was proof that NGOs lie when they say they have no money. I looked it over: the document was a sheet bearing the insignia of the ARS, outlining the stipends to which recognized refugees are entitled if they qualify for an EU assistance program, and the process for claiming them was laid out at the bottom of the page. This was not an internal NGO document, as Bashir had interpreted it, but informational material for recognized refugees themselves distributed by the ARS social service department. However, for Bashir, who had "found" the document (he did not say how), this paper served as "proof" of the money that the *ARS* was supposed to give to refugees.

In considering Bashir's use of documents in the service of a politics of exposure, I do not want to get hung up on distinguishing between "real" and "false" interpretations of this ARS document. Rather, the flexible meanings this document can take on, and the diversity of its uses, highlight how documentary forms—like the pink card—persistently take on new lives. This is what Hetherington (2011) calls the "duplicitousness" of documents: the open-ended ways in which documents can always be put to new uses, for contradictory projects and politics. While in one context this sheet is merely informational, for Bashir it gives testament to funds that, thanks to the circuitousness of bureaucratic practices and the poor availability of information, he certainly never received—from NGOs or the state. Moreover, we also see here how *mythopoesis*, the search for sense and truth through the production of, often phantasmagorical, forms of knowledge, is crucial for those on all sides of the asylum process. Just as service providers employ forms of *mythopoesis* to produce knowledge about claimants, asylum seekers themselves devise ways of rendering bureaucracy and bureaucrats knowable (see Graeber 2006). While often reflecting larger structural truths, such knowledge may not be materially reliable in its details, a fact that itself points to the veiled nature of these bureaucratic encounters and the epistemic gaps that they generate. Yet Bashir was going that very afternoon to present this document to the social worker who had "lied" to him, to show her, quite simply, that he *knew,* and moreover, that he had *proof.*

Later that afternoon I left Greece, and despite a number of attempts to reach Bashir by phone (he did not have email) I could not contact him to find out what happened in his meeting (an unfortunate limitation of such serendipitous ethnographic encounters). But I want to highlight Bashir's participation in a wider move toward values of transparency and accountability emerging among both *citizens* and *aliens*. The rumor about money that somehow disappears haunts a variety of bureaucracies in Greece, both governmental and nongovernmental. The "refugee" version of this rumor, while directed toward NGOs, bespeaks a wider culture of suspicion toward bureaucracy in general—among both Greek and migrant Athenians—which reached its zenith in the financial controversy wracking the Greek state. With the financial crisis, and the revelation that politicians *were* pocketing or at least misusing state funds, those rumors long thought to be true but which, hitherto, had lacked confirmation were exposed in an international public sphere. Such tactics can be deployed in the service of a number of different political aims. Though their goals and audiences are different, Bashir's move toward exposure echoes that of an angry Greek populace demanding services and accountability from their state. Yet the demands of transparency can also discipline and subjugate these very populations. Asylum seekers must expose, substantiate, and prove themselves through the asylum process; as part of the austerity measures, Greeks now face a variety of, often enormously exploitative, policies and practices meant to increase the accountability of taxpayers (Placas 2009). The politics of exposure are flexible. Yet despite his own "alienness," Bashir's insistence on bureaucratic transparency and accountability is at the heart of current citizenship practices in Greece.

Dialogue

I first met Azar, an Afghan of Hazara descent, in 2007; he was a recognized refugee, working as a part-time interpreter at the ARS. This occasional work supplemented his full-time employment at a private medical clinic in the Athens city center, where he had worked for a number of years. He had studied medicine in Afghanistan, and he had almost completed the second year of his residency or "practical" training when he was forced to flee. In Greece, however, his former training was not recognized, and in order to become a physician he would have had to start again from scratch; hence, he settled for a job as a physician's assistant, though he planned eventually to accredit himself in Greece. He left Afghanistan in 2001, after being tortured by local Taliban leaders. Long before that, in the early 1990s, he had also been caught up in violence between warring *mujahedeen*, when he worked as an interpreter with an international humanitarian aid organization.

In an interview that we did together in 2008, he told me that he was generally happy in Greece, largely because he found Greece more "Eastern," not European. He highlighted that people in Greece were friendlier and, he added, also less racist than in the European North: "I have friends in Germany, and no one wants to sit next to them on the bus. Here, there is no problem." He also hinted that in Greece the very differences that had divided Afghans could be, in a way, forgotten; another Afghan he had met in Greece confessed to having been one of the people who had tortured him, and they had become friends: "The war is another time," he added. And so, despite limitations in his professional life, in Athens Azar had found a somewhat stable and, moreover, friendly new home, where he could start over—a refugee success story.

In July 2011, we spoke for the first time in three years, but I had been following his work from afar. In 2009, he had founded an Afghan community organization in Athens, and their regularly updated website, combined with his blog and Facebook page, provided detailed accounts of their current activities and projects. I was eager to learn the story behind these new changes in his life. We met in the Plateia Exarcheion at 10:30 p.m., after he had finished work at the clinic which was just a few blocks away, though his energetic smile and clean white shirt belied the long day he had just passed. He began chattering away immediately, updating me on the news I had missed, as he led me to a nearby café, where a young, black bartender in trendy jeans and a button-down shirt greeted Azar warmly in perfect, accent-less Greek. Azar introduced him as Petros; he was originally from Kenya but had grown up in Greece. We took a table by the window and Petros brought us some wine, and then Azar recounted how he had become active politically.

In addition to founding an Afghan community organization, Azar sat on the recently established Migrants Council for the city of Athens,[5] advising the city government on migration-related issues. He had gotten married to an Afghan who worked for the UN in Pakistan. While he was still fairly at home in Greece, he emphasized that the major element that has changed since the crisis is the racism, and the frequent and violent attacks directed toward persons of color, very often explicitly toward Afghans. During the pogroms of May 2011, he himself had been attacked, along with numerous other Afghans, and the community organization had been vandalized. Most horrible, he explained, was how children and families had also been attacked. A three-year-old Hazara boy who had been sleeping in the park with his homeless family was abducted and raped. This rise of race-related violence in formerly "friendly" Athens, and the exposure of fellow Afghans not just to social exclusion but also to physical violence, was a driving force in Azar's political transformation.

Petros came over and joined us, and Azar clarified that they sat together on the Athens Migrants' Council. According to its mandate, the Migrants' Council, established in 2010, is composed largely of *polites metanastes* [πολίτες μετανάστες] (citizen immigrants), who, irrespective of their formal citizenship status, "acquire organic ties with Athens and actively participate in the economic and social life of the city." Although the formulation "citizen immigrant" itself suggests that persons of non-Greek origin remain forever "immigrants," the Council is focused on bringing the perspectives of migrants into projects of "integration." Speaking collaboratively, like people accustomed to talking and working together, Azar and Petros analyzed the problem of race-related violence in terms of the state's unwillingness to address it: because immigration is seen as a problem by the state, these attacks are not framed as a problem, so the state does not make a real effort to punish those responsible for the attacks. It is as if, explained Petros, "immigrants somehow must experience these things *because* they are immigrants." For instance, he added, on television there was footage of someone attacking a migrant-owned business, and the attacker's face was clearly visible, but still no one was held accountable. Azar likened this moment to the period in 1990–1991 when mass Albanian immigration to Greece began and Albanians were viewed with fear; now, he explained, Albanians participate in attacks against new foreigners, as a way to show they are "inside the society." In addition to the problem of racism, they both highlighted the general need to have "a state that works," and social services for asylum seekers and refugees—though this, Azar emphasized, was an "old story."

Azar's advocacy work focused on both the issue of racism and the ongoing need for services, as he and his colleagues and collaborators sought to take into their own hands the work of a broken state. With regard to services, both Azar and Petros noted the effectiveness of lateral grassroots support both within and across various communities of migrants. The Migrant Council planned to establish a phone chain of people to help receive new arrivals in Athens, assisting with legal and bureaucratic issues as well as more material forms of support. The Afghan community organization strives to collect resources from its members and provide assistance to those who need it, in particular clothing and food. Yet it is worth noting that such forms of lateral support have limits (and, no doubt, dilemmas) not unlike those faced by ARS workers and other nongovernmental service providers. When I asked Azar if they ever provide assistance with housing or beds, he shook his head: "No, we can't." He added that he had even thought of changing his phone number, owing to all the calls he receives from people asking for help, at all hours of the day and night.

As head of the community organization, Azar also focused on creating and participating in forums for education, intercultural exchange, and debate in Athens and even other sites in Greece and Europe, as a way of overcoming palpable forms of *ratsismos*. The community organization had a "cultural space" near Plateia Attikis, a neighborhood where many migrants live, but after it was vandalized they rented a new space near Omonia Square. One of his primary goals, he explained, was to educate Athenians about Afghan culture and people, "to show them who we are." "Many Greeks think we all support the Taliban, et cetera, and that we want to take over Greece. But how can you say that a woman on the street with two kids wants to take over Greece?" So he wanted to show that Afghanistan has its own rich history and culture. He also sought to educate Afghans themselves so as not to be so "closed," sponsoring language instruction and lessons about Greek culture, as well as dance classes and music concerts involving both Afghans and Greeks.

Azar had also, in the course of these projects, become a public figure, a representative for Afghan and refugee interests in Greece and in Europe more broadly. He had collaborated with the UNHCR, organizing a conference about Afghan refugees in Greece, flying in Afghan intellectuals from throughout the world. A powerful European advocacy NGO had brought him to Brussels for a working group, and he was scheduled to attend a training in Prague for representatives of refugee communities. In Greece, he has been invited to speak in Parliament and to do interviews on TV. When I pushed him a little on how he had taken on this leadership role, he explained that while he had not been "active" before, little by little he had become this way. Moreover, since he had been in Greece for a long time, he felt a sense of responsibility, since he could do things that others could not. But also, he explained with a grin, "I like it"; he enjoys this work and it excites him, because he likes to talk and to discuss. He then told me an extraordinary story of how he had gone to speak with a group of Golden Dawn members, emphasizing that it was the most interesting discussion in which he had ever taken part. He went to one of their meeting spaces and demanded twenty minutes to speak to them: at first, they threw things at him and shouted, but after ten minutes they listened to him.

Azar's political engagement also involves a politics of exposure, bringing to light things that, in the current political and economic climate in Athens, remain hidden: the problems of social support and racism, and the everyday violence that threatens the bodies of foreign residents, even Azar himself. As a kind of cultural broker, he also seeks to paint a more "real," layered picture of both Afghan and Greek culture and history to these divided audiences. Yet while Bashir's politics of exposure centered on transparency and accountability, Azar seeks to bring to light and transform the "crazy situation" in Greece through *dialogue*: forms of education, communication, and debate.

Azar employs values of intercultural communication and multiculturalism coherent with those dominant in the NGO world and Greek leftist politics. His tactic of encouraging open dialogue is framed as a method through which problems of racism can be exposed, recognized, and perhaps also alleviated. He actively seeks discussions with governmental officials, NGO leaders, and those who disagree with him (including the Far Right); he, in turn, is actively sought out, a soft-spoken, well-groomed, educated "citizen immigrant," who speaks fluent Greek and English. Yet through his own position at the relative inside of the body politic, he seeks a space for alien residents of Athens, who are not just disenfranchised but often homeless, undocumented or in legal limbo, and vulnerable to ongoing attacks that have made fear for bodily integrity a part of daily life. He explicitly claims a presence not just for himself or a group of individuals but for a *community* of Afghans, which bridges ethnic boundaries and the divisions wrought through past experiences of war, and who—like him—may be in Athens to stay.

Exposed Bodies and Lives

"A Witness"

In July 2008, before his political transformation, I met with Azar on a Saturday evening in the city center near the neighborhood of Psiri, which was bustling with club goers and young people. After making a quick trip to his car to pick up some file folders (he said he had brought some things to show me), we sat at a rickety table at a small outdoor café, and he took out a folder and began to sort through its contents. This was a mini archive not unlike that which Bashir later shared with me, but Azar had brought along not just bureaucratic documents but also records of other memories, from both Greece and Afghanistan. He handed me a newspaper article in which he had been featured, as well as photos of his young son from his first wife, also from Afghanistan, from whom he had recently been divorced; both she and his son also lived in Athens. He then presented me with some papers from his original case folder at the ARS from 2001, when he too had sought help there. He emphasized—with more than a hint of pride—that he had represented himself in the asylum process, with successful results. An ARS lawyer accompanied him to his asylum hearing, even though he had never met the lawyer before, but in the end he told his story himself despite the lawyer's interference. Not surprisingly, Azar had been a canny self-advocate in his encounters with bureaucracy and law.

Finally he pulled out a pile of photographs and held them to his chest, hiding them from view. He explained that these were photos he had taken when he was working for a mobile medical unit in Afghanistan in the early 1990s. When they arrived at sites where there had been fighting between *mujahadeen*, he often took pictures, *san martiras* [σαν μάρτυρας] (as a witness), he explained. He warned me softly: "perhaps you don't want to see these photographs? They are very grim." But when I assented, he presented the photographs one by one, with reverence: First, there were photos of fighters—young Hazara boys and men with guns; a picture of a young man with a rifle and a skull cap and a serious expression (Azar laughed that this boy thought he was really tough). But then we arrived at a photo of two young girls lying next to each other, their bodies in an advanced stage of decomposition, dressed in ornate traditional garb with brightly colored scarves on their heads. *Koritsia* (girls), he breathed. Each successive photo was a document of death: bodies in the houses where they had been found, at the morgue, and at hospitals. Finally, a picture of a young man lying dead in the street while others passed by on foot, in cars, one person on a bicycle—a quotidian routine of death: "They are so used to it, you see."

Azar, in his new life as community leader, has continued this project of witnessing that he began so many years ago. When I visited him at the new Afghan cultural center in Omonia in July 2011, we huddled in front of his laptop as he showed me multiple digital folders of photos documenting in livid detail the recent beatings of Afghans that have taken place. He even showed me pictures of the young Hazara boy who had been raped, a wide-eyed toddler like any other, except for a faded bruise on his face. On his Facebook page, Azar also posted a series of photographs of a young Afghan who had lost nearly every tooth in his mouth in the pogroms of 2011. He reports to Athens newspapers and on the internet the beatings that take place, along with these photographic proofs, seeking to bring these events out of the realm of hearsay and expose them to a wider audience.

These photographs of exposed and mangled bodies bear forensic witness to violence that remains unaccounted for and unrecognized by the state and wider Greek and more global publics. Being "alien" in Greece has, in fact, become an issue of life and death. This is no longer the slow wasting away that accompanies projects of mere survival, as Bashir described, but instead entails brutal forms of "making die" through which the frustrations of an angry crisis-ridden populace are beaten into the bodies of foreigners. Petryna (2002) writes of how images of deformity and illness were key to how the state of Ukraine projected images of victimhood, "laying bare" the obstructed and degraded life at the core of contemporary Ukrainian citizenship. Through images exposing the bodies of victims, alien and foreign residents of Athens also attempt to claim a kind of citizenship: they lay bare the brutalized life that has now come to constitute their everyday experience in Greece, seeking recognition that their own bodies have the same value, the same humanity, as those of Greek citizens.

Such images are predicated on an assumption that the suffering human body will have emotional resonance with the viewer, engendering a sense of shared human citizenship that transcends the limits of ethnonational belonging. Lori Allen (2009) describes similar aesthetic tactics in the context of the second Palestinian Intifada, which drew on notions of common humanity and the affective power of images to carve out space for Palestinians as subjects entitled to human rights: "Through a focus on the blood, guts, and flesh . . . the physical common denominators that all human beings share are thrust before the world's eyes" (162). As Allen highlights, these aesthetic politics hinge on the question "what counts as proof of suffering and the presumed connection between suffering and political entitlement" (162). The human being, when exposed in its aspect of extreme suffering, becomes visible as a universal human and, through the logic of rights, a kind of universal citizen. These aesthetics of suffering may invoke increasingly dominant, international norms of rights-based entitlement, with their own exclusionary potential. Yet as a form of political action they also disrupt and expose the limits of national citizenship, which confines those outside the body politic to the margins of life.

Proofs

I now want to return to the Iranian hunger strike in the context of this aesthetic politics of exposure. While its scale was much smaller than the "300," the hunger strike enacted by 49 Iranians—including Bashir—in front of the University of Athens in October 2010 was highly organized and achieved relatively widespread publicity. Bashir highlighted that, in fact, international news channels covered the strike, whereas the Greek media neglected to report it, thus keeping the strikers, their protest, and their demands "hidden" from "normal Greeks." This hunger strike was meant to combat an exceptional—and untenable—situation: the struggle for mere survival that shaped these asylum seekers' everyday lives. In material terms, however, the strikers sought legal recognition (asylum) and, by extension, social services and support. When I asked him why he went on strike, Bashir explained:

"You are frustrated. They are frustrated. . . . And we didn't ask something, you know, special. We didn't ask some castle for us, you know. . . . something you know like kings or something like that. Just a piece of document. A piece of I don't know, something else, a little bit social services."

Hunger striking has a storied twentieth-century history as a form of nonviolent action that carries what Gene Sharp (2005), the scholar of protest, has described as a highly *coercive* element, putting time-sensitive pressure on both public opinion and the intended target of the protest—in this case, state and NGO bureaucracies in Greece. Prisoners have often used this tactic—in Ireland, Iran, and, of course, at Guantanamo—and here we see it used by "prisoners" of bureaucracy and law, who have no other leverage than their own bodies. In an important sense, however, these Iranian hunger strikers also employed their suffering bodies to expose and render *transparent* the hidden violence instantiated through bureaucracy and law.

The strike was regularly chronicled in a blog. Textually and visually, the blog focuses on the bodies of the strikers, and in particular, their sewn mouths. Daily updates center on their deteriorating physical conditions, with a great many entries announcing when someone has "gone to hospital." There are multiple photos of strikers in hospital beds. These aesthetic and narrative details highlight the urgency of the strikers' claims for legal recognition and the violence entailed in remaining in limbo. The protest, as chronicled visually, serves in a way to re-perform the asylum claim itself: these men and women place their bodies and their lives in urgent danger—and fear for one's life and body is a primary criterion for assessing asylum applications. Interestingly, the most visible presence on the website is a young, striking woman, with short dyed blond hair, who sewed her mouth along with the men—the only woman who enacted this radical bodily technique. While she is identified as the first person to be taken to the hospital, her image—with her sharp features, determined expression, and the two threads that mar her lips—is repeatedly enlisted to convey the strength of the entire group of strikers, a moving trope of gendered sacrifice and power.

Among these many accounts of the strikers' bodily health, there are a few entries that focus on "revealing" what the strikers describe as Greece's suspiciously close relationship with the government of Iran. One entry, entitled "revealing the relations," includes the following video: In an incongruously jovial atmosphere at the *propylaia* (monumental gateway) of the University of Athens, where a small crowd has gathered to support the hunger strikers, a bearded young man with glasses talks to the camera against background noise that, after a few moments, becomes audible as Iggy Pop's "The Passenger." He explains that they have a number of pictures to "show the world that Iran and Greece do have a very close relationship." He then gestures to three photographs, which have been enlarged for public exhibition, and the camera zooms in on each one as the speaker narrates: one image of a Greek writer dining at the Iranian embassy in Athens in 2010; one image of then prime minister Papandreou shaking the hand of Ahmadeenajad on a diplomatic mission; and finally, a photo of the former Greek Minister of Citizen Protection, Eleftherios Oikonomou, in a chummy pose with the Iranian Ambassador to Greece and Mohsen Rezaee, an Iranian politician and former military leader, whom the speaker describes as the "Iranian head of police." The speaker asks rhetorically how the leaders who have persecuted Iranian seekers of freedom can be greeted so warmly by the Greek government.

In placing such visual "proofs" of collusion between the Greek and Iranian governments alongside images of failing bodies which, in turn, expose the hidden violence of law and bureaucracy, the blog combines an aesthetics of suffering with transparency politics. The images of the strikers' sewn mouths expose and render transparent political and legal violence, while images of friendly meetings between Greek and Iranian leaders serve to expose "lies," not unlike the corruption that Bashir described among service providers. The blog thus highlights the entwinement of diverse forms of action in the politics of exposure; more mundane tactics such as auditing, through photographs and documents, unfold alongside dramatic images of sewn mouths and failing bodies.

The hunger strike, as a bodily technique, could in some ways be taken to represent the overwhelming politicization of life: the subsuming of individual and collective bodies, in their suffering, into the legal, political, and social order. For Bashir and his compatriots, their suffering bodies provided a way into the terrain of legal belonging. Yet as a form of witnessing—not unlike Azar's photographs—the hunger strike exposes both the trenchant persistence and the limits of legal violence, highlighting the capacity of human life and personhood to exceed the boundaries of the political and social body (Douzinas 2013: 3). Throughout this book, I have shown that even in sites where personhood and human life are at their most vexed and most susceptible to management, ineffable forms of sociality and ethical consciousness arise. Here, however, I have sought to articulate an emergent radical politics, a form of witnessing that exposes the violence at the core of social life, which Veena Das (2007: 71) describes as "the criminality of the social order itself."

Athina Athanasiou (2007) suggests that the ultimate political management of otherness takes place through a jurisdiction over "life at its limits": the governance of suffering, vulnerable, displaced, or disarticulated bodies. Yet she shows that even amid this politicization of life, there is always a surplus, an excess, which creates a space for more meaningful politics and solidarities, particularly in sites of crisis (Athanasiou 2012). Witnessing takes place at this site of excess, the point of opening between the political order and the person. This is the threshold at the limits of life, where the human as a sociopolitical being, subject to sharp demarcations of inclusion and exclusion, transforms into something terrible, rending, beautiful, and perhaps unrecognizable.

The Journeys, and the Dramas, Continue

"And the journey continues. . . ." So reads the final entry of the blog of the "300," followed by a spread of photos of smiling strikers and supporters, and finally, a small group in front of the port of Piraius taken before they headed back to Crete. The caption celebrates the successful end to the 40-day strike, while also recognizing the need for ongoing political action. The "300" garnered material forms of success with their hunger strike, achieving—though in limited and ad hoc ways—legalization for the strikers. The Iranian Hunger Strikers' blog, in contrast, concludes with a group photo of those who sewed their mouths, flashing peace signs, and the statement: "43 days passed and yet no response from the Greek government." Bashir, however, explained that in practice, the strike had worked: he and a number of other strikers acquired refugee status.

Unlike the 300, the Iranian hunger strikers did not receive an official statement from the Greek government explaining the decision to issue legalizations, but Bashir insisted that he would never have received asylum otherwise. The highly public nature of the state's response to the 300, versus the more veiled, procedural response to the Iranians (if their recognitions were indeed a result of the strike), may be grounded in important distinctions between the two groups of strikers. For the 300, legalization took place outside an existing legal process, since no such process had been available to them; the state enacted ad hoc regularization, grounded on a clause that allows for such actions in certain (exceptional) circumstances. The Iranian hunger strikers, instead, demanded that to which they were formally entitled even within the purview of the Greek system: to have their asylum claims examined.

Bashir's insistence that the strike was integral to his ultimate acquisition of refugee status points to another, perhaps unpredictable, consequence of such forms of political action: despite their effectiveness in achieving particular goals, they may in fact complement and work within an existing Greek ethos of bureaucracy, rather than challenging or transforming more entrenched, systemic practices. As I discussed in Chapter 2 through the lens of the pink card, the asylum process in Greece unfolds through pervasive forms of mystification that encourage ad hoc and often seemingly arbitrary decisions from bureaucrats. When the asylum process proved impossible for these Iranian refugees, they turned to an exceptional form of political action to expose and address an untenable and exceptional situation. Such exceptionality is, however, very much in the spirit of how the asylum process has worked in Greece, with its ethos of mystification, unpredictability, and arbitrariness. We can surmise that for the Greek asylum bureaucracy in the last months of 2010 (before the reform process began), a series of recognitions issued to a small group of Iranian asylum seekers were, in many ways, as ad hoc and arbitrary as any other decision.

Perhaps owing to the pervasive sense among asylum seekers that bureaucracy and law are not viable pathways to make claims to recognition and entitlement in Greece, hunger striking has become an even more widespread form of political action, even an alternative way to claim status and services. The strikes continue. In July 2011, I met a group of Afghans hunger striking in front of the Propylaia, with a sign reading *Zitame politiko asylo* [ζητάμε πολιτικό άσυλο] (we request political asylum) serving as a centerpiece for their small group of tents. An informational booth, staffed day and night, displayed pictures of mangled bodies—images of the war. I also found, to my surprise, a small group of hunger strikers, also Iranian, camped in front of the ARS, as well as a group in front of the UNHCR offices in Athens. Some of them had, in fact, been on strike with Bashir and, like him, had received asylum. Despite the change in their legal status, these now recognized refugees found that the material facts of their everyday lives had not changed: they still remained without services and without support, struggling with mere survival.

In late 2010, one of Bashir's companion strikers, who had received asylum, came to the ARS and, brandishing a knife, took workers hostage and threatened to commit suicide. Thankfully, he and everyone inside were

Figure 4. Afghan asylum seekers hunger striking in Athens, July 2011.

Figure 5. Images of suffering and maimed bodies accompanying the Afghan hunger strike, July 2011.

ultimately safe (owing largely to a quick response by local community members in Exarcheia), but this event brought the desperation on the street into the ARS offices in an immediate and violent way. Workers underwent follow-up counseling care, while the young man was temporarily placed in a mental health facility. The workers I spoke with chalked this event up to mental instability and terrible frustration wrought through years in Greece. Yet they emphasized that his anger toward the ARS and its employees was misplaced, much in the vein of the disconnects between workers and clients that I described in Chapter 3. When I spoke to Bashir about this event, however, he explained that though this man had received asylum he still could not claim services, not even from NGOs. And so he "protested again" as a way—to quote Bashir—to "stand up for his rights."

The further dilemma, then, is that for many of those who achieve formal recognition as refugees in Greece, their lives may not be substantively different from before. Roya, discussed in Chapter 2, ultimately received asylum with her husband, but when she read my analysis of her case, she asked me to emphasize that "nothing has really changed." Social services for recognized refugees are only slightly more generous than those for asylum seekers. Moreover, although they receive travel documents, recognized refugees cannot relocate permanently within the EU, attesting to ongoing limitations in mobility. "Responsibility" for refugees in the EU is determined on a national basis, and one may relocate only under special circumstances, such as close family ties in another EU country. Otherwise, one must reapply for asylum in a new European country *and* demonstrate that Greece did not adequately provide protection. While occasionally such tactics are met with success, it is particularly difficult to make such a claim when one has, in fact, been offered protection in Greece through the assignation of refugee status. Unlike MSS, whose claim had not even been examined, recognized refugees have, at the very least, a travel document and legal permission to stay, though refugee travel documents often prove a mystery to those at the airport. Melike, for instance, explained that even after more than twenty years as a refugee in Greece, she always has to plan extra time at the airport to educate the authorities about her status.

The "journey," nonetheless, does continue, in spite of formal and informal impediments. As might be expected, many recognized refugees do resettle informally, though this has its own hazards, since it is not legally sanctioned and they cannot claim the benefits of residence in the new member state. Yet many take their chances and leave. Omar wrote me in fall 2012 explaining that he did not care about the risks—he simply could not stay in Greece any longer. Shortly afterward, he went to the Netherlands, where he has a nephew, and applied for asylum—almost ten years after he was first recognized as a refugee in Greece. His claim was rejected, and he was returned to Greece in spring 2013; he is now in his mid-seventies, struggling just to keep a roof over his head, and increasingly fearful for his safety on the streets of Athens. Bashir, likewise, explained that most of his fellow strikers had left Greece, with their newly minted travel documents, and he was planning to leave soon. "This is not my dead end, not my destiny. . . . In few days I will leave this country forever."

With the fragmentation of the state and the breakdown of political entitlements accompanying the financial crisis, the conditions of exception and exclusion– so familiar to asylum seekers and refugees—are becoming, more and more, dominant modes of political belonging in Greece, for both "citizens" and "aliens." Indeed, the larger terrain of citizenship in Greece is increasingly up for grabs. I have often heard Athenians of Greek origin ask: "How can *kseni* expect to find help here? Not even Greeks have services." Implicit in this reminder is not just a commentary on the failures of the Greek state (on which Greeks and foreigners alike might agree), but also the question of why should "strangers" be able to live in Greece? This final question is what is at stake in the politics of exposure that I have described here. Bashir, Azar, and their compatriots struggle to make claims to life that transcend the refugee's alienness. Unlike both the practice of humanitarian aid and the legal framework of asylum, which offer life only by virtue of the claimant's alien origins, these political actions assert a new vision of civic entitlement: an image of shared human citizenship and human life that transcends the stranger's position at the margins of the *polis*.

The Machine

When Orestes, polluted through his act of matricide, asks for refuge in Athens from the persecuting Furies, clasping his arms around Athena's ancient image, he seeks not simply redemption but "good judges." The Furies, themselves the embodiment of chthonic pollution, alien beings who do not belong within the city walls yet simultaneously represent the ancient laws of blood, seek something similar: judges. In the *Eumenides*, Athena's subsequent unveiling, in which she exposes her true form, has often been identified as the first known use of the "god in the machine," the *deus ex machina*, or the Μηχανή (*Mikhani*) in ancient Greek. In tragic drama, a god was often raised onto the stage by a crane at the end of the action, divine intervention emerging as the only way to conclude, to undo the indissoluble tensions in which all actors have been caught. Yet the *Eumenides* is notable for the undeniably secular quality of this *Mikhani*. Athena immediately institutes a jury, "good" but human judges, citizens of Athens who assemble on the rock of judgment above the city. She grants her authority to them, voting alongside these citizens, a good judge who is perhaps, in her own way, no less human. Yet even as she votes to redeem Orestes she also provides a threshold to those persecuted, persecuting Furies, who, finding refuge beneath the great rock, become kindly but remain terrifying, new guardians of the city and its citizens. This afterthought, with a hint of the grace of *filoksenia*, is part and parcel of the work of judgment; it is also revolutionary, a line of flight from the machine of law, putting new faces on both gods and citizens, enacting radical transformation from the inside out.

Greece, its citizens (strangers and insiders alike), and Europe remain very much in the balance, clinging to various images of the divine. The failures of the asylum process, the brutalized bodies of "aliens" (not just their images), and the ghosts that law has produced serve to expose how regimes of rights and humanitarianism are increasingly fraught with tensions and tragedies that are untenable for all involved. Yet the intimacies and engagements that tragedy engenders, and the creative ways in which people respond to its constraints, provide thresholds into transformative, even revolutionary, work: at the level of individual ethics, community politics, and national and supranational governance, contest, and collaboration. This is "something like [but not quite] hope" (Clifford 1997): those elements of personhood, law, sociality, and politics that perpetually evade visibility, knowledge, and writing, but which remake the world from within. Lights vanishing into darkness, and their promise of transformation.

Notes

Introduction

1. Throughout the book, I draw on the translation of *The Oresteia* by David Grene and Wendy Doniger O'Flaherty (1989).

2. Following intensified efforts by both EU and Greek authorities, including the mobilization of the EU border management agency Frontex and an additional 1,881 police officers in the Evros region near Turkey, the number of undocumented persons detected crossing the Greek/Turkish border decreased by 44 percent between 2011 and 2012 (Frontex 2013). Data released by Frontex in 2013 regarding the "Eastern Mediterranean Migration Route," which entails entries to Greece, Bulgaria, and Cyprus, showed a decrease of 57,025 detected entries to 37,224 in 2012. Most of those apprehended are from Afghanistan, Syria, Pakistan, and Bangladesh. Moreover, according to statistics from the Greek Ministry of Public Order and Citizen Protection, the numbers of those arrested by police and port authorities for illegally crossing the border decreased from 146,377 in 2008 and 132, 524 in 2010 to 76,878 in 2012.

3. When I began my research in 2004, the Ministry of Public Order processed asylum claims; in 2007 the Ministry of Public Order was subsumed into the Ministry of the Interior. It has since been reorganized and renamed the Ministry of Public Order and Citizen Protection.

4. It is important to note that those awarded refugee status had rarely lodged an application the same year in which they received a positive decision; rather, positive decisions were most often awarded to persons whose claims had been in process for a year or more and often for many years.

5. Gluckman (2006 [1965]) highlights how the "stranger," someone from outside, often rearticulates or makes clear the internal values of the group. Gluckman specifically refers to the role of arbiters, or institutionalized practices through which people are brought from outside to weigh in on specific situations. This is, I think, interesting when placed alongside Herzfeld's analysis of the foreigner (*ksenos*) in tourism contexts in Greece, where the host community becomes, at least formally, more cohesive through its encounters with foreigners. Mae Ngai (2004), more radically, shows how the whole premise of citizenship is grounded on the position of *aliens* on U.S. territory.

6. "Superfluities," for Marx, refer to people and things that may be deemed expendable but which are nonetheless constitutive of relationships of power and capital (see Mbembe 2004). For Arendt (1976 [1951]), "superfluity" describes the destitution and debasement of "superfluous men," wage labor and bodies ripe for exploitation.

7. For an outstanding in-process and interactive map of Athens, see the open-source mapping project, Map the Commons: http: //mappingthecommons.wordpress.com/.

8. In a previous publication (Cabot 2013b), I referred to the NGO as the Athens Refugee Center (ARC), a pseudonym that was much too close to the name of Helping Hands: The Athens Refugee Ministry, known informally as the Athens Refugee Center.

9. See, for instance, the extraordinary work done on the island of Leros, in which community members and local advocates have frequently come together to house and care for new arrivals.

Chapter 1. European Moral Geographies

1. The administrative deportation order issued by the Greek police during that period asked individuals to leave voluntarily, most often without specifying where they had to go, or how.

2. See the documentary *Dublin's Trap: Another Side of the Greek Crisis* (Carter 2012), for a remarkably informative and balanced account of the "MSS" decision and the events surrounding it.

3. According to the decision, "relevant" legislation includes international human rights law (the 1951 Geneva Convention on the Status of Refugees); European Community law that reasserts the value of human rights (in particular, the European Convention on Human Rights); EC law focused on both safeguarding and regulating access to asylum (including the Dublin and Eurodac systems, as well as EU directives on asylum matters); and European soft law, consisting of recommendations from the European Commissioner for Human Rights.

4. According to the Frontex website, these teams are composed of experts in different areas of border management, including land and sea border surveillance, dog handling, identification of false documents, and second line activities such as establishing nationalities of irregular migrants detected at the border (http://www.frontex.europa.eu/).

5. Under international law, asylum seekers may only be transferred to another country if they have previously found protection there, or, in certain circumstances, if it is a "safe third country" which will take responsibility for their asylum claim. A "safe third country" transfer of responsibility is only justified when the applicant has meaningful links or connections (e.g., family or cultural ties, or legal residence) with that country and when there are guarantees that the asylum seeker will be readmitted to that country, enjoy effective protection against refoulement, and be able to seek asylum. In most cases, Turkey does not meet these criteria, particularly since it only recognizes refugees fleeing events in Europe; as a result, the UNHCR processes most of the asylum applications in Turkey and resettles those whom it grants asylum.

6. When I conducted follow-up fieldwork in July 2010 and 2011, NGO workers, researchers, and asylum seekers I met attested that there were fewer recent reports of this practice. Nevertheless, during the period of my primary fieldwork (2006–2008), this practice was widely reported and discussed in advocacy circles and also in the European Parliament, when I attended a session of the Committee on Civil Liberties in July 2007.

7. I urge any readers interested in an authoritative analysis of the current state of the legislative apparatus of asylum in Greece to look beyond this book. Not only is a full discussion of asylum law in Greece beyond the purview of my analysis, but the asylum process is constantly changing; information presented here will surely be outdated, even in the lag between writing and publication. As much as possible, I take account of the shifting scenario of asylum in Greece, but I also refer to practices and policies that may have changed or been eradicated altogether. For excellent recent accounts of Greek asylum law written in English, which also discuss the last few years of rapid change from a broader European perspective, see Mcdonough and Tsourdi 2012; and Papageorgiou 2013.

8. In 2010, the Administrative Cassation Court of Appeals (Dhikitiko Akirotiko Efetio; Διοικητικό Ακυρωτικό Εφετείο) assumed jurisdiction for such procedural examinations of the asylum process.

9. For those interested in the details of the new asylum process as it is envisioned in law 3907/2011 (though only partially functioning in practice), key changes are as follows: the applicant goes to the regional office of the new asylum service and files an asylum application, and s/he is given a date for a first interview. The interview is performed by a civil servant (no longer from the police authority), who issues the first-instance decision. If this decision is negative, then the applicant has the right to appeal; the appeal goes to the Appeals Authority, where a rapporteur makes a recommendation to a committee, which examines the case only on the basis of the documents in the file. There is no further interview with the applicant at this stage, except if and only if the rapporteur proposes an interview. The committee then issues a decision which, if it is negative, can be appealed by the applicant to the Athens Cassation Court of Appeals. Importantly, while regional offices for first instance applications are opening in the border cities of Alexandroupoli and Oresteiada, as well as in Thessaloniki, the second instance examimation committees are located in Athens. Thus, appeals also take place in Athens, under the jurisdiction of the Athenian appeals court.

10. For a comprehensive discussion of the emergence of Greek asylum law see Sitaropoulos 2000.

11. Note that even though we spoke in Greek, "advocacy" was coded in English (as opposed to the Greek *sinighoria*; συνηγορία), attesting, I would suggest, to how it is often seen to circulate in an English-dominated international sphere.

Chapter 2. Documenting Legal Limbo

1. The new asylum authority opened its doors in June 2013, and this is now where first instance applications are lodged.

2. During fieldwork in Lesbos in June 2008, when I spoke with a group of lawyers assisting asylum seekers in detention, they expressed excitement and satisfaction that they had recently been able to assist five asylum applicants in lodging applications and receiving pink cards from this island border.

3. There are two forms of deportation in Greece: one entails "penal" deportation, the other "administrative." The expulsion order discussed here and most commonly issued entails the process of administrative deportation.

4. See Elizabeth Dunn's work on humanitarian aid and refugees in Georgia (Dunn 2012).

5. As I discuss in Chapter 3, this stasis changed dramatically in spring 2008, when, in response to international critiques regarding the situation of Iraqi asylum seekers in Greece, the Ministry awarded asylum to dozens of Iraqis over the space of a few months. Most were Chaldean Christians, however, and most of these cases dated from before 2002 and even earlier (1998/1999). Many other long-standing Iraqi applicants have still not received decisions on their claims.

6. Immigration law in Greece is not consistent or comprehensive but depends on an often changing legislative scenario dictated through a series of presidential decrees (*proedhrika dhiatagmata* [προεδρικά διατάγματα]) that sometimes build on each other and at other times, cancel each other out. Depending on when one enters Greece and what the most recent presidential decree states, the requirements for regularization can change. At the time of Kamir's application, he had to be able to prove—not with his pink card but with other documents, such as work papers—that he had been living and working in Greece for an extended period of time. Currently, the relevant law for regularization of migrants in Greece is 3386–2005, amended in 2007; it remains highly restrictive.

7. Presidential Decree 220/2007 in fact states that those asylum seekers who do not have housing will be provided shelter, though this was rarely the case in practice. "Σε αιτούντα ο οποίος δε διαθέτει στέγη ή επαρκείς πόρους για να καλύψει τις ανάγκες στέγασής του, παρέχεται στέγη σε Κέντρο Φιλοξενίας ή άλλο χώρο" (To the applicant who does not have at his disposal shelter or adequate resources to meet his housing needs, shelter will be provided at a Hospitality Center or other space.")

Chapter 3. Engaging Tragedy

1. Phoevi, who speaks perfect English, most often spoke to me in English when we were in one-on-one conversation.

2. Interestingly, this institutional focus on limitation and lack is congruent with many state bureaucratic offices, as any trip to a Greek hospital or immigration office will tell you.

3. Faubion uses the term "themitical" to describe the homeostatic and reproductive elements of ethics, drawing on the ancient Greek *themitos*: "allowed by the gods and of men, righteous" (27).

4. The distinction between an NGO lawyer and a "private" lawyer is by no means

clear. Many ARS lawyers worked in other offices or consortiums serving private clients (though, to my knowledge, not asylum seekers), in order to supplement salaries. Moreover, one in particular moved on to open his own "private" firm but, nonetheless, took on significant numbers of pro bono clients—or rather, as he described them, clients who did not (or could not) pay. He made the important observation that even the performance of being a paying client increased the trust between himself and those he represented, since they approached him as "their" lawyer, as opposed to someone merely granting them assistance, as at the ARS.

5. The stamp states: "The applicant has not expressed any fear of persecution whatsoever and, according to his statements, he left his country of origin solely for economic reasons and to improve his living conditions."

6. The forms of temporary protection offered vary according to the host country, even within Europe. In Greece, both humanitarian protection and subsidiary protection have been used to provide temporary status to persons deemed to represent part of a mass-influx of people, owing to violence in the home country that would make return unsafe or to incidences of *force majeure*. While refugee status and subsidiary protection are housed in international and EU law, however, humanitarian status is inscribed in Greek national law. For a full discussion see Magliveras 2011.

7. *Malakia* refers to the act of masturbation, but *malakies* functions similarly to the way "bullshit" functions in English.

8. Such characterizations of the state long preceded the recent Greek financial crisis, with roots in the Civil War and its aftermath and the Junta, but they have been greatly exacerbated amid the current financial difficulties.

9. Donnelly (2003) also draws a distinction between rights and "benefits," which makes having a right very different from simply being the "(rights-less) beneficiary" of kindness or charity (10).

Chapter 4. Images of Vulnerability

1. These aesthetic factors also reflect the increasing racialization and criminalization of sex work in Greece. This is a complex topic, which I can only touch on here: Sex workers have occupied an important, and not necessarily dangerous, place in Greek public consciousness (see, e.g., Melina Mercouri's much-loved character in the classic film *Never on Sunday*; Dassin 1960). Currently, Greece has a legal, regulated sex industry, in which workers, many of them of non-Greek origin, are subject to state biopolitics aimed toward monitoring a legal, healthy, and productive population. Regulatory measures include mandatory testing for disease. Yet unregulated sex work has also increased, a phenomenon that, among dominant publics, is associated with the intensified visibility of the racialized bodies of women of color (primarily of African origin) on Athens streets. The (actual or perceived) loosening state grip on the sex industry is caught up in public anxieties and increasingly violent and militarized attempts at regulation. Such anxieties were thrown into particularly high relief when the Athens police posted the names and photos of sex workers who had been found to

be HIV positive; these workers were also charged with the intent to cause grievous bodily harm.

2. According to the 2011 U.S. Department of State Trafficking in Persons Report, "tier 2" refers to "countries whose governments do not fully comply with the U.S.'s Trafficking Victim's Protection Act's [TVPA] minimum standards but are making significant efforts to bring themselves into compliance with those standards." While the TVPA is U.S. legislation, it has had a significant role in articulating international parameters for the protection of trafficking victims. Before September 2003, Greece was, in fact, classified as "tier 3," designating countries that "ignore or promote" trafficking. Following the approval of comprehensive legislation to protect victims of labor and sex trafficking (Presidential Decree 223/2003 and law 3386/2005), Greece was upgraded to "tier 2" and remains so classified. Other relevant legislation includes the UN Protocol to Prevent, Suppress and Punish Trafficking in Persons, especially Women and Children (otherwise known as the Trafficking Protocol, UN TIP Protocol, or "Palermo" Protocol), adopted in Palermo, Italy, in 2000 (see Warren 2007 for a full discussion), as well as EU legislation on the prevention of trafficking and the protection of victims. Other EU countries currently listed as "tier 2" are Bulgaria, Estonia, Latvia, Portugal, Hungary, Romania, Malta, and Cyprus ("tier 2 watch list").

3. See, for instance, France Terre d'Asile, Institute for Rights, Equality, and Diversity, and Consiglio Italiano per i Rifugiati (2010); Human Rights Watch (2008, 2013).

4. Susan Bibler Coutin employs the notion of "resolution" as both a legal and visual descriptor to characterize the unresolved status of Salvadoran migrants to the United States. She writes, "Just as a photographic image with low resolution produces a blurry picture, these migrants had difficulty clarifying their legal status, social location, and individual futures" (2007: 117).

Chapter 5. Recognizing the Real Refugee

1. According to data from the Greek Ministry of Public Order, in 2006 there were 3,750 asylum applicants from Bangladesh (30.57% of the total number of applications received), and 2,378 from Pakistan (19.39%). In 2007, there were 9,144 applicants from Pakistan (36.41%), and 2,965 from Bangladesh (11.81%).

2. I am extremely grateful to my friend and interlocutor, lawyer Maria Malikouti, for her insights into the backhanded ways in which the Simvoulio tis Epikratias rules on the merits of asylum cases.

3. I should note that a great many of the visitors to the ARS claimed to be only minimally literate even in their own languages; lack of formal education was a challenge for many ARS clients and potential clients (not just those from Bangladesh).

Chapter 6. Rearticulating the Ethnos

1. Prior to the 2010 citizenship bill, children born in Greece to migrant parents could not apply for citizenship until their eighteenth birthday, and even then had to demonstrate continuous legal residence in Greece for at least ten of the twelve years

preceding their application. The amended bill, however, made citizenship available to alien residents who had been legally present in Greece for at least seven years, and to children whose parents had been residing in Greece legally for five or more years, or who had successfully completed at least six years of school.

2. The text of the decision is fascinating for how it draws unselfconsciously on metaphors of timeless, deep rooted, and robust tradition, linking culture to generational descent through either family relationship or state educational institutions. It represents a powerful example of what Stolcke (1995) and Herzfeld (2002) would call "cultural fundamentalism," through which the domain of culture becomes pragmatically and metaphorically linked to blood, descent, and entrenched notions of identity. Race thus finds its way in through the back door, so to speak, in the guise of "culture." The decision cites, as a prerequisite for citizenship, "the existence of a real bond of the alien to the Greek state and the Greek society, which are not invertebrate organisms and ephemeral creations but represent timeless unity with a definite cultural foundation, a community with relatively stable mores, a shared language with a long tradition, elements that are passed down from generation to generation with the help of smaller social units (family) and organized state units (education)" (Council of State, 460/2013) ["... η ύπαρξη γνησίου δεσμού του αλλοδαπού προς το ελληνικό κράτος και την ελληνική κοινωνία, τα οποία δεν είναι οργανισμοί ασπόνδυλοι και δημιουργήματα εφήμερα αλλά παριστούν διαχρονική ενότητα με ορισμένο πολιτιστικό υπόβαθρο, κοινότητα με σχετικώς σταθερά ήθη και έθιμα, κοινή γλώσσα με μακρά παράδοση, στοιχεία τα οποία μεταβιβάζονται από γενεά σε γενεά με την βοήθεια μικρότερων κοινωνικών μονάδων (οικογένεια) και οργανωμένων κρατικών μονάδων (εκπαίδευση)" (Σ.τ.Ε. 460/2013)].

3. See the informative blog, "Accept Pluralism," managed by migration scholar Anna Triandafillydou: "The reasoning of the State Council judges was that voting rights of whichever type are for citizens only even if the Constitution does not specify this as regards local election. In addition they sustained that the new provisions for naturalization of first or second generation migrants are against the Constitution because they disregard that naturalization can only happen if there is a 'real bond' between the foreigner and the Greek nation. Such 'real bond' cannot be ascertained, they argue, by formal legal requirements such as the length of residency or the fact of being born in Greece or the fact of having studied at a Greek school for 6 years," http://www.rscas.org/accept/blog/?p=182, accessed November 30, 2012.

4. The racist, masculinist brutality of Golden Dawn is directed not just toward migrants and foreigners, but toward women and those on the political left as well (Avdela and Psarra 2012): in June 2012, Golden Dawn MP Ilias Kasidiaris assaulted Communist Party member Liana Kanelli on live television during a debate. Significant numbers of the Athens police force are said to support the party.

5. Over the past thirty years, there have been discussions and even introduction of multiple laws to initiate building a mosque in central Athens (for instance Law 2833, in 2000, providing for establishment of a mosque in the eastern suburb of Paiania). These initiatives have not, however, been realized in practice.

Chapter 7. Citizens of Athens

1. For critical anthropological accounts of the diversity of movements invoking a "direct democracy" model, see for instance Graeber 2013; Juris 2013; Razsa and Kumik 2012.

2. The law granting "asylum" to protesters at Greek universities dates to 1982, when students were granted freedom of speech on campus, partly owing to the history of repression of students during the Junta (which ended in 1974). The law was repealed in October 2011, owing largely to "non-student abuse" of the privilege (the hunger strike being cited as a prime example).

3. Indymedia, or the Independent Media Center (IMC), is a transnational network of independent journalists who write on social justice issues. With its inception in the Seattle anti-World Trade Organization protests in 1999, Indymedia is generally highly critical of neoliberalism and capitalist intervention.

4. Even the recent discussions regarding how EU austerity measures exact unjust tolls on the Greek populace bear similarities to this account, in that it is seen to be unjust, and thus, a kind of "theft."

5. The Συμβούλιο Ένταξης Μεταναστών [Council for the Integration of Migrants] for the city of Athens was established in 2010, by order of Presidential Decree 3852/2010, "ως συμβουλευτικό όργανο του δήμου, για την ενίσχυση της ένταξης των μεταναστών στην τοπική κοινωνία" [as an advisory body of the municipality, for the reinforcement of the integration of immigrants in the local community] (see official website of the city of Athens: cityofathens.gr/node/384, accessed November 27, 2012). The official city website describes the council as composed of important advisors for the new multicultural city that Athens has become: Η πόλη της Αθήνας, τα τελευταία χρόνια, χρωματίζεται από ένα πολύχρωμο, πολυπολιτισμικό καμβά. Στην Αθήνα διαβιούν πολίτες μετανάστες, που εργάζονται, αποκτούν βιοτικούς δεσμούς με την Αθήνα και συμμετέχουν ενεργά στην οικονομική και κοινωνική ζωή της πόλης [The city of Athens, during the last few years, is being colored by a multicolored, multicultural canvas. In Athens live citizen immigrants, who work, acquire organic ties with Athens, and actively participate in the economic and social life of the city].

Bibliography

Aeschylus. 1989. *The Oresteia*. Trans. David Grene and Wendy Doniger O'Flaherty. Chicago: University of Chicago Press.

Agamben, Giorgio. 1998. *Homo Sacer: Sovereign Power and Bare Life*. Trans. David Heller-Roazen. Stanford, Calif.: Stanford University Press.

———. 2009. *What Is an Apparatus and Other Essays*. Stanford, Calif.: Stanford University Press.

Agathangelou, Anna. 2004. *The Global Political Economy of Sex: Desire, Violence, and Insecurity in Mediterranean Nation States*. New York: Palgrave Macmillan.

Agustín, Laura María. 2007. *Sex at the Margins: Migration, Labour Markets and the Rescue Industry*. London: Zed Books.

Ahearn, Laura. 2001. "Language and Agency." *Annual Review of Anthropology* 30: 109–37.

Alivizatos, Nikos. 1996. *The Political Institutions in Crisis, 1922–1974*. Athens: Themelio.

Allen, Lori. 2009. "Martyr Bodies in the Media: Human Rights, Aesthetics, and the Politics of Immediation in the Palestinian Intifada." *American Ethnologist* 36: 161–80.

Alexandrakis, Othon. 2013. "Neoliberalism and the New Agora: Exploring Survival, Emergence, and Political Subjectivity Among Pluralized Subaltern Communities in Athens, Greece." *Anthropological Quarterly* 86, 1: 77–105.

Althusser, Louis. 1971. *Lenin and Philosophy and Other Essays*. Trans. Ben Brewster. New York: Monthly Review Press.

Améry, Jean. 1980. *At the Mind's Limits: Contemplations by a Survivor on Auschwitz and Its Realities*. Trans. Sidney Rosenfeld and Stella P. Rosenfeld. Bloomington: Indiana University Press.

Antoniou, Dimitris. 2005. "Western Thracian Muslims in Athens: From Economic Migration to Religious Organization." *Balkanologie* 4: 79–101.

———. 2010. "The Mosque That Wasn't There: Ethnographic Elaborations on Orthodox Conceptions of Sacrifice." In *Orthodox Christianity in 21st Century Greece: The Role of Religion in Culture, Ethnicity and Politics*, ed. Victor Roudometof and Vasilios Makrides. Farnham: Ashgate.

Arendt, Hannah. 1976 [1951]. *The Origins of Totalitarianism*. New York: Harcourt.

———. 1998 [1958]. *The Human Condition*. Chicago: University of Chicago Press.

Ascherson, Neal. 1995. *Black Sea*. 1st American ed. New York: Hill and Wang.

Athanasiou, Athina. 2007 *Ζωή στο οριο* [Life at the Limit]. Athens: Ekkremes.

———. 2012. *Η κρίση ως κατάσταση "'εκτακτης ανάγκης"* [The Crisis as "State of Emergency"]. Athens: Savvalas.

Athanassopoulou, Effie. 2002. "An 'Ancient' Landscape: European Ideals, Archaeology, and Nation Building in Early Modern Greece." *Journal of Modern Greek Studies* 20.

Austin, J. L. 2001 [1962]. *How to Do Things with Words*. Cambridge, Mass.: Harvard University Press.

Avdela, Effie, and Angelika Psarra. 2012. "Απόκρυφες πτυχές της μελανής ψήφου." [Arcane Aspects of the Black Vote]. *Η Αυγή*, January 7.

Babül. Elif. 2012. "Training Bureaucrats, Practicing for Europe: Constitutive Bureaucratic Imaginaries in Turkey." *Political and Legal Anthropology Review* 35.

Balibar, Étienne. 1998. "The Nation Form: History and Ideology." In *Race, Nation, Class: Ambiguous Identities*, ed. Étienne Balibar and Immanuel Wallerstein. London: Verso.

———. 2004. *We, the People of Europe? Reflections on Transnational Citizenship*. Princeton, N.J.: Princeton University Press.

Ballinger, Pam. 2003. *History in Exile: Memory and Identity at the Borders of the Balkans*. Princeton, N.J.: Princeton University Press.

Bastea, Eleni. 2000. *The Creation of Modern Athens: Planning the Myth*. Cambridge: Cambridge University Press.

Bateson, Gregory. 1972. *Steps to an Ecology of Mind: Collected Essays in Anthropology, Psychiatry, Evolution, and Epistemology*. Chandler Publications for Health Sciences. San Francisco: Chandler.

Bauman, Richard, and Charles Briggs. 1990. "Poetics and Performance as Critical Perspectives on Language and Social Life." *Annual Review of Anthropology* 19: 59–88.

Benjamin, Walter. 1986 [1936]. "The Work of Art in the Age of Mechanical Reproduction." In *Illuminations: Essays and Reflections*, ed. Hannah Arendt, 217–53. New York: Schocken.

———. 1999. "Critique of Violence." In *Selected Writings*, vol. 1, *1913–1926*, 236–52. Cambridge, Mass.: Belknap Press of Harvard University Press.

———. 2002. "The Storyteller: Observations on the Works of Nikolai Leskov." In *Selected Writings*, vol. 3, *1935–1938*, ed. Michael W. Jennings, 143–67. Cambridge, Mass.: Belknap Press of Harvard University Press.

Biehl, Joao, and Peter Locke. 2010. "Deleuze and the Anthropology of Becoming." *Current Anthropology* 50: 317–51.

Blommaert, Jan. 2001. "Analyzing African Asylum Seekers' Stories in Belgium." *Discourse and Society* 12: 413–49.

Bohmer, Caroline, and Amy Shuman. 2008. *Rejecting Refugees: Political Asylum in the 21st Century*. New York: Routledge.

Bourdieu, Pierre. 1977. *Outline of a Theory of Practice*. Cambridge Studies in Social Anthropology 16. Cambridge: Cambridge University Press.

Bowker, Geoffrey, and Susan Leigh Star. 1999. *Sorting Things Out: Classification and Its Consequences*. Cambridge, Mass.: MIT Press.

Brenneis, Donald L. 1987. "Performing Passions: Aesthetics and Politics in an Occasionally Egalitarian Community." *American Ethnologist* 14: 236–50.

———. 2007. "Reforming Promise." In *Documents: Artifacts of Modern Knowledge*, ed. Annelise Riles. Ann Arbor: University of Michigan Press.

Brenneis, Donald L., and Alessandro Duranti, eds. 1986. "The Audience as Co-Author." *Text* 6, 3.

Bubant, Nils. 2009. "From the Enemy's Point of View: Violence, Empathy, and the Ethnography of Fakes." *Cultural Anthropology* 24: 553–88.

Butler, Judith. 1997. *Excitable Speech: A Politics of the Performative*. New York: Routledge.

———. 2000. *Antigone's Claim: Kinship Between Life and Death*. New York: Columbia University Press.

———. 2004. *Precarious Life: The Powers of Mourning and Violence*. London: Verso.

Cabot, Heath. 2012. "The Governance of Things: Documenting Limbo in the Greek Asylum Procedure." *Political and Legal Anthropology Review* 35: 11–29.

———. 2013a. "Engagements and Interruptions: Mapping Emotion at an Athenian NGO." In *Careful Encounters: Ethnographies of Support*, ed. Friederike Fleischer and Markus Schlecker. London: Palgrave Macmillan.

———. 2013b. "The Social Aesthetics of Eligibility: NGO Aid and Indeterminacy in the Greek Asylum Process." *American Ethnologist* 40: 452–66.

Cabot, Heath, and Ramona Lenz. 2012. "Borders of (in)Visibility in the Greek Aegean." In *Culture and Society in Tourism Contexts*, ed. Antonio Miguel Nogués-Pedregal. Tourism Studies Series. Bingley, UK: Emerald Press.

Calabresi, Guido, and Phillip Bobbitt. 1978. *Tragic Choices*. Fels Lectures on Public Policy Analysis. New York: Norton.

Calavita, Kitty. 2005. *Immigrants at the Margins: Law, Race, and Exclusion in Southern Europe*. Cambridge: Cambridge University Press.

Campbell, James K. 1964. *Honour, Family, and Patronage: A Study of Institutions and Moral Values in a Greek Mountain Community*. Oxford: Oxford University Press.

Candea, Matei, and Giovanni Da Col. 2012. "Special Issue: The Return to Hospitality: Strangers, Guests, and Ambiguous Encounters." *Journal of the Royal Anthropological Institute* 18: Siii–Siv, S1–S217.

Carter, Bryan, dir. 2012. *Dublin's Trap: Another Side of the Greek Crisis*. Films Transit International.

Cavanaugh, Jillian. 2009. *Living Memory: The Social Aesthetics of Language in a Northern Italian Town*. Oxford: Wiley Blackwell.

Chakrabarty, Dipesh. 2000. *Provincializing Europe: Postcolonial Thought and Historical Difference*. Princeton Studies in Culture/Power/History. Princeton, N.J.: Princeton University Press.

Chandler, David. 2001. "The Road to Military Humanitarianism: How the Human

Rights NGOs Shaped a New Humanitarian Agenda." *Human Rights Quarterly* 23: 678–700.

Chatterjee, Partha. 1993. *Nationalist Thought and the Colonial World: A Derivative Discourse*. Minneapolis: University of Minnesota Press.

Cheliotis, Leonidas. 2013. "Behind the Veil of Philoxenia: The Politics of Immigration Detention in Greece. *European Journal of Criminology* 10, 6: 739–59.

———. Manuscript in progress. *Immigrants and the Penal State: Exploring the Psychosocial Bases of Punitiveness in the Margins of Europe.*

Christou, Anastasia. 2006. "Deciphering Diaspora: Translating Transnationalism: Family Dynamics, Identity Constructions and the Legacy of 'Home' in Second-Generation Greek-American Return Migration." *Ethnic and Racial Studies* 29: 1040–56.

———. 2009. "No Place Is (Like) Home: Mobilities, Memories and Metamorphoses of Greek Migrants in Denmark." In *Greek Diaspora and Migration Since 1700: Society, Politics and Culture*, ed. Dimitris Tziovas, 83–95. Aldershot: Ashgate.

Clifford, James. 1988. *The Predicament of Culture: Twentieth-Century Ethnography, Literature, and Art*. Cambridge, Mass.: Harvard University Press.

———. 1997. *Routes: Travel and Translation in the Late Twentieth Century*. Cambridge, Mass.: Harvard University Press.

Cohen, Robin. 1991. *Contested Domains: Debates in Contemporary Labour Studies*. London: Zed Books.

Cohn, Bernard. 1987. *An Anthropologist Among the Historians and Other Essays*. New York: Oxford University Press.

Cole, Simon A. 2001. *Suspect Identities: A History of Fingerprinting and Criminal Identification*. Cambridge, Mass.: Harvard University Press.

Comaroff, Jean, and John Comaroff. 1991. *Of Revelation and Revolution: Christianity, Colonialism, and Consciousness in South Africa*. Chicago: University of Chicago Press.

Conley, John M., and William M. O'Barr. 1998. *Just Words: Law, Language, and Power*. Chicago: University of Chicago Press.

Cooper, Frederick, and Ann Laura Stoler. 1997. *Tensions of Empire: Colonial Cultures in a Bourgeois World*. Berkeley: University of California Press.

Coutin, Susan. 2000. *Legalizing Moves: Salvadoran Immigrants' Struggle for U.S. Residency*. Ann Arbor: University of Michigan Press.

———. 2005. "Being en Route." *American Anthropologist* 107: 195–206.

———. 2007. *Nations of Emigrants: Shifting Boundaries of Citizenship in El Salvador and the United States*. Ithaca, N.Y.: Cornell University Press.

Coutin, Susan, and Barbara Yngvesson. 2006. "Backed by Papers: Undoing Persons, Histories, and Return." *American Ethnologist* 33: 177–90.

Cowan, Jane K. 2001. "Ambiguities of Emancipatory Discourse: The Making of a Macedonian Minority in Greece." In *Culture and Rights: Anthropological Perspectives*, ed.

Jane K. Cowan, Marie-Benedicte Dembour, and Richard A. Wilson, 152–76. Cambridge: Cambridge University Press.

———. 2008. "Fixing National Subjects in the 1920's Southern Balkans." *American Ethnologist* 35: 338–56.

Crapanzano, Vincent. 1980. *Tuhami: Portrait of a Moroccan.* Chicago: University of Chicago Press.

De Certeau, Michel. 1984. *The Practice of Everyday Life.* Berkeley: University of California Press.

Danforth, Loring M. 1995. *The Macedonian Conflict: Ethnic Nationalism in a Transnational World.* Princeton, N.J.: Princeton University Press.

Danforth, Loring M., and Riki van Boeschoten. 2011. *Children of the Greek Civil War: Refugees and the Politics of Memory.* Chicago: University of Chicago Press.

Daniel, E. Valentine, and John R. Knudson. 1995. *Mistrusting Refugees.* Berkeley: University of California Press.

Darian-Smith, Eve. 1999. *Bridging Divides: The Channel Tunnel and English Legal Identity in the New Europe.* Berkeley: University of California Press.

———. 2007. *Ethnography and Law.* International Library of Essays in Law and Society. Burlington, Vt.: Ashgate.

Das, Veena. 2004. "The Signature of the State: The Paradox of Illegibility." In *Anthropology in the Margins of the State*, ed. Veena Das and Deborah Poole, 225–52. Oxford: James Currey.

———. 2007. *Life and Words: Violence and the Descent into the Ordinary.* Berkeley: University of California Press.

Dassin, Jules, dir. 1960. *Never on Sunday.* 91 min. Lopert Pictures. Los Angeles.

Davis, Elizabeth Anne. 2011. *Bad Souls: Madness and Responsibility in Modern Greece.* Durham, N.C.: Duke University Press.

Debono, Daniela. 2011. "'Not Our Problem': Why the Detention of Irregular Migrants Is Not Considered a Human Rights Issue in Malta." In *Are Human Rights for Migrants? Critical Reflections on the Status of Irregular Migrants in Europe and the United States*, ed. Marie-Benedicte Dembour and Tobias Kelly, 146–62. London: Routledge.

Deleuze, Gilles. 1998. "What Children Say." In Deleuze, *Essays: Critical and Clinical.* Trans. Daniel W. Smith and Michael A. Greco, 61–68. London: Verso.

Deleuze, Gilles, and Felix Guattari. 1987. *A Thousand Plateaus: Capitalism and Schizophrenia.* Trans. Brian Massumi. Minneapolis: University of Minnesota Press.

Derrida, Jacques. 1992. "Force of Law: The Mystical Foundation of Authority." In *Deconstruction and the Possibility of Justice*, ed. Drucilla Cornell, Michel Rosenfield, and David Gray Carlson, 3–67. London: Routledge.

Dirks, Nicholas. 2001. *Castes of Mind: Colonialism and the Making of Modern India.* Princeton, N.J.: Princeton University Press.

Donnelly, Jack. 2003. *Universal Human Rights in Theory and Practice*. Ithaca, N.Y.: Cornell University Press.

Douglas, Mary. 1966. *Purity and Danger: An Analysis of Concepts of Pollution and Taboo*. London: Routledge.

Douzinas, Costas. 2012. "Stasis Syntagma: The Names and Types of Resistance." In *New Critical Legal Thinking Law and the Political*, ed. Matthew Stone, Illan Wall, and Costas Douzinas, 32–46. London: Routledge.

———. 2013. *Philosophy and Resistance in the Crisis: Greece and the Future of Europe*. Cambridge: Polity Press.

Douzinas, Costas, and Ronnie Warrington. 1994. *Justice Miscarried: Ethics and Aesthetics in Law*. Postmodern Theory. New York: Harvester Wheatsheaf.

Dubisch, Jill, ed. 1986. *Gender and Power in Rural Greece*. Princeton, N.J.: Princeton University Press.

———. 1993. "'Foreign Chickens' and Other Outsiders: Gender and Community in Greece." *American Ethnologist* 20: 272–87.

Duffield, Mark R. 2007. *Development, Security and Unending War: Governing the World of Peoples*. Cambridge: Polity.

Dunn, Elizabeth. 2012. "The Chaos of Humanitarian Aid: Adhocracy in the Republic of Georgia." *Humanity: An International Journal of Human Rights, Humanitarianism, and Development* 3: 1–23.

Eco, Umberto. 1998. *Serendipities: Language and Lunacy*. New York: Columbia University Press.

Engel, David M., and Frank W. Munger. 2003. *Rights of Inclusion: Law and Identity in the Life Stories of Americans with Disabilities*. Chicago: University of Chicago Press.

Evans-Pritchard, E. E. 1937. *Witchcraft, Oracles and Magic Among the Azande*. Oxford: Clarendon.

Fassin, Didier. 2005. "Compassion and Repression: The Moral Economy of Immigration Policies in France." *Cultural Anthropology* 20: 362–87.

———. 2007. "Humanitarianism as a Politics of Life." *Public Culture* 19: 499–520.

———. 2011. *Humanitarian Reason: A Moral History of the Present*. Berkeley: University of California Press.

Fassin, Didier, and Estelle d'Halluin. 2005. "The Truth from the Body: Medical Certificates as Ultimate Evidence for Asylum Seekers." *American Anthropologist* 107: 507–608.

Fassin, Didier, and Richard Rechtman. 2010. *The Empire of Trauma: An Inquiry into the Condition of Victimhood*. Trans. Rachel Gomme. Princeton, N.J.: Princeton University Press.

Faubion, James D. 2011. *An Anthropology of Ethics*. New Departures in Anthropology. Cambridge: Cambridge University Press.

Feldman, Gregory. 2012. *The Migration Apparatus: Security, Labor, and Policymaking in the European Union*. Stanford, Calif.: Stanford University Press.

Feldman, Ilana. 2008. *Governing Gaza: Bureaucracy, Authority, and the Work of Rule, 1917–1967*. Durham, N.C.: Duke University Press.

Feldman, Ilana, and Miriam Iris Ticktin. 2011. *In the Name of Humanity: The Government of Threat and Care*. Durham, N.C.: Duke University Press.

Ferguson, James. 1994. *The Anti-Politics Machine: "Development," Depoliticization, and Bureaucratic Power in Lesotho*. Minneapolis: University of Minnesota Press.

Fisher, William. 1997. "Doing Good? The Politics and Anti-Politics of Ngo Practices." *The Annual Review of Anthropology* 26.

Fortun, Kim. 2001. *Advocacy After Bhopal: Environmentalism, Disaster, New Global Orders*. Chicago: University of Chicago Press.

France Terre d'Asile, Institute for Rights, Equality, and Diversity, and Consiglio Italiano per i Rifugiati. 2010. "The Reception and Care of Unaccompanied Minors in Eight Countries of the European Union."

Foucault, Michel. 1978. *The History of Sexuality*. New York: Pantheon.

———. 1980 [1977]. *The Confession of the Flesh*. In *Power/Knowledge: Selected Interviews and Other Writings, 1972–1977*, ed. and trans. Colin Gordon. New York: Pantheon.

———. 1991. "Governmentality." In *The Foucault Effect: Studies in Governmentality*, ed. Burchell, Graham, Colin Gordon, and Peter Miller, 87–105. Chicago: University of Chicago Press.

———. 2009 [2004]. *Security, Territory, Population: Lectures at the Collège de France, 1977–78*. Trans. Graham Burchell. Picador Reading Group. New York: Picador.

Friedrich, Paul. 1986. *The Language Parallax: Linguistic Relativism and Poetic Indeterminacy*. Austin: University of Texas Press.

Frontex. 2013. Annual Risk Analysis, April. www.frontex.europa.eu.

Gilroy, Paul. 1987. *"There Ain't No Black in the Union Jack": The Cultural Politics of Race and Nation*. Chicago: University of Chicago Press.

———. 2004. *After Empire: Melancholia or Convivial Culture?* London: Routledge.

Gluckman, Max. 2006 [1965]. *Politics, Law, and Ritual in Tribal Society*. New Brunswick, N.J.: Transaction.

Good, Anthony. 2011. "Witness Statements and Credibility Assessments in the British Asylum Courts." In *Cultural Expertise and Litigation: Patterns, Conflicts, Narratives*, ed. Livia Holden, 94–122. London: Routledge.

Goodale, Mark. 2009. *Surrendering to Utopia: An Anthropology of Human Rights*. Stanford Studies in Human Rights. Stanford, Calif.: Stanford University Press.

Gordillo, Gaston. 2006. "The Crucible of Citizenship: I.D. Paper Fetishism in the Argentinean Chaco." *American Ethnologist* 33: 162–76.

Gourgouris, Stathis. 1996. *Dream Nation: Enlightenment, Colonization, and the Institution of Modern Greece*. Stanford, Calif.: Stanford University Press.

Graeber, David. 2006. "Beyond Power/ Knowledge: An Exploration of the Relation of Power, Ignorance and Stupidity." Annual Malinowski Memorial Lecture, May 25, London School of Economics and Political Science.

———. 2013. *The Democracy Project: A History, a Crisis, a Movement*. New York: Spiegel and Grau.

Gramsci, Antonio. 1992. *Prison Notebooks*. Ed. Joseph A. Buttigieg, trans. Joseph A.

Buttigieg and Antonio Callari. European Perspectives. New York: Columbia University Press.

Green, Sarah. 2010. "Performing Border in the Aegean: On Relocating Political, Economic, and Social Relations." *Journal of Cultural Economy* 3.

Greene, Molly. 2000. *A Shared World: Christians and Muslims in the Early Modern Mediterranean*. Princeton, N.J.: Princeton University Press.

Greenhouse, Carol. 1996. *A Moment's Notice: Time Politics Across Cultures*. Ithaca, N.Y.: Cornell University Press.

Hall, Stuart. 1990. "Cultural Identity and Diaspora." In *Identity, Community, Culture, Difference*, ed. James Rutherford. London: Lawrence and Wishart.

Hamilakis, Yannis. 2007. *The Nation and Its Ruins: Antiquity, Archaeology and National Imagination in Greece*. Oxford: Oxford University Press.

Harding, Susan. 2000. *The Book of Jerry Falwell: Fundamentalist Language and Politics*. Princeton, N.J.: Princeton University Press.

Hathaway, James. 1984. "The Evolution of Refugee Status in International Law: 1920–1950." *International and Comparative Law Quarterly* 33, 2: 348–80.

Heidegger, Martin. 1962. *Being and Time*. Trans. John Macquarrie and Edward Robinson. New York: Harper and Row.

Herzfeld, Michael. 1982. *Ours Once More: Folklore, Ideology, and the Making of Modern Greece*. Austin: University of Texas Press.

———. 1985. *The Poetics of Manhood: Contest and Identity in a Cretan Mountain Village*. Princeton, N.J.: Princeton University Press.

———. 1987a. *Anthropology Through the Looking-Glass: Critical Ethnography on the Margins of Europe*. Cambridge: Cambridge University Press.

———. 1987b. "'As in Your Own House': Hospitality, Ethnography, and the Stereotype of Mediterranean Society." In *Honor and Shame and the Unity of the Mediterranean*, ed. David Gilmore, 75–89. Special Publication 22. Washington, D.C.: American Anthropological Association.

———. 1992. *The Social Production of Indifference: Exploring the Symbolic Routes of Western Bureaucracy*. Oxford: Berg.

———. 1997. *Cultural Intimacy: Social Poetics in the Nation State*. Oxford: Berg.

———. 2002a. "The Absent Presence: Discourses of Crypto-Colonialism." *South Atlantic Quarterly* 101: 900–926.

———. 2002b. "Cultural Fundamentalism and the Regimentation of Identity: The Embodiment of Orthodox Values in a Modernist Setting." In *The Postnational Self: Belonging and Identity*, ed. Ulf Hedetoft and Mette Hjort. Minneapolis: University of Minnesota Press.

Hetherington, Kregg. 2011. *Guerrilla Auditors: The Politics of Tranparency in Neoliberal Paraguay*. Durham, N.C.: Duke University Press.

Hirsch, Susan. 1998. *Pronouncing and Persevering: Gender and the Discourses of Disputing in an African Islamic Court*. Chicago: University of Chicago Press.

Hirschon, Renée. 1998. *Heirs of the Greek Catastrophe: The Social Life of Asia Minor Refugees in Piraeus*. 2nd ed. Oxford: Berghahn.

———, ed. 2003. *Crossing the Aegean: An Appraisal of the 1923 Compulsory Population Exchange Between Greece and Turkey*. New York: Berghahn.

Hoag, Colin. 2010. "The Magic of the Populace: An Ethnography of Illegibility in the South African Immigration Bureaucracy." *Political and Legal Anthropology Review* 33: 6–25.

Howell, Signe. 1997. *The Ethnography of Moralities*. London: Routledge.

Hull, Matthew S. 2003. "The File: Agency, Authority, and Autography in an Islamabad Bureaucracy." *Language and Communication* 23: 287–314.

———. 2012. *Government of Paper: The Materiality of Bureaucracy in Urban Pakistan*. Berkeley: University of California Press.

Human Rights Watch. 2008. "Left to Survive: Systematic Failure to Protect Unaccompanied Migrant Children in Greece." December 22.

———. 2013. "Turned Away: Summary Returns of Unaccompanied Migrant Children and Adult Asylum Seekers from Italy to Greece." January 22.

Hyndman, Jennifer. 2000. *Managing Displacement: Refugees and the Politics of Humanitarianism*. Borderlines. Minneapolis: University of Minnesota Press.

Jakobson, Roman. 1990 [1957]. *On Language*. Cambridge, Mass.: Harvard University Press.

Joppke, Christian. 1998. "Why Liberal States Accept Unwanted Immigration" *World Politics* 50: 266–93.

Juris, Jeffrey. 2012. "Reflections on Occupy Everywhere: Social Media, Public Space, and Emerging Logics of Aggregation." *American Ethnologist* 39: 259–79.

Just, Roger. 1989. "The Triumph of the Ethnos." In *History and Ethnicity*, ed. Elizabeth Tonkin, Mayron McDonald, and Malcolm Chapman, 71–88. ASA Monographs. London: Routledge.

———. 2000. *A Greek Island Cosmos: Kinship and Community in Meganisi*. Oxford: James Currey.

Kant, Immanuel. 1987. *Critique of Judgment*. Trans. Werner S. Pluhar. Indianapolis, Ind.: Hackett.

Karakasidou, Anastasia. 1997. *Fields of Wheat, Hills of Blood: Passages to Nationhood in Greek Macedonia, 1870–1990*. Chicago: University of Chicago Press.

Keane, Webb. 2010. "Minds, Surfaces, and Reasons in the Anthropology of Ethics." In *Ordinary Ethics*, ed. Michael Lambek, 64–84. New York: Fordham University Press.

Kearney, Michael. 1991. "Borders and Boundaries of the State and Self at the End of Empire." In *Migrants, Regional Cultures and Latin American Cities*, ed. Lane Hirabayashi and Teófilo Altimarano, 149–66. Washington, D.C.: Society for Latin American Anthropology and American Anthropological Association.

Kelly, Tobias. 2011. *This Side of Silence: Human Rights, Torture, and the Recognition of Cruelty*. Philadelphia: University of Pennsylvania Press.

Kobelinsky, Carolina. 2010. *L'accueil des demandeurs d'asile: Une ethnographie de l'attente*. Paris: Éditions du Cygne.

Kostopoulou, Elektra. 2009. "The Muslim Millet of Autonomous Crete: An Exploration into Its Origins and Implications." Ph.D. dissertation, Bogazici University of Istanbul.

Lacan, Jacques. 1992. *The Ethics of Psychoanalysis, 1959–1960*. Seminar of Jacques Lacan 7. New York: Norton.

Laidlaw, James. 2002. "For an Anthropology of Ethics and Freedom." *Journal of the Royal Anthropological Institute* 8: 311–32.

Laing, R. D. 1983 [1967]. *The Politics of Experience*. New York: Pantheon.

Laliotou, Ioanna. 2004. *Transatlantic Subjects: Acts of Migration and Cultures of Transnationalism Between Greece and America*. Chicago: University of Chicago Press.

Lambek, Michael, ed. 2010. *Ordinary Ethics: Anthropology, Language, and Action*. New York: Fordham University Press.

Laqueur, Thomas. 1989. "Bodies, Details, and the Humanitarian Narrative." In *The New Cultural History*, ed. Lynn Hunt, 176–205. Berkeley: University of California Press.

Latour, Bruno. 2005. *Reassembling the Social: An Introduction to Actor-Network Theory*. Oxford: Oxford University Press.

Lauth Bacas, Jutta. 2011. "No Safe Haven: The Reception of Irregular Boat Migrants in Greece." *Ethnologia Balkanica* 14.

Lawrence, Christopher M. 2007. *Blood and Oranges: European Markets and Immigrant Labor in Rural Greece*. Dislocations 2. New York: Berghahn.

Llewellyn, Karl N., and E. Adamson Hoebel. 1941. *The Cheyenne Way: Conflict and Case Law in Primitive Jurisprudence*. Civilization of the American Indian Series 21. Norman: University of Oklahoma Press.

———. 2002. *The Cheyenne Way: Conflict and Case Law in Primitive Jurisprudence*. Buffalo, N.Y.: W.S. Hein.

Loizos, Peter, and Euthymios Papataxiarchis, eds. 1991. *Contested Identities: Gender and Kinship in Modern Greece*. Princeton, N.J.: Princeton University Press.

Mackridge, Peter. 1985. *The Modern Greek Language: A Descriptive Analysis of Standard Modern Greek*. Oxford : Oxford University Press.

Magliveras, Konstantinos D. 2011. *Migration Law in Greece*. Alphen aan den Rijn: Kluwer Law.

Mahmood, Saba. 2005. *Politics of Piety: The Islamic Revival and the Feminist Subject*. Princeton, N.J.: Princeton University Press.

Malkki, Liisa. 1995a. *Purity and Exile: Violence and National Cosmology Among Hutu Refugees in Tanzania*. Chicago: University of Chicago Press.

———. 1995b. "Refugees and Exile: From 'Refugee Studies' to the National Order of Things." *Annual Review of Anthropology* 24: 495–523.

Mamdani, Mahmood. 1996. *Citizen and Subject: Contemporary Africa and the Legacy of Late Colonialism*. Princeton, N.J.: Princeton University Press.

Matoesian, Gregory M. 1993. *Reproducing Rape Domination Through Talk in the Courtroom*. Chicago: University of Chicago Press.

———. 1997. "'You Were Interested in Him as a Person?': Rhythms of Domination in the Kennedy Smith Rape Trial." *Law and Social Inquiry* 22: 55–93.

———. 2001. *Law and the Language of Identity: Discourse in the William Kennedy Smith Rape Trial*. Oxford: Oxford University Press.

Mbembe, Achille. 2004. "Aesthetics of Superfluity." *Public Culture* 16: 373–405.

Mcdonough, Paul, and Evangelia Lilian Tsourdi. 2012. "The "Other" Greek Crisis: Asylum and EU Solidarity." *Refugee Survey Quarterly* 31: 67–100.

McKinley, Michelle. 1997. "Life Stories, Disclosure, and the Law." *Political and Legal Anthropology Review* 20: 70–82.

Menz, George. 2009. *The Political Economy of Managed Migration: Nonstate Actors, Europeanization, and the Politics of Designing Migration Policies*. Oxford: Oxford University Press.

Mitchell, Katharyne. 1997. "Transnational Discourse: Bringing Geography Back In." *Antipode* 29: 101–14.

Moore, Sally Falk. 1978. *Law as Process: An Anthropological Approach*. New Brunswick, N.J.: Transaction.

Mountz, Alison. 2010. *Seeking Asylum: Human Smuggling and Bureaucracy at the Border*. Minneapolis: University of Minnesota Press.

Mountz, Alison, Richard Wright, Ines Miyares, and Adrian J. Bailey. 2002. "Lives in Limbo: Temporary Protected Status and Immigrant Identities." *Global Networks* 2: 335–56.

Muehlebach, Andrea. 2007. "On Affective Labor in Post-Fordist Italy." *Cultural Anthropology* 26: 59–82.

Ngai, Mae M. 2004. *Impossible Subjects: Illegal Aliens and the Making of Modern America*. Politics and Society in Twentieth-Century America. Princeton, N.J.: Princeton University Press.

Nuijten, Monique. 2003. *Power, Community, and the State: The Political Anthropology of Organization in Mexico*. London: Pluto Press.

Nussbaum, Martha. 2001 [1986]. *The Fragility of Goodness: Luck and Ethics in Greek Tragedy and Philosophy*. New York: Cambridge University Press.

Ong, Aihwa. 1999. *Flexible Citizenship: The Cultural Logics of Transnationality*. Durham, N.C.: Duke University Press.

———. 2003. *Buddha Is Hiding: Refugees, Citizenship, the New America*. Berkeley: University of California Press.

Ortner, Sherry. 1984. "Theory in Anthropology Since the 1960s." *Comparative Studies in Society and History* 26: 126–66.

———. 2006. *Anthropology and Social Theory: Culture, Power, and the Acting Subject*. Durham, N.C.: Duke University Press.

Panourgia, Neni. 1995. *Fragments of Death, Fables of Identity: An Athenian Anthropography*. Madison: University of Wisconsin Press.

———. 2009. *Dangerous Citizens: The Greek Left and the Terror of the State*. New York: Fordham University Press.

———. 2011. "The Squared Constitution of Dissent." *Fieldsights—Hot Spots: Cultural Anthropology Online, October 29.*

Papageorgiou, Ioannis. 2013. "The Europeanization of Immigration and Asylum in Greece (1990–2012)." *International Journal of Sociology* 43: 72–90.

Papageorgiou, Ioannis, and Giorgia Dimitropoulou. 2008. "Unaccompanied Minors Asylum Seekers in Greece: A Study on the Treatment of Unaccompanied Minors Applying for Asylum in Greece." UN High Commissioner for Refugees in Greece.

Papailias, Penelope. 2004. *Genres of Recollection: Archival Poetics and Modern Greece.* Anthropology, History, and the Critical Imagination. New York: Palgrave Macmillan.

Papataxiarchis, Euthymios. 2006. *Περιπέτειες της ετερότητας: Η παραγωγή της πολιτισμικής διαφοράς στη σημερινή Ελλάδα.* [Adventures of Alterity: The Production of Cultural Difference in Contemporary Greece]. Athens: Alexandria.

Paxson, Heather. 2004. *Making Modern Mothers: Ethics and Family Planning in Urban Greece.* Berkeley: University of California Press.

Petronati, Marina. 2000. "Culture as Resistance. The Transformation of Eritrean Refugees' Rootlessness." In *Population Movements and Development.* Vgenopoulos C.47–55. Athens: Papazisis.

Petryna, Adriana. 2002. *Life Exposed: Biological Citizens After Chernobyl.* Princeton, N.J.: Princeton University Press.

Pietz, William. 1985. "The Problem of the Fetish, I." *Res: Anthropology and Aesthetics* 9: 5–17.

Placas, Aimee J. 2009. "The Emergence of Consumer Credit in Greece: An Ethnography of Indebtedness." Doctoral dissertation, Rice University.

Rabinow, Paul. 1977. *Reflections on Fieldwork in Morocco.* Quantum Book. Berkeley: University of California Press.

Ramji-Nogales, Jaya, Andrew Ian Schoenholtz, and Philip G. Schrag. 2009. *Refugee Roulette: Disparities in Asylum Adjudication and Proposals for Reform.* New York: New York University Press.

Razsa, Maple, and Andrej Kumik. 2012. "The Occupy Movement in Žižek's Hometown: Direct Democracy and a Politics of Becoming." *American Ethnologist* 39: 238–58.

Redclift, Nanneke. 2005. *Contesting Moralities: Science, Identity, Conflict.* London: UCL Press.

Redfield, Peter. 2005. "Doctors, Borders and Life in Crisis." *Cultural Anthropology* 20: 328–61.

Richland, Justin B. 2010. "'They Did It like a Song:' Ethics, Aesthetics, and Tradition in Hopi Legal Discourse." In *Ordinary Ethics: Anthropology, Language, and Action*, ed. Michael Lambek. New York: Fordham University Press.

Riles, Annelise, ed. 1997. *Documents: Artifacts of Modern Knowledge.* Ann Arbor: University of Michigan Press.

———. 2001. *The Network Inside Out.* Ann Arbor: University of Michigan Press.

Robbins, Joel. 2004. *Becoming Sinners: Christianity and Moral Torment in a Papua New*

Guinea Society. Ethnographic Studies in Subjectivity 4. Berkeley: University of California Press.

Rofel, Lisa. 2007. *Desiring China: Experiments in Neoliberalism, Sexuality, and Public Culture*. Durham, N.C.: Duke University Press.

Rosen, Tracy. *2011*. "The "Chinese-ification" of Greece." *Fieldsights—Hot Spots, Cultural Anthropology Online, October 30*.

Rouse, Roger. 1991. "Mexican Migration and the Social Space of Postmodernism." *Diaspora: A Journal of Transnational Studies*: 8–23.

Rozakou, Katerina. 2006. "Street Work: Όρια και αντιφάσεις των συναντήσεων Ελλήνων εθελοντών και προσφύγων. ["Street Work: Boundaries and Contradictions of the Encounters Between Greek Volunteers and Refugees"]. In *Περιπέτειες της ετερότητας: η παραγωγή της πολιτισμικής διαφοράς στη σημερινή Ελλάδα*. [Adventures of Alterity: The Production of Cultural Difference in Contemporary Greece], ed. Euthemios Papataxarchis, 325–55. Athens: Alexandria.

———. 2012. "The Biopolitics of Hospitality in Greece: Humanitarianism and the Management of Refugees." *American Ethnologist* 39, 3: 562–77.

Sapir, Edward. 1921. *Language: An Introduction to the Study of Speech*. New York: Harcourt Brace.

Sassen, Saskia. 1996. *Losing Control? Sovereignty in an Age of Globalization*. University Seminars/Leonard Hastings Schoff Memorial Lectures. New York: Columbia University Press.

Scarry, Elaine. 1985. *The Body in Pain: The Making and Unmaking of the World*. New York: Oxford University Press.

Scott, James. 1998. *Seeing like a State: How Certain Schemes for Improving the Human Condition Have Failed*. New Haven, Conn.: Yale University Press.

Seremetakis, Nadia. 1996. *The Senses Still: Perception and Memory as Material Culture in Modernity*. Chicago: University of Chicago Press.

Sharp, Gene, and Joshua Paulson. 2005. *Waging Nonviolent Struggle: 20th Century Practice and 21st Century Potential*. Boston: Extending Horizons Books.

Shore, Cris. 2000. *Building Europe: The Cultural Politics of European Integration*. London ; New York: Routledge.

Simmel, Georg. 1950. "The Stranger." In *The Sociology of Georg Simmel*, 402–8. New York: Free Press.

Sitaropoulos, Nicholas. 2000. "Modern Greek Asylum Policy and Practice in the Context of the Relevant European Developments." *Journal of Refugee Studies* 12: 105–17.

Soysal, Yasemin Nuho Glu. 1994. *Limits of Citizenship: Migrants and Postnational Membership in Europe*. Chicago: University of Chicago Press.

Stewart, Charles. 1991. *Demons and the Devil: Moral Imagination in Modern Greek Culture*. Princeton Modern Greek Studies. Princeton, N.J.: Princeton University Press.

Stolcke, Verena. 1995. "Talking Culture: New Boundaries, New Rhetorics of Exclusion in Europe." *Cultural Anthropology* 36: 1–24.

Stoler, Ann Laura. 2008. *Along the Archival Grain: Epistemic Anxieties and Colonial Common Sense*. Princeton, N.J.: Princeton University Press.

Tadiar, Neferti. 2005. *Fantasy-Production: Sexual Economies and Other Philippine Consequences for the New World Order*. Hong Kong: Hong Kong University Press.

Taussig, Michael. 1997. *The Magic of the State*. New York: Routledge.

———. 2004. *My Cocaine Museum*. Chicago: University of Chicago Press.

Ticktin, Miriam. 2006. "Where Ethics and Politics Meet: The Violence of Humanitarianism in France." *American Ethnologist* 33: 33–49.

———. 2011. *Casualties of Care: Immigration and the Politics of Humanitarianism in France*. Berkeley: University of California Press.

Torpey, John. 2000. *The Invention of the Passport: Surveillance, Citizenship, and the State*. Cambridge: Cambridge University Press.

Triandafyllidou, Anna and Ruby Gropas. 2009. "Constructing Difference: The Mosque Debates in Greece." *Journal of Ethnic and Migration Studies* 35: 957–75.

Tsimouris, Giorgos. 2001. "Reconstructing 'Home' Among the 'Enemy': The Greeks of Goceada (Imvros) After Lausanne." *Balkanologie*.

———. 2007. *Ίμβριοι: Φυγάδες απ' τον τόπο μας ομηροι στηνπατρίδα* [Imvri: Fugitives from Our Place Hostages in the Homeland]. Athens: Ellinika Grammata.

——— 2013. "Casino Capitalism, Fascism, and the Re-Bordering of Immigration: Welcome to Greece." COST Action IS0903 Working Paper. Berlin: EastBordNeted.

Tsing, Anna. 2005. *Friction: An Ethnography of Global Connections*. Princeton, N.J.: Princeton University Press.

Tsitselikis, K. 2004. "Η θρησκευτική ελευθερία μεταναστών: Η περίπτωση των Μουσουλμάνων" [The Religious Freedom of Immigrants: The Case of Muslims]. In *The Greece of Migration*, ed. Mihalis Pavlos and Dimitris Christopoulos, 267–303. Athens: Kritiki.

Turner, Victor W. 1967. *The Forest of Symbols: Aspects of Ndembu Ritual*. Ithaca, N.Y.: Cornell University Press.

———. 1974. *Dramas, Fields, and Metaphors: Symbolic Action in Human Society*. Symbol, Myth, and Ritual. Ithaca, N.Y.: Cornell University Press.

Volpp, Leti. 2012. "Imaginings of Space in Immigration Law." *Law, Culture and the Humanities*.

Unamuno, Miguel de. 1954. *Tragic Sense of Life*. New York: Dover.

UNHCR. 2010. "2009 Global Trends: Refugees, Asylum-Seekers, Returnees, Internally Displaced and Stateless Persons." United Nations High Commissioner for Refugees, Division of Programme Support and Management. Country Data Sheet, June 15.

Vance, Carole S. 1984. *Pleasure and Danger: Exploring Female Sexuality*. London: Pandora.

Veesman, Cornelia. 2008. *Files: Law and Media Technology*. Stanford, Calif.: Stanford University Press.

Verinis, James. 2011. "New Immigrants and Neo-Rural Values: The Small Non-Greek Farmers of Global Greek Countrysides." *Anthropological Journal of European Cultures* 20: 46–68.

Voutira, Eftihia. 2003. "Refugees: Whose Term Is It Anyway? Emic and Etic Constructions of 'Refugees' in Modern Greek." In *The Refugee Convention at Fifty: A View from Forced Migration Studies*, ed. Joanne Van Selm et al., 65–81. Lanham, Md.: Lexington Books.

Wallace, Helen. 2000. "Europeanisation and Globalisation: Complementary or Contradictory Trends?" *New Political Economy* 5: 369–82.

Warren, Kay. 2007. "The 2000 UN Human Trafficking Protocol: Rights, Enforcement, Vulnerabilities." In *The Practice of Human Rights*, ed. Sally Engle Merry and Mark Goodale, 242–69. Cambridge: Cambridge University Press.

White, Luise. 2000. *Speaking with Vampires: Rumor and History in Colonial Africa*. Berkeley: University of California Press.

White, Richard. 1991. *The Middle Ground: Indians, Empires, and Republics in the Great Lakes Region, 1650–1815*. Cambridge Studies in North American Indian History. Cambridge: Cambridge University Press.

Xenakis, Sappho. 2012. "A New Dawn? Change and Continuity in Political Violence in Greece." *Terrorism and Political Violence* 24, 3: 437–64.

Xenakis, Sappho, and Leonidas Cheliotis. 2013. "Spaces of Contestation: Challenges, Actors, and Expertise in the Management of Urban Security in Greece." *European Journal of Criminology* 10: 297–313.

Yalouri, Eleana. 2001. *The Acropolis: Global Fame, Local Claim*. Oxford: Berg.

Yiakoumaki, Vassiliki. 2006a. "'Local,' 'Ethnic' and 'Rural' Food: On the Emergence of 'Cultural Diversity' in Post-EU-Accession Greece." *Journal of Modern Greek Studies* 24: 415–45.

———. 2006b. "Ethnic Turks and "Muslims" and the Performance of Multiculturalism: The Case of the Drómeno of Thrace." *South European Society and Politics* 29, 1: 1058–79.

———. 2006c. "Περί (Δια)Τροφής Και Εθνικής Ταυτότητας: Οι Διαστάσεις Μιας Νέας "Πολιτισμικής Ποικιλότητας" Στη Σημερινή Ελλάδα." [About Nutrition and National Identity: The Dimensions of a New "Cultural Diversity" in Contemporary Greece]. In *Περιπέτειες της ετερότητας: η παραγωγή της πολιτισμικής διαφοράς στη σημερινή Ελλάδα*. [Adventures of Alterity: The Production of Cultural Difference in Contemporary Greece], 105–38. Athens: Alexandria.

Zarkia, Cornelia. 1996. "*Philoxenia*: Receiving Tourists—Not Guests—on a Greek Island." In *Coping with Tourists: European Reactions to Mass Tourism*, ed. Jeremy Boissevain. Oxford: Berghahn.

Zavos, Alexandra. 2011. "Hunger Striking for Rights: The Alien Politics of Immigrant Protest." *Fieldsights— Hot Spots, Cultural Anthropology Online*, October 27, 2011.

Zigon, Jarrett. 2007. "Moral Breakdown and Ethical Demand: A Theoretical Framework for an Anthropology of Moralities." *Anthropological Theory* 7: 131–50.

———. 2008. *Morality: An Anthropological Perspective*. Oxford: Berg.

———. 2010. "Moral and Ethical Assemblages: A Response to Fassin and Stoczkowski." *Anthropological Theory* 10: 3–15.

Zilberg, Elana. 2011. *Space of Detention: The Making of a Transnational Gang Crisis between Los Angeles and San Salvador*. Durham, N.C.: Duke University Press.

Zinn, Dorothy Louise. 2001. *La raccomandazione: Clientelismo vecchio e nuovo*. Rome: Donzelli.

Žižek, Slavoj. 1989. *The Sublime Object of Ideology*. London: Verso.

———. 2000 [1992]. *Looking Awry: An Introduction to Jaques Lacan through Popular Culture*. Cambridge, Mass.: MIT Press.

Zolberg, Aristide R., Astri Suhrke, and Sergio Aguayo. 1989. *Escape from Violence: Conflict and the Refugee Crisis in the Developing World*. New York: Oxford University Press.

Index

Note: A *t* following a page reference indicates a table. Unless otherwise indicated, all locations are in Greece.

Acknowledgments

Particularly in this historical moment, when debt has become a marker of structural violence, I will not say that I have incurred "debts" in the writing of this book. Nevertheless, I have had ample opportunity to develop my sense of gratitude: to the people who have offered me their assistance, kindness, critique, and support; and to the fates and fortune, for the incredible privileges to which I have been party and which this book, of course, directly reflects. My Greek interlocutors always tell me I say "thank you" too much. In that spirit, then:

My thanks, above all, to those who shared their lives with me and who let me into their worlds, sharing in dialogue and dialectic, correcting my mistakes, and offering me insight, friendship, and often protection. While I do not want to name them here, I hope they will know who they are and will find my account of our time spent together to reflect my gratitude, admiration, and the enormous pleasure, and indeed love, that I have in felt writing about these shared experiences.

My thanks to the funding bodies that made this research even a viable possibility: the U.S. National Science Foundation, the Wenner-Gren Foundation for Anthropological Research, the Fulbright Foundation in Greece, and the Woodrow Wilson National Fellowship Foundation. A postdoctoral fellowship at Princeton's Seeger Center for Hellenic Studies was instrumental in allowing me to develop this work.

Many generous interlocutors have offered their thoughtful feedback on this work, in its many iterations. Donald L. Brenneis, Susan Bibler Coutin, Lisa Rofel, and Melissa L. Caldwell, have asked the right questions, made the right critiques, and given praise when it was sorely needed. With regard to the book, specifically, I am grateful to Penn Press Editor Peter Agree for believing in and supporting this project since before it was even a book. James Faubion, Jessica O'Reilly, and Barbara Yngvesson read the manuscript in its entirety and provided detailed and invaluable feedback; I cannot thank them enough for their time and generosity. Michael Herzfeld not only read two versions of the manuscript, but he was instrumental even in the minutiae of revisions. My deep appreciation for the insights of my wonderful *parea* of fellow anthropologists of Greece, of my generation, whose work and conversation have been instrumental to the development of this manuscript: Othon Alexandrakis, Dimitris Dalakoglou, Toby Lee, Kostis Kalantzsis, Aimee Placas, Tracey Rosen, Katerina Rozakou, and Tina Palivos. Others provided crucial comments on versions of these chapters, either more formally in writing, as discussants, or as participants in workshops: Gregory Feldman, Michelle McKinley, Elizabeth Mertz, Leti Volpp, Jeremy Campbell, Didier Fassin, Kregg Hetherington, Colin Hoag, Tobias Kelly, Carolina Kobelinsky, Sarah Willen, Lori Allen, Jane Cowan, Penelope Papailias, Neni Panourgia, Miriam Ticktin, and Heather Turcotte. Finally, thank you to Matthew Wolf-Meyer for his invaluable mentorship with regard to the "book process."

At Princeton, Elizabeth Ann Davis, Carol J. Greenhouse, João Biehl, and Molly Greene were important and welcoming mentors, while Karen Emmerich, Marek Meško, Elektra Kostopoulou, Dimitris Kousouris, Peter Locke, Ramah Mckay, Lou Ruprecht, Erica Weiss, and William Vega were crucial conversation partners. Dimitris Gondicas, in his ineffable way, managed to create one of the most lively and supportive academic communities in which I have had the pleasure to take part. At the College of the Atlantic, colleagues provided support and conversation that were crucial to helping me stitch this together, especially John Anderson, Molly Anderson, J. Gray Cox, Catherine Clinger, Bonnie Tai, Karen Waldron, and John Visvader. A number of extraordinary undergraduates have helped me hone and develop not just my ideas for this book but my capacities as a scholar and a teacher, in particular Amber Igasia, Alistaire McKemy, and Graham Reeder. Bronwyn Clement, Addie Namnoum, and Nathan Thanki not only shared important insights but also graced me with their incredible proofreading skills as deadlines were pending.

The author expresses appreciation to the Schoff Fund at the University Seminars at Columbia University for their help in publication. The ideas presented have benefited from discussions in the University Seminars on Modern Greek Studies.

Some of the material in Chapters 2 and 4 appeared in articles in *Political and Legal Anthropology Review* and *American Ethnologist*, respectively.

My thanks and love to dear friends and family, all over the world, whose support and conversation has been crucial: Hussein Elfil, Giorgos Sourmelis, Oya Fidan, Alexia Vasiliou, Ali Ahmed, Eleni Maliou and Vasilis Terzides, Maria Malikouti, Richard Williams, Qiamy Hafiz, Edward and Sarah Germain, Bill, Brett, Emily, and Susie Tyne, Linda Farrer, Julia Crothers, Anna Shneiderman, Colin DeYoung, Chuck Lucasey, Paul Soter, Maureen Griffin, Janel Obenchain, Klara Takas, Maria Lewis, Virginia Gardiner, Emily Herzog, Joan and Fred Gardiner (who first sparked my interest in Greece through the priceless gift of *D'Aulaires' Book of Greek Myths*), Ellen Cabot, John, Laura, and Campbell Kinnard; and my grandmothers, Ruth McDowell Kinnard and Virginia Ward Cabot, now passed on, but who have been some of my most important intellectual mentors. Grazie mille ai miei carissimi suoceri, Gianna Cumerlato e Rino Poier.

To my parents, Judith and Christopher Cabot, and my sister, Elizabeth Cabot, for more than I could ever articulate: in particular, for putting up with me and supporting my interests in philosophy, religion, culture, and now law, for thirty plus years, without ever suggesting that there was a limit to what I could desire or accomplish. A belly rub to Fritz, who spent many a day on my lap as I wrote and made changes. And finally to Salvatore Poier: my thanks, my love, and a breeze on the top of the Summano; a river in Berlin; a sunset above Xanthi; and a morning cup of Café Carraro. All that and more, my amore.

www.ingramcontent.com/pod-product-compliance
Lightning Source LLC
Chambersburg PA
CBHW020844270326
41928CB00006B/538

* 9 7 8 1 5 1 2 8 2 5 2 1 3 *